Race, Religion & Racism

RACE, RELIGION & RACISM

Volume Three

Jesus, Christianity & Islam

Frederick K.C. Price

FAITH ONE
PUBLISHING

Faith One Publishing
Los Angeles, California

Race, Religion & Racism, Volume Three
Jesus, Christianity & Islam
ISBN 1-883798-53-1
Library of Congress Catalog Card Number: 99-75670
Copyright © 2002 by
Frederick K.C. Price
P.O. Box 90000
Los Angeles, CA 90009

Published by Faith One Publishing
7901 South Vermont Avenue
Los Angeles, California 90044

Publisher's Cataloging-in-Publication
(Provided by Quality Books, Inc.)

Price, Frederick K. C.
    Race, religion & racism. Vol. 3, Jesus, Christianity
& Islam / Frederick K.C. Price. -- 1st ed.
    p. cm.
    Includes bibliographical references and index.
    LCCN 99-75670
    ISBN 1-883798-53-1

    1. Race--Religious aspects--Christianity. 2. Racism
--Religious aspects--Christianity. 3. Jesus Christ--
Islamic interpretations. 4. Islam--Relations--
Christianity. 5. Christianity and other religions--
Islam. I. Title

    BT734.2.P75 2002   261.8'34
                              QBI01-700962

Table of Contents

Preface

In this, the third volume of *Race, Religion & Racism*, I explore the religion section of this study, especially the allure of Islam for black Americans. Although this is out of the title's sequence — I have already dealt with race and racism in the previous two volumes of this series — the Lord led me to approach the subject in this order.

Race, Religion & Racism began in 1991 when God gave me an assignment to speak about racial issues. And a year later, a white minister with whom I had a long fellowship, made a racist comment to his congregation which was caught on tape. Despite being confronted with the evidence, and notwithstanding my urging, this minister refused to recant his statements publicly. This incident accelerated my research into racism in America, especially as it related to the church.

The teaching series started on Ever Increasing Faith television in October 1997, and two years later, Faith One published Volume 1 of *Race, Religion & Racism* as part of a three-part book series. That volume surveyed race and racism in America, especially as it related to slavery. In Volume 2, published in 2001, I focused on racism's origins in America, its role in the church (including a detailed examination of the *Dake's Annotated Reference Bible*), an analysis of the concept of reconciliation, and an examination of the "curse of Ham." Either of these first two volumes may be read independently.

In this final volume, *Jesus, Christianity & Islam*, the Lord has called me to deal with the challenge to Christianity, especially in the black community, from Islam. Large numbers of American Blacks are embracing Islam, especially the sect of Islam known as the Nation of Islam. We want to know, what does the Nation of Islam teach? If people are making a decision to leave Christianity for Islam, do they have all the information they need?

Even more important, we want to know, What is Islam? Are Jehovah and Allah merely different names for the same God? What do Islam's prophets and proponents say about it? What are the claims made by some of its leaders? What do the *Koran* and the other holy books of Islam say about such issues as slaves, the place of women, and the character (and skin color) of the Prophet Muhammad? What does Islam say about Jesus? In each case, I want to compare what the prophets and primary sources of Islam say to what is said in the Bible. When we are finished, I think you will see that Jehovah-God and Allah can't possibly be the same person, and that what these prophets have to say about the person of Jesus requires that people make a choice about who they serve.

In 1991 I was also led to investigate the predominant portrayal in western societies of Jesus as a European white man. What color was Jesus? What was His bloodline, His DNA, if you will? Was He the "black Jesus" that some African-American churches have been claiming recently? Or was He the Hollywood Jesus with blond hair and blue eyes?

Finally, to wrap up the series, since one of the major problems faced by African Americans devolving from slavery has been low self-esteem and poor image as a race, I examine people of color in America who produced great scientific and business achievements. Some of these may surprise or even shock you. But surely you will be inspired.

Throughout, the message is that God loves all His children equally. There is no segregation in heaven, and no second best that came from the hand of the Maker. Our challenge is to see things the way they really are, then transform them into the way God intends them to be.

— Frederick K.C. Price, D.D.

Acknowledgments

First, I must thank my heavenly Father; my Savior and Lord Jesus Christ, the head of the Church; and the Holy Spirit, under whose inspiration I wrote this volume.

In addition, a large and diverse team contributed to the editing, research, printing, and marketing involved in producing this book. While I cannot name everyone who had a hand in this, I would like to take note of several people specifically:

Professor Larry Schweikart of the University of Dayton (Ohio) served as my chief editor and researcher, and I thank him for all of his tireless efforts and the extraordinary work of his researcher Julia Cupples.

Stanley O. Williford of Vision Publishing served as editor, and I am always amazed at his ability to capture the essence of my thoughts so accurately on paper.

Larry and Stanley worked closely with my in-house publishing arm, Faith One Publishing, and together they have clearly conveyed what God put in my heart regarding this portion of *Race, Religion & Racism*. Thank you, Faith One Publishing team. Your diligent efforts are greatly appreciated.

To Nitza Wilon, our copy editor; Vickie Agee, our indexer; Alan and Maggy Graham, our typesetters; and Doris Pettigrew, our transcriber: I could not have asked for a better production team.

Overseeing a book project takes superior organization, detailed coordination, and excellent time management, and I am happy to have a staff that could master such tasks. A special thank you to A. Michael Evans Jr., vice president of marketing; Jennette Fant, special assistant to the president for executive administration; Velda Fennell, director of marketing and project manager; and Michelle McIntosh, publications coordinator.

To our attorneys, Norma Williams and Freya Christian, who carefully reviewed the book, your input and advice were invaluable.

As always, to my wife, Betty, and children, your undying and prayerful support has been a pillar of strength in all my endeavors.

Finally, to the congregation of Crenshaw Christian Center and the loyal viewers of Ever Increasing Faith Ministries, I can only echo the words of my Lord, "Well done, thy good and faithful servants!" May you reap the bountiful harvest that you have sown with your contributions and support of the ministry.

—Frederick K.C. Price, D.D.
Los Angeles

1

The True Message to the
Black Man and Woman

In the previous two volumes of this series, we have looked at the issues of race and racism. This volume — the grand finale, if you will — addresses religion. In recent years, I have become concerned about the inroads that Islam has made into the black community. I have laid the groundwork for discussing this by looking at race and racism in the first two volumes of this series. There is no question that racism in the church — racism by Christians — has caused some Blacks to conclude that if this is the way Christianity treats people, then Christianity isn't for them.

Maybe Islam is. *USA Today* recently noted that although in the 1930s there were only a few dozen black Muslims in the United States, today about 2.5 million American Blacks classify themselves as Muslims.[1] *U.S. News* on-line placed the number even higher, at 5 million to 6 million, while a more conservative — and probably low — estimate made by Daniel Pipes, an Arab scholar, places the figure at 1 million.[2] If the higher number is accurate, it would mean

---

[1] Edward Blum and Marc Levin, "Islam Challenges Black Churches," *USA Today*, July 19, 2000.

[2] Jonah Blank, "The Muslim Mainstream: Islam Is Growing Fast in America and its Members Defy Stereotypes," *www.usnews.com/issue/980720/20isla.htm*; Daniel Pipes, "How Elijah Muhammad Won,"

1

that "Muslims in America already outnumber Presbyterians, Episco-palians, and Mormons...." They are also "more numerous than Quakers, Unitarians, Seventh-day Adventists, Mennonites, Jehovah's Witnesses, and Christian Scientists combined."[3] The Website www.adherents.com, which uses Gallup Poll numbers as a measure of the size of religious groups in America, listed Islam at 5.27 million in 1990 (the last census), or about 5 percent of the U.S. population. This is a far cry from the 151 million American Christians, but it is still a significant number of people. Some writers project that if conver-sion rates remain unchanged, Islam will be the dominant religion in black urban areas in 20 years.

Even if the lower numbers are accurate, it is clear that Islam is growing in America, and especially among Blacks. So we need to exam-ine this and find out what the attraction is.

If you just look at Islam superficially, you might get the impression that it is much like Christianity: There is a God named Allah whom some say is just another name for Jehovah; it has a prophet named Muhammad; and it does not seem to — again, on the surface — attack Jesus as a person.[4] After all, it is said the Muslims accept Jesus as a prophet. It also seems that Islam is less racist than

---

Commentary, Vol. 109, no. 5, June 2000, 31-36. The Website *www.adherents.com/rel_USA.html* refers to both census data and the *Yearbook of American and Canadian Churches*, and states that while the American Muslim Council routinely claims more than 6.5 million members, nothing close to this number has been verified by independent sources. The *Yearbook* places the number of American Muslims at 3.9 million, or slightly larger than the African Methodist Episcopal (AME) Church. See *Churches and Church Membership in the United States, 1990* (Mars Hill, North Carolina: Glenmary Research Center, 1991), 1-3.

[3] Blank, *passim*.

[4] Much of this perception that God equals Allah equals Jehovah comes from the writings of Elijah Muhammad, *Message to the Blackman in America* (Newport News, Virginia: United Brothers Communications

Christianity, especially toward people of color, because most Muslims are darker-skinned people. Islam has thus been painted as a religion that is more tolerant of black people.

These messages must be getting through, because many young black men in particular have been drawn to Islam. A typical attitude was expressed by a Baptist woman whose son converted to Islam: "This Islam sounds like true religion to me. They don't believe in smoking dope, drinking liquor and no adultery. I say we could use more teaching like that.... I enjoy listening to [my son] talk about [Islam], and how it came out of Africa, and that sounds pretty good."[5] But there is more to committing your life to Islam — or Jesus Christ — than not doing drugs and staying away from liquor! Much more. So my question is: Are these people drawn to Islam getting accurate information? Do they really know the choice they are making — and the evidence on which they make that choice?

Today, the Muslim movement among Blacks in America consists of several major denominations or groups, of which one of the most prominent (though possibly not the largest) is the Nation of Islam.[6] However, until well after Elijah Muhammad's death, the term

---

Systems, 1992 [reprint of 1965 edition]) where he states, "This mighty One, is known under many names. He has no equal. There never was one like Him. He is referred to in the Bible as God Almighty, and in some places as Jehovah, the God of Gods, and the Lord of Lords. The Holy Qur-an refers to Him as Allah, the One God.... He, also, is referred to as the Christ the second Jesus. The Son of Man, who is wise and all-powerful," 111. Notice especially "second Jesus."

[5] This woman is quoted in Pipes, 36.

[6] The Black Muslim movement originated before World War I with the Moorish Science Temple of America, founded in 1913 by Prophet Drew Ali (Timothy Drew). Wallace D. Fard took over the movement when Ali died, and in 1930 founded the first known Black Muslim mosque in Detroit, formally starting the Nation of Islam. Fard himself is called God, Allah, or the Great Mahdi by Black Muslims. In 1933, Elijah Muhammad (originally Elijah Poole [also spelled "Pool"], b. 1897)

Black Muslim meant one group — the Nation of Islam. Other major Islamic groups in America include the "Five Percenters," Ansaar Allah (Islamic Party of North America), Dar Ul-Islam, the Islamic Brotherhood, the United Nation of Islam, the Hanafi Movement, and no doubt many others. While *imam* [prayer leader] Warith Deen Muhammad, the son of Elijah Muhammad, is reportedly the "man who attracts the greatest following among American Muslims…," he apparently has no denominational affiliation and has instructed Muslims to attend any mosque.[7] Therefore, because the Nation of

---

founded a mosque in Chicago, and upon Fard's disappearance in 1934, assumed the leadership of the Nation of Islam (NOI). Muhammad led the Black Muslims until the 1960s, when Malcolm X, head of the New York mosque, challenged his leadership. Malcolm X, also known as El-Hajj Malik El-Shabazz (born Malcolm Little) was the son of a Baptist preacher who was killed, most likely by Whites, because of his social activism. After going to prison for burglary, Malcolm X studied the so-called Black Muslims. Unlike traditional Islam, the Black Muslims viewed Whites as "devils" and predicted a future race war. When Malcolm X was released from prison, he abandoned his "slave name" and rose rapidly in the Detroit organization. He rejected the main objectives of the Civil Rights Movement, and where Dr. Martin Luther King said, "I have a dream," Malcolm X said that other black people were having nightmares. The Black Muslims emphasized segregation and separation from white society, and under Malcolm X they called for a revolution and bloodshed. In 1964, Malcolm X publicly broke with the Black Muslims and formed his own movement. A year later, men said to be Black Muslims shot him. (See *The Autobiography of Malcolm X*, with the assistance of Alex Haley [New York: Ballantine, 1973 (1965)]). Wallace Muhammad, who succeeded Elijah Muhammad in 1975, de-emphasized the "white hatred" aspects of the movement and moved Black Muslims toward Sunni Islamic practices, taking the name American Muslim Mission. In the late 1970s, Louis Farrakhan (b. 1933) revived the earlier Nation of Islam name and again stressed black separatism.

[7] Blank, passim.

Islam (NOI) has been the most prominent, and because of its leaders —
Elijah Muhammad, Malcolm X, and today, Louis Farrakhan — I will be
dealing predominantly with the Black Muslim movement as presented in
the doctrines of the Nation of Islam, which numbers some 20,000 to
50,000 members.[8]

Let me make a disclaimer right off the bat. I am not interested in "bashing" anyone, or in offending anyone's faith. I am not
attacking any particular person or minister. I do not mean to give
offense to the many brothers in prison who have become involved in
the Black Muslim movement. But often — not all the time, but often
— people latch onto something without fully exploring what it means,
or what it stands for. Just as many Christians never pick up a Bible
and have little idea what Christianity is all about. For example, we
know from one study that even though many people claim to go to
church regularly, in fact when you ask them if they went to church
last week, it turns out that not nearly as many did.[9]

In other words, many "Christians" are Christians in name
only, and don't really know what Christianity is all about. So, too,
many Black Muslims in America probably do not know what their
holy books really say, or what their prophets — the messengers of
Allah — have said.

Islam seems to be, in many respects, similar to Christianity.
It is a monotheistic religion, but instead of Jehovah God, the Muslims have Allah. Isn't it the same person? We'll examine that.

---

[8] In 1975, Imam Warith renounced most of the doctrines of Elijah
Muhammad, and in 1985 "disbanded" the Nation of Islam, although
clearly the organization still exists, and arguably thrives, today. For
an overview of the history of Black Muslims, see C. Eric Lincoln, *The
Black Muslims in America*, 3rd ed., (Grand Rapids: William B. Eerdmans
Publishing Company, 1994 [1961]) 63-129, 177-209.

[9] C. Kirk Hadaway and Penny Long Marler, "Did You Really Go to Church
This Week? Behind the Poll Data," *The Christian Century*, Vol. 115,
no. 14, May 6, 1998, 472-475.

But whereas the Christian church in America has had a history of racism, and where, as we have seen, many aspects of Christian life today still have trappings of this racism, it becomes quite tempting for young black men to say, in essence, "I don't need that garbage," and look around for something else. They see Islam, which seems to favor people of color, and they see books, such as the one we will examine by Elijah Muhammad, called *Message to the Blackman in America,* and they think, "Hey, this is for me."

But what is Islam all about, especially the Black Muslim movement in America that has been so attractive to black people? I want to begin this section of the book by examining the teachings of Elijah Muhammad, the fountainhead of the modern Nation of Islam. The eminent scholar Daniel Pipes of the University of Pennsylvania argued that without Elijah Muhammad, the million or so African Americans who are now Muslims would probably still be Christians.[10]

In 1965, Elijah Muhammad published *Message to the Blackman in America.*[11] (By the way, this is how it is spelled in his title: "Blackman"). In this, we find some startling statements on the subject of God. For instance, writing under the heading "Allah is God: The Coming of the Son of Man — The Infidels Are Angry," Elijah Muhammad says:

> Who is His Father if God is not His Father? God is His Father, but the Father is also a man. You have heard of old that God prepared a body, or the expected Son of Man; Jesus is a specially prepared man to do a work of

---

[10] Pipes, "How Elijah Muhammad Won," *Commentary,* Vol. 109, no. 6, June 2000, 31-36.

[11] For *Message to the Blackman in America,* see publishing information in footnote 4. Two recent biographies of Elijah Muhammad include Karl Evanzz, *The Messenger: The Rise and Fall of Elijah Muhammad* (New York: Pantheon, 1999), and Claude Andrew Clegg, III, *An Original Man: The Life and Times of Elijah Muhammad* (New York: St. Martin's, 1997).

redeeming the lost sheep (the so-called Negro). He had to have a body that would be part of each side (black and white), half and half. Therefore, being born or made from both people, He is able to go among both black and white without being discovered or recognized. This He has done in the person of Master W. F. Muhammad, the man who was made by His Father to go search for the lost members of the Tribe of Shabazz. Master W. F. Muhammad is that Son of Man whom the world has been expecting to come for 2,000 years, seeking to save that which was lost.[12]

We are going to investigate these comments in detail, but let's begin with the statement, "…but the Father is also a man…." This is referring to Allah, the God of Islam. Many people, black and white, believe that because Islam is monotheistic, Muslims must worship the same God as Christians, but under a different name. Allah, they think, is the same as Jehovah God of the Jews and Christians.

It is interesting that both Elijah Muhammad and Muhammad the Messenger of Allah quote the Bible, and since the Bible came before Muhammad, then the Bible is the first source. Therefore, we must go back and refer to the oldest source rather than to the newest source, because the youngest source is supposed to be a product of the older source. If anything that Muhammad says doesn't fit the Bible, then we have to reject it. We know that God is not the author of confusion, and if Jehovah of the Bible is the same person as Allah of Islam, then the Bible and the Koran would have to say the same thing.

Elijah Muhammad says that "the Father is also a man." Look closely at what it says: "Allah is God. The coming of the Son of Man — the Infidels Are Angry: Who is His father if God is not His father? God is His father, but the Father is also a man…."

---

[12] Muhammad, 19-20.

Note that it did not say that Allah manifested himself in the "form of a man." Elijah Muhammad said, "…the Father is also a man…." That's different than saying someone manifested himself in the form of a man.

What does the Bible say? In Numbers 23:19, it is written:

"God is not a man, that He should lie, nor a son of man, that He should repent. Has He said, and will He not do? Or has He spoken, and will He not make it good?"

Just the first part of the verse is the key part: **"God is not a man, that He should lie…."** Yet, we have Elijah Muhammad, who came after the Bible, saying "…the father is also a man…." The Bible says, **"God is not a man…."**

Mr. Muhammad goes on to write under the heading "Allah is God: If God was your Father, you would love me."[13] Elijah Muhammad quoted Jesus saying this from John 8:42 in the Bible:

"If God were your Father, you would love Me…."

Again, Elijah Muhammad says Allah is God, so my perception of this is that he would be saying to Fred Price, "If God were your Father, then you would love Me, Elijah Muhammad." That puts Elijah Muhammad in the same relationship to Allah as Jesus is to God. Mr. Muhammad goes on to address Christians: "Read and study the above chapter of John 8:42, all of you, who are Christians, believers in the Bible and Jesus, as you say. If you understand it right, you will agree with me that the whole Caucasian race is a race of devils."[14] Those are powerful words indeed!

Let's go on, though. Mr. Muhammad continues his discussion of Allah in "Allah is God: The Coming of God and the Gathering Together of His People," saying:

---

[13] Muhammad, 23.
[14] Muhammad, 23.

> Allah came to us from the Holy City Mecca, Arabia, in
> 1930. He used the name Wallace D. Fard, often signing
> it W. D. Fard, in the third year (1933). He signed his
> name W. F. Muhammad which stands for Wallace Fard
> Muhammad. He came alone. He began teaching us the
> knowledge of ourselves, of God and the devil, of the
> measurement of the earth, of other planets, and of the
> civilization of some of the planets other than earth.... I
> asked him, "Who are you, and what is your real name?"
> He said, "I am the one that the world has been expect-
> ing for the past 2,000 years."[15]

If I understand the Bible correctly, based on what Mr.
Muhammad said, he's actually saying that he — Wallace Fard
Muhammad — is the Messiah, because that's what the world has
been waiting for 2,000 years, the return of the Messiah. He goes on
to write, "I said to Him again, 'What is your name?' He said, 'My
name is Mahdi; I am God....'"[16] This was Wallace D. Fard, better
known as W. F. Muhammad, speaking to Elijah Muhammad. And
Elijah Muhammad said to him:

> "What is your name?" He said, "My name is Mahdi; I
> am God,..." He spoke with authority, not as one who is
> under authority but as one independent. He said the
> world's time was out in 1914, but people could get an
> extension of time, depending upon their treatment of
> the righteous.... Islam is our salvation....The greatest
> hindrance to the truth of our people is the preacher of
> Christianity.[17]

---

[15] Muhammad, 16-17.

[16] Muhammad, 17.

[17] Muhammad, 17-18. Among the more bizarre statements in this
passage is the introduction of something Minister Louis Farrakhan
would later call the "mothership" or the "mother wheel": "He
[meaning Mahdi, speaking to W. F. Muhammad] pointed out that a
destructive, dreadful-looking plane that is made like a wheel is in
the sky today. It is a half-mile by a half-mile square; it is a humanly

If Elijah Muhammad is right, then Jesus was not the Son of God or the redeemer of mankind. Jesus was not the Messiah, and we have to look for another. Moreover, Mr. Fard told Elijah Muhammad that he (Wallace Fard) was God. But what does the Bible says about these claims?

Mr. Muhammad says, *"Allah came to us from the Holy City of Mecca, Arabia, in 1930."* In Matthew 1:18-23, it is written:

> **18**   **Now the birth of Jesus Christ was as follows: After His mother Mary was betrothed to Joseph, before they came together, she was found with child of the Holy Spirit.**
>
> **19**   **Then Joseph her husband, being a just *man*, and not wanting to make her a public example, was minded to put her away secretly.**
>
> **20**   **But while he thought about these things, behold, an angel of the Lord appeared to him in a dream, saying, "Joseph, son of David, do not be afraid to take to you Mary your wife, for that which is conceived in her is of the Holy Spirit.**
>
> **21**   **"And she will bring forth a Son, and you shall call His name Jesus, for He will save His people from their sins."**

---

built planet. It is up there and can be seen twice a week; it is no secret." Ibid., 17-18. This is an astounding statement for two reasons. First, no astronomers of whom I am aware have ever noted seeing this vehicle. Certainly, the United States Air Force would be concerned about such a ship. No person I have ever known has seen this, even though it "is up there and can be seen twice a week...." Second, if it is humanly built, and this was written in 1965, then it contradicts a statement we will see later made by Mr. Muhammad that such satellites were impossibilities. Mr. Muhammad claims that "Ezekiel saw it a long time ago. It was built for the purpose of destroying the present world," Ibid., 18.

22   So all this was done that it might be fulfilled which was spoken by the Lord through the prophet, saying:

23   *"Behold, the virgin shall be with child, and bear a Son, and they shall call His name Immanuel,"* which is translated, "God with us."

Putting that together with Luke 2:1-11, we find:

1   And it came to pass in those days *that* a decree went out from Caesar Augustus that all the world should be registered.

2   This census first took place while Quirinius was governing Syria.

3   So all went to be registered, everyone to his own city.

4   Joseph also went up from Galilee, out of the city of Nazareth, into Judea, to the city of David, which is called Bethlehem, because he was of the house and lineage of David,

5   to be registered with Mary, his betrothed wife, who was with child.

6   So it was, that while they were there, the days were completed for her to be delivered.

7   And she brought forth her firstborn Son, and wrapped Him in swaddling cloths, and laid Him in a manger, because there was no room for them in the inn.

8   Now there were in the same country shepherds living out in the fields, keeping watch over their flock by night.

9   **And behold, an angel of the Lord stood before them, and the glory of the Lord shone around them, and they were greatly afraid.**

10   **Then the angel said to them, "Do not be afraid, for behold, I bring you good tidings of great joy which will be to all people.**

11   **"For there is born to you this day in the city of David a Savior, who is Christ the Lord."**

The city of David is also known as Bethlehem, and Bethlehem is not in Arabia, but in Palestine. This was the Bible's prophecy of how the Messiah would come, but Mr. Muhammad says that he came from the city of Mecca, in Arabia, in 1930. How can that be, when Luke's Gospel was written long before 1930? And if Allah gave Mr. Muhammad this, and Allah is the same as Jehovah God, and Jehovah God is the author of the Bible, then Jehovah and Allah are both confused!

It is also interesting to note that Luke meticulously establishes the historical circumstances surrounding the birth of Jesus, relating it to events in the Roman Empire. In Luke 2:1, it says: **"And it came to pass in those days...."** If it had just said, "It came to pass in those days," then we might not know when "those days" were. But the Holy Spirit gives us a further line of demarcation in Luke 2:1-3:

1   *...that* **a decree went out from Caesar Augustus that all the world should be registered.**

2   **This census first took place while Quirinius was governing Syria.**

3   **So all went to be registered, everyone to his own city.**

What's interesting about that? It is that Caesar Augustus was emperor from 30 B.C. until 14 A.D. Quirinius was governor of Syria from 10 B.C. to 7 B.C. and later served a second term from 6 A.D. to 9 A.D. Jesus was born (or came) somewhere between 6 and 14 A.D — not 1930! And we have historical documentation to prove this by virtue of the evidence relating to those in power at the time, both in Rome and Judea.

Mr. Muhammad further wrote, "Islam is our salvation."[18] If Mr. Muhammad was writing under inspiration from Allah, and the Bible is written under the inspiration of Jehovah God, then I don't know how they can be the same person when they are giving us conflicting information. Generally speaking, when using historical evidence, the document that comes first carries the greatest weight — has more authenticity — simply because it came first. So when Mr. Muhammad wrote "Islam is our salvation," then Muhammad must be our savior. If that is true, the Bible should say the same thing.

But it doesn't say the same thing. In Acts 4:12, we find:

> **"Nor is there salvation in any other, for there is no other name** [i.e., other than Jesus Christ] **under heaven given among men by which we must be saved."**

Again, the context makes clear that the phrase "no other name" refers to no other name except Jesus Christ, not W. D. Fard. My question is, "Whose report will you believe?"

Mr. Muhammad goes on to write, "…the greatest hindrance to the truth of our people is the preacher of Christianity." But the Bible says in Romans 10:13-15:

> **13**   For *"whoever calls on the name of the Lord shall be saved."*

> **14**   **How then shall they call on Him in whom they have not believed? And how shall they believe**

---

[18] Muhammad, 18.

> in Him of whom they have not heard? And
> how shall they hear without a preacher?

> **15**   And how shall they preach unless they are
> sent? As it is written: *"How beautiful are the
> feet of those who preach the gospel of peace,
> who bring glad tidings of good things!"*

I don't know how Allah, if he is Jehovah, would write something
that would say that the greatest hindrance is the preacher of Christianity, in
the face of the Bible saying **"…how shall they preach unless they are
sent?"** or **"…how shall they hear without a preacher?"** That seems to
me to be in conflict with what Mr. Muhammad said.

Mr. Muhammad goes on to write under the heading, "The
Coming of Allah (God)": "…If we believe that He is a spirit and not
a man, then we can never expect to have any knowledge of Him
except by sense of feel.…"

Just in passing, you do know, don't you, that "feelings" are
not the same as "spirit?" Feeling is a sensory perception. The phi-
losopher John Locke once wrote in the *Essay Concerning Human
Understanding* that we can't know anything except by the five senses,
and this gave people all sorts of strange reasons to try to find God
through nature and the senses.[19]

But your spirit is not the same as your physical senses. The
spirit world is completely different from the material world of the
senses. That is why believing is completely different from seeing,
and 2 Corinthians 5:7 says, **"For we walk by faith, not by sight,"**
which means there must be a difference between "faith" and "sight."
Put another way, "We walk by faith, not by our sensory perceptions of the physical world." So right there you know something is

---

[19] John Locke, *An Essay Concerning Human Understanding*, abridged
and edited by A.S. Pringle-Pattison (Oxford, Clarendon Press, 1924),
17 and passim.

wrong with Mr. Muhammad's comment that "…we can never expect to have any knowledge of Him [meaning God] except by the
sense of feel…." Anyway, to continue, with Mr. Muhammad's
words:

> We cannot see a spirit; therefore, the teachings of His
> coming would be false. The spirit of life is and has been
> with us all of our lives. God is in person among us to-
> day. *He is a man,* [emphasis mine] He is in His time. God
> sees, hears, knows, wills, acts and is a person (man).
> The evil workings of the devil MUST come to an end.[20]

Before we look at anything else, note that Mr. Muhammad
says of God, "He is a man." Yet Jesus said of God, "God is a Spirit."
In John, Chapter 4, Jesus is talking to the woman at the well in
Samaria, and for this passage I want to use the King James, not the
New King James, version of the Bible, because it gives a clearer
picture based on our knowledge about spirits. Jesus says to the woman
in John 4:24:

> **God *is a* Spirit: and they that worship him must wor-
> ship *him* in spirit and in truth.**

Elijah Muhammad says God is a man. Jesus said God is a
Spirit. That's conflicting. The only thing we need to do is ask the
question, Who lived first and who was with God first, Elijah
Muhammad or Jesus? The revelation that Mr. Muhammad received,
he received from Wallace Fard Muhammad, who came on the scene
in 1930. This is approximately 1,930 years after Jesus Christ said,
"God is a Spirit…." Mr. Muhammad comes later and says, "God is a
man and not a spirit…." The next question would simply be: Who
was with God in the beginning to know who and what God is and
what God is not? In John 1:1, it is written: **In the beginning….** How

---

[20] Muhammad, 15.

far back is the beginning? It's at the beginning, and that means it's starting out.

It says: **In the beginning was the Word.…** If you look at the word *Word* in the original Greek language, it is the word *logos*, and it refers to Jesus Christ in eternity past. It does not refer to the physical flesh-and-blood Jesus who walked the earth, who turned the water into wine, who cleansed the lepers, who was crucified and died on the cross, but the Jesus who dwelt in that physical body of the one we've come to know as Jesus the Christ. He was already in existence before He came to this life and took upon Himself a physical body. He's called the *logos*, the second person of the Godhead, who was with God in eternity past.

We could say it like this: "In the beginning was the Word (Jesus) and the Word (Jesus) was with God, and the Word (Jesus) was God." Now I have found no writings or teachings where Mr. Elijah Muhammad claimed to be with Allah in the beginning. But the Bible says that Jesus was with the Father in the beginning. So if Jesus was with God in the beginning, and Mr. Elijah Muhammad didn't come along until 1,930 years after the flesh-and-blood Jesus was born, it would seem reasonable to me to believe that whoever was with God in the beginning ought to know who God is and who God is not! The one who was with Him (Jesus) said, **"God *is* a Spirit.…"** The one who "was not" with God in the beginning, Mr. Muhammad, said, "God is a man.…" There seems to be a conflict between Jesus and Mr. Elijah Muhammad. They couldn't be representing the same God. Whose report will you believe?

Mr. Muhammad tells us, quoting Matthew 24:27, in "Allah is God: The Coming of the Son of Man, the Great Mahdi": **"For as the lightning cometh out of the east, and shineth even unto the west, so shall also the coming of the Son of man be."** He then writes:

> You must forget about ever seeing the return of Jesus, Who was here 2,000 years ago. Set your heart on seeing the One that He prophesied would come at the end of the present world's time (the white race's time). He is

called the "Son of Man," the "Christ," the "Comforter."
You are really foolish to be looking to see the return of
the Prophet Jesus. It is the same as looking for the return of Abraham, Moses and Muhammad. All of these
prophets prophesied the coming of Allah or one with
equal power, under many names. You must remember
that Jesus could not have been referring to Himself as
returning to the people in the last days.[21]

Once again, if Jehovah and Allah are the same God,
manifesting themselves through the Bible and the Koran, then
Jehovah and Allah won't contradict each other.

Mr. Muhammad says, "...You must forget about ever seeing
the return of Jesus, Who was here 2,000 years ago.... You must remember that Jesus could not have been referring to Himself as returning to the people in the last days." Yet these statements are beyond belief, in light of Bible statements to the contrary. For instance,
Jesus, speaking in John 14:1-3, says:

1   **"Let not your heart be troubled; you believe
     in God, believe also in Me.**

2   **"In My Father's house are many mansions; if
     it were not so, I would have told you. I go to
     prepare a place for you.**

3   **"And if I go and prepare a place for you, I will
     come again and receive you to Myself....**

The question, is who ought to know more about a person —
the person himself or someone living 1,930 years later? Jesus Himself
said, **"I will come again."** Mr. Elijah Muhammad says, "...forget about
ever seeing the return of Jesus, Who was here 2,000 years ago...."
So we know he's talking about the same Jesus Christ who was here
2,000 years ago, according to the Bible.

---

[21] Muhammad, 10.

Not only did Mr. Muhammad say that "You must forget about ever seeing the return of Jesus," but he also wrote that "You must remember that Jesus could not have been referring to Himself as returning to the people in the last days."[22]

That's a strong statement. In essence, Mr. Muhammad is saying Jesus didn't mean what He said. And let's be honest here, this isn't a matter of interpretation, in that Jesus used plain language: **"...I will come again and receive you to Myself."** So we have what Mr. Muhammad says to the black man in America.

But what does the Bible say to the black man in America? In the Book of Acts 1:1-11, we find:

1   **The former account I made, O Theophilus, of all that Jesus began both to do and teach,**

2   **until the day in which He was taken up, after He through the Holy Spirit had given commandments to the apostles whom He had chosen,**

3   **to whom He also presented Himself alive after His suffering by many infallible proofs, being seen by them during forty days and speaking of the things pertaining to the kingdom of God.**

4   **And being assembled together with *them*, He commanded them not to depart from Jerusalem, but to wait for the Promise of the Father, "which," *He said*, "you have heard from Me;**

5   **"for John truly baptized with water, but you shall be baptized with the Holy Spirit not many days from now."**

---

[22] Muhammad, 10.

6   Therefore, when they had come together,
      they asked Him, saying, "Lord, will You at
      this time restore the kingdom to Israel?"

7   And He said to them, "It is not for you to
      know times or seasons which the Father has
      put in His own authority.

8   "But you shall receive power when the Holy
      Spirit has come upon you; and you shall be
      witnesses to Me in Jerusalem, and in all Judea
      and Samaria, and to the end of the earth."

9   Now when He had spoken these things, while
      they watched, He was taken up, and a cloud
      received Him out of their sight.

10   And while they looked steadfastly toward
      heaven as He went up, behold, two men stood
      by them in white apparel,

11   who also said, "Men of Galilee, why do you
      stand gazing up into heaven? This *same* Jesus,
      who was taken up from you into heaven, will
      so come in like manner as you saw Him go into
      heaven."

Mr. Muhammad says to forget about ever seeing the Man again, while the two angels said, "This same Jesus shall come!" Whose report will you believe?

The Bible says in 2 Corinthians 13:1, *"By the mouth of two or three witnesses every word shall be established."* I've given you John, where Jesus Himself said He was coming back, and Acts, where the angels said He was coming back. But I want to give you a third witness, from 1 Corinthians 11:23-26:

23   For I received from the Lord that which I also
      delivered to you: that the Lord Jesus on the

same night in which He was betrayed, took
bread;

24 and when He had given thanks, He broke *it* and
said, "Take, eat; this is My body which is broken
for you; do this in remembrance of Me."

25 In the same manner *He* also *took* the cup after
supper, saying, "This cup is the new covenant
in My blood. This do, as often as you drink *it*,
in remembrance of Me."

26   For as often as you eat this bread and drink
this cup, you proclaim the Lord's death till He
comes.

Will you please tell me what **till He comes** means? Doesn't
that imply that He plans to come back? And He wants you to do this
until He gets back? Mr. Muhammad said, "…you must forget about
ever seeing the return of Jesus…." Whose report will you believe?

Mr. Muhammad continues writing under the heading "Allah
is God: The Origin of God as a Spirit and Not a Man": "Take heed to
yourselves, that your hearts be not deceived, and you turn aside, and
serve other gods; worship them." Again, Mr. Muhammad quotes the
Bible — in this case, the book of Deuteronomy 11:16. He writes:

The great archdeceivers (the white race) were taught by
their father, Yakub, 6,000 years ago, how to teach that
God is a spirit (spook) and not a man. In the grafting of
his people (the white race), Mr. Yakub taught his people
to contend with us over the reality of God by asking us
[meaning black people] of the whereabouts of that first One
(God) who created the heavens and the earth, and that,
Yakub said, we cannot do. Well, we all know that there
was a God in the beginning that created all these things
and do know that He does not exist today. But we know
again that from that God the person of God continued
until today in His people, and today a Supreme One

(God) has appeared among us with the same infinite wisdom to bring about a complete change.... If Jesus were a Son of God, what about Moses and the other prophets? Were they not His Sons since they were His prophets?[23]

Let me note here that just because someone is a prophet that doesn't make him your son. But to continue, Mr. Muhammad contends, "...we all know that there was a God in the beginning that created all these things and do know that He does not exist today." So I have a question: Does the Bible have anything to say about this assertion by Mr. Muhammad? In Genesis 1:1, it is written:

In the beginning God created the heavens and the earth.

Well, Mr. Muhammad said that God was the Creator in the beginning, so the Bible says the same thing. But Mr. Muhammad then said, "He does not exist today." Oh really? What does the Bible say? Genesis 21:33 records this:

Then *Abraham* planted a tamarisk tree in Beersheba, and there called on the name of the Lord, the Everlasting God.

Mr. Muhammad says that God doesn't exist today, but the Bible says He's everlasting. If He's an everlasting God, He has to exist today. Again, following the biblical pattern, we need to give more than one witness. So we find, in Exodus 3:15:

Moreover God said to Moses, "Thus you shall say to the children of Israel: 'The LORD God of your fathers, the God of Abraham, the God of Isaac, and the God of Jacob, has sent me to you. This *is* My name forever, and this *is* My memorial to all generations.' "

---

[23] Muhammad, 9.

If God does not exist today, then how can He be forever and how can it accrue to all generations? It would have to have stopped when He stopped being God, correct? **"This *is* My name forever, and this *is* My memorial to all generations."** How many generations are left out of "all generations?" Not one. In fact, aren't we, in our time, a generation? So this applies to us, too, doesn't it? Then God must exist today if it's all generations. But Mr. Muhammad said: "...we all know...He does not exist today...."

I have yet another witness for you, though. In Exodus 15:18, it says, **"The Lᴏʀᴅ shall reign forever and ever."** Don't you know that it would have been enough to say, "The Lord shall reign forever." Doesn't that tell you that forever is forever? Now, my understanding in English of the meaning of forever is that it doesn't stop. And notice God's superlatives. He says: **"The Lᴏʀᴅ shall reign forever and ever."** He didn't have to say "and ever," because forever is ever. But he wanted us to know it in a way that we wouldn't forget that He is the Lord who reigns forever *and* ever.

In Deuteronomy 33:27, the Bible makes this startling statement:

> **The eternal God *is your* refuge, and underneath *are* the everlasting arms; He will thrust out the enemy from before you, and will say, 'Destroy!'**

Now notice what He calls Himself. He doesn't say the "sometime God," the "short-version God" or the God "until"; He says **"the eternal God."** Eternal means forever! Notice the next clause: **"...and underneath are the everlasting arms...."** Now how long is everlasting? If Allah is the same God that the Christians follow, we've got a real problem here, because one of these gods is confused. I didn't say which one; I'll let you make that decision. In Psalm 90:1-2, we have another revealing statement:

> 1   **Lᴏʀᴅ, You have been our dwelling place in all generations.**

2   **Before the mountains were brought forth, or ever
You had formed the earth and the world, even
from everlasting to everlasting. You *are* God.**

Notice that the verse didn't say, "You *were* God," past tense,
but rather, **You *are* God,** present tense. Mr. Muhammad said: "…we
all know that there was a God in the beginning that created all these
things and do know that He does not exist today." We will look now
at Isaiah 40:28:

> **Have you not known? Have you not heard? The ever-
> lasting God, the LORD, the Creator of the ends of the
> earth, neither faints nor is weary. His understanding
> is unsearchable.**

Now get this: We know that this is the same God that Mr.
Elijah Muhammad is referring to because he admitted that He (God)
was the Creator and created all these things. He said it:

> "…we all know that there was a God…that created all
> these things and do know that He does not exist today."

But we just read Isaiah, where it is written, **Have you not
known? Have you not heard? The everlasting God, the LORD, the
Creator of the ends of the earth….**

This is the same God that Elijah Muhammad is talking about,
and He says, in His word, that He is "everlasting." Now how can He
be everlasting and Mr. Muhammad says, "He does not exist today?"
I have a problem with that. Either one of the two witnesses, Isaiah or
Elijah Muhammad, is mistaken or lying, because each of them,
speaking prophetically, gives a different account.

According to Mr. Muhammad, "…we all know that there
was a God in the beginning that created all these things and do know
that He does not exist today." The One who "created" all things —
that's the word that ties it together. We know we're talking about the
same God. I have one more passage of Scripture that I think puts the
icing on the cake concerning this issue. It's found in Jeremiah 10:10:

But the LORD *is* the true God; He *is* the living God and the everlasting King. At His wrath the earth will tremble, and the nations will not be able to endure His indignation.

Let's consider this phrase, **But the LORD is the true God; He is the living God....**

Apparently, there are some false gods, because if there were no false gods, Jeremiah wouldn't have to qualify God with "true." Also, notice that it says "living God." So there must be some dead gods. I wonder which God is the true and living God — Allah or Jehovah? It's your call.

Mr. Muhammad says that the Creator God, who was in the beginning, doesn't exist today. But the true God says He does exist today! Moreover, the Scripture in Jeremiah also says, **But the LORD *is* the true God; He *is* the living God and the everlasting King....** If He is everlasting, He must still exist today. So again we have a conflict between what Mr. Muhammad says about God and what God says about Himself.

Mr. Muhammad goes on to state under the heading "Allah is God, Who is That Mystery God? Part II": "Did God say that He was a Mystery God, or did someone say it of Him? Did God say that He was only a Spirit, or did someone say it of Him? If He were a Spirit and not a man, we would all be spirits and not human beings!"[24] It appears Mr. Muhammad has not accurately read the Bible, which clearly states that God is a Spirit, and so is man. If Mr. Muhammad were a true prophet sent from God, "Allah," and if Allah was the true God, the living God, the everlasting God, wouldn't the true God know what He had created? Wouldn't He know whether He had created us as spirits or just human beings?

In John 4:24 (KJV), it records the fact that Jesus, speaking to the woman at the well in Samaria, referred to God as follows: **"...God**

---

[24] Muhammad, 4-5.

is a Spirit…." John also says, in Chapter 1, Verse 1, **In the beginning was the Word,** [*logos* in Greek, which refers to Jesus, the second person of the Godhead in eternity past] **and the Word was with God….** If the Word, Jesus, was "with God," then the Word should know who, or what, God was or wasn't. In John 4:24, which we just read, Jesus Himself said, **"…God is a Spirit…."** But Mr. Muhammad says, "God is a man and not a spirit…." Jesus says God is a Spirit. Somebody is confused here.

There is still more to this, though. Mr. Elijah Muhammad says that we are human beings and not spirits. The Bible says otherwise. In 1 Thessalonians 5:23, it is written:

> **Now may the God of peace Himself sanctify you completely;** [King James Version says "wholly," which means completely] **and may your whole spirit, soul, and body be preserved blameless at the coming of our Lord Jesus Christ.**

This means that man is a tripartite being, composed of three parts: spirit, soul, and body. Notice that spirit comes first. Remember, Jesus said, **"God is a Spirit."** So if God is a Spirit, and not a man, then God would always start with where and Who He is and move out to what He isn't. God always starts with spirit. Man always starts with the body and attempts to work to the inside and never gets there.

Do you recall earlier that Mr. Elijah Muhammad said that "…we can never expect to have any knowledge of Him [God] except by *sense of feel* [emphasis added]"? Here again, feelings are of the body — the outside, working in — while God deals with people through the spirit, working out. Mr. Muhammad says that if God were a spirit, then we would be spirits and not human beings.

The Bible, in fact, says we *are* spirits, we *have* souls, and we *live* inside bodies. What you see when you look at Fred Price is not me. You only see the house I live in. It is true that our bodies must have some characteristics of our spirit, because we know we will recognize people in heaven, so our spirits must look something like

25

our physical bodies. But we are not bodies, nor are we souls. We are spirits, and God is a Spirit.

Genesis 1:26 gives further illumination on this subject:

> **Then God said, "Let Us make man in Our image, according to Our likeness; let them have dominion over the fish of the sea, over the birds of the air, and over the cattle, over all the earth and over every creeping thing that creeps on the earth."**

Notice in the first part of the verse it is written: **Then God said, "Let Us make man in Our image, according to Our likeness…."** So I must look like God, because I'm made in His image. Jesus said God is a Spirit. If God made me in His image, then, I must be like God, and that means I must be a spirit.

In order to live in the three-dimensional earth realm, you need an "earth suit," which is called the body. You don't need a body to be you, but you do need a body to live here. I'll repeat that. You do not need a body to be you. But to live on earth as God created you requires a body. In Numbers 23:19, we find:

> **"God *is* not a man, that He should lie, nor a son of man, that He should repent. Has He said, and will He not do? Or has He spoken, and will He not make it good?"**

Read again part of that 19th Verse: **"God *is* not a man…."** Yet, Elijah Muhammad said that God is a man and not a spirit. The Bible says otherwise: In 1 Samuel 15:28-29, it is written:

> **28   So Samuel said to him** [Saul], **"The LORD has torn the kingdom of Israel from you today, and has given it to a neighbor of yours, *who is* better than you.**
>
> **29   "And also the Strength of Israel will not lie nor relent. For He *is* not a man, that He should relent."**

So again, Elijah Muhammad says God is a man, and that He's not a Spirit. The Bible says repeatedly that God is not a man, and that He is a Spirit. Whose report will you believe?

To continue our analysis of *Message to the Blackman in America*, Mr. Muhammad makes an astounding statement about who was the first man, under the heading, "Original Man: Who is the Original Man?":

> The original man, Allah has declared, is none other than the black man. The black man is the first and last, maker and owner of the universe. From him came all brown, yellow, red and white people. By using a special method of birth control law, the black man was able to produce the white race.[25]

This is an astounding statement! I don't know when the material contained in this book was first proclaimed by Mr. Muhammad, but what is vitally important is the fact that he states many things in his 1965 edition relative to historical events that places the credibility of everything he says in doubt. He is called the messenger of God (Allah), and therefore, I would think that if he were Allah's messenger, he would be getting his message directly from Allah or God, whoever God is. God is divine and should know the future as easily as we humans know the past. Based on that, God's messenger, speaking on behalf of God, could never predict or prophesy something that would be proven historically untrue.

In *Message to the Blackman in America*, Mr. Muhammad makes a statement that illustrates my point. I think it is vitally important that every Christian, Muslim, and those who would become members of the Nation of Islam, examine this statement closely. He writes, under the heading, "Devil: The Making of Devil":

---

[25] Muhammad, 53.

> She [America] holds a whole nation (so-called Negroes), prisoner, and refuses to open the door of freedom, justice, and equality to them. She threatens to go to war against other nations who hold any of her citizens prisoners. They now boast of building rockets to land on our moon (which *can't and won't be done)*; [emphasis mine] and to build a small contraption to try circling the earth like our moon, which *we have made to revolve around the earth* [emphasis mine].[26]

I hope you read that carefully. People are making decisions about their eternal future — about Christianity or Islam. These are life choices. Now, if this man is speaking as the messenger of Allah, as he claims, it would seem to me that Allah would have known that in 1969 Neil Armstrong would set foot on the moon, and therefore Allah would not have put something false in print for all posterity to read. Keep in mind, Mr. Muhammad wrote this — supposedly under inspiration from Allah — in 1965 or earlier.

Again, let me be clear: I'm not coming against the man. But if he were a messenger of Allah and he's giving me a message, because I'm a black man in America, and he wants me to follow his message, then he better give me some information that can be validated. For Mr. Muhammad to make a statement such as the one we just read — that there will be no moon voyages (let alone the subsequent statement that humans — "we" — made the moon to revolve around the earth — places Mr. Muhammad in the light of a false prophet. I'm not calling him one, but his statement places him in that position. Deuteronomy 18:20-22 comments on this:

> **20**   **'But the prophet who presumes to speak a word in My name, which I have not commanded him to speak, or who speaks in the name of other gods, that prophet shall die.'**

---

[26] Muhammad, 110.

21   "And if you say in your heart, 'How shall we know the word which the LORD has not spoken?'

22   "when a prophet speaks in the name of the LORD, if the thing does not happen or come to pass, that *is* the thing which the LORD has not spoken; the prophet has spoken it presumptuously; you shall not be afraid of him."

Likewise, we find in Jeremiah 28:9:

"As for the prophet who prophesies of peace, when the word of the prophet comes to pass, the prophet will be known *as* one whom the LORD has truly sent."

In other words, the prophecies of a prophet who claims to be of God or a prophet of Allah must come to pass if we are to validate that he is truly sent.

Mr. Muhammad says that "they" are thinking about building rockets to go to the moon *"(which can't and won't be done)."* The man who is the fountainhead from which the Nation of Islam has sprung prophesied that sending a rocket to the moon could not be done. His prophecy has proven by facts to be inaccurate. Which of his other prophecies or teachings are inaccurate, or just plain wrong? He has already said that we humans "have made [the moon] to revolve around the earth." Excuse me? Where is that found? I never saw in Genesis where God authorized man to tell the stars and planets and moon what to do. God made the heavens and the earth, and since He set everything in motion, it is obvious that God, not "we" (humans), made the moon to revolve around the earth.

Let's be generous. There are those "conspiracy theorists" who claim that the Apollo moon landing never took place — that it was faked in some television studio. Never mind that Neil Armstrong, many astronauts after him, and thousands of support people at the

Johnson Space Center in Houston have personal eyewitness evidence of having landed on the moon, and have mountains of scientific data from the moon landings. Let's leave that aside for a minute.

How about Mr. Muhammad's statement, again, in 1965 when it was published, that "Now they boast of building rockets to land on our moon (which *can't and won't be done* [emphasis mine]) and to build a small contraption to try circling the earth like our moon...."

The history books that I can find on almost any shelf show that eight years before this book was published — in 1957 — the Soviet Union placed in orbit around the earth the first satellite, called *Sputnik.* Just a few years later, they placed the first man, Yuri Gagarin, in orbit around the earth, and we followed that by sending John Glenn up to orbit the earth. Now they could track these objects, and track these men, maintaining constant visual and radio communication with them. There is no way those orbits were faked. Now, it's bad enough that Mr. Muhammad couldn't get the future right, but here it appears he didn't even know the recent past!

I would think that God would not give His messenger a message that would prove over time to be inaccurate, or that contradicts history that so many people alive today would have lived through. But here we have two completely inaccurate predictions: 1) that men would not land on the moon — they did; and 2) that men would not put a contraption, as he called it, around the earth to circle like our moon — which they did.

In fact, for many years the Soviet Union had in permanent orbit around the earth a primitive space station that had people in it at all times, and our own astronauts docked there, working with those Russians, on many occasions.

As astounding as what we have already found out regarding Mr. Elijah Muhammad's prophecies, I have even more shocking information for your consideration. In 1997, *Message to the Blackman in America* was reprinted. The copyright page reads as follows: "*Message to the Blackman in America*, copyright 1965, by Elijah Muhammad; published and reprinted 1997 by Messenger

Elijah Muhammad Propagation Society (M.E.M.P.S.)."[27] What is interesting about this reprint is that there is a *glaring* omission of a statement by Mr. Muhammad, which I believe damages his credibility as a *true* prophet of God (Allah). I want to quote again from the 1965 edition, just so you have it fresh in your memory. You recall that Mr. Muhammad made a bold *prophetic* declaration about satellites and moon landings under the heading, "Devil: The Making of Devil":

> She holds a whole nation, (so-called Negroes) prisoner, and refuses to open the door of freedom, justice and equality to them. She threatens to go to war against other nations who hold any of her citizens prisoners. They now boast of building rockets to land on our moon (which can't and won't be done); and to build a small contraption to try circling the earth like our moon, which we have made to revolve around the earth.

Now look at the 1997 edition, on the same page:

> She holds a whole nation (so-called Negroes) prisoner, and refuses to open the door of freedom, justice and equality to them. She threatens to go to war against other nations who hold any of her citizens prisoner. They now boast of building rockets to land on the moon, and to build a small contraption....

Do you see anything missing? Did you notice that the statement "(which can't and won't be done)" was eliminated? In fact, the way it now reads, it's as if Mr. Muhammad admits that they have built rockets to land on the moon. Why? If that 1965 message was from Allah, through the messenger of Allah, would you have to take out a phrase? Do you know why the editors took out that phrase?

---

[27] Elijah Muhammad, *Message to the Blackman in America* (Messenger Elijah Muhammad Propagation Society (M.E.M.P.S.), 1997), claiming to be a reprint of the 1965 edition.

Because by 1997, we had landed many men on the moon, and this would make the prophet a false prophet. Does this mean that many black people are following a false prophet who changes his mind? You be the judge.

What does the Bible say about God changing the message that He gives His prophets? In Malachi 3:6, we see that God says, **"For I *am* the LORD, I do not change...."** It is interesting that this statement is not in the Koran. Nowhere in the Koran does it say anything to the effect that Allah does not change, and I've read it cover to cover. I've read every jot and tittle, every semicolon. In the Old Testament, there are all kinds of predictions. Some have already come to pass and are historically documented — the destruction of Jerusalem in 70 A.D., for example, the Babylonian captivity of the Jews, the restoration of the nation of Israel in 1947. Other prophecies are still yet to be fulfilled. But Mr. Muhammad said, "(which can't and won't be done)," so that is a categorical statement and he is supposedly speaking for Allah. Well, if he was wrong on that point, who's to say he isn't wrong on others? And when you say you are the messenger of Allah, and put something in print that is wrong, you're in trouble unless you retract your statement.

But there is more evidence of questionable prophetic powers on the part of Mr. Muhammad. Under the heading, "The Judgment: The Day of America's Downfall," he writes, "The years 1965 and 1966 are going to be fateful for America, bringing in the 'Fall of America'."[28] So apparently America fell. You didn't know that? America fell in 1965 or 1966, so we're not actually here. I mean, we cannot be in America, because America fell. I don't know about you, but on July 4th, of the year 2000, I watched celebrations across this country marking the 224th birthday of the United States. So it must have been some other America that fell, because this one — warts and all — is still here.

---

[28] Muhammad, 270.

This is not to belittle Mr. Muhammad, but when you purport to speak on behalf of God, you better know what you are talking about and you better be able to prove it. Moses would have looked stupid if he threw down his staff in Pharaoh's court and it stayed a hunk of wood. Mr. Muhammad was wrong about moon landings, wrong about orbiting satellites, wrong about the fall of America. What else is he wrong about?

Under the heading "Prayer Service: The Opening," Mr. Muhammad says:

> And now, take notice of those who call themselves Christians going astray from the right path (Islam). Notice them going to the extreme by worshiping Jesus: first by falsely accusing Jesus of being the Son of Allah (God) born without the agency of man, thus accusing God of an act of adultery. They preach the rightful laws of God, but practice the laws of Satan and now have become the world's greatest trouble makers (war makers), and have caused the nations to deviate from the path of Allah (God). And now they are heading the entire world into total destruction.[29]

Notice what Mr. Muhammad says: "…Christians…accusing Jesus of being the Son of Allah (God)…." His statement is not accurate! Christians did not come up with the idea of calling Jesus the Son of God — both God and Jesus did! Let's let the Bible speak on this issue. In Matthew 3:13-17, it is written:

13   **Then Jesus came from Galilee to John at the Jordan to be baptized by him.**

14   **And John *tried to* prevent Him, saying, "I need to be baptized by You, and are You coming to me?"**

---

[29] Muhammad, 151.

15   But Jesus answered and said to him, "Permit *it to be so* now, for thus it is fitting for us to fulfill all righteousness." Then he allowed Him.

16   When He had been baptized, Jesus came up immediately from the water; and behold, the heavens were open to Him, and He saw the Spirit of God descending like a dove and alighting upon Him.

17   And suddenly a voice *came* from heaven, saying, "This is My beloved Son, in whom I am well pleased."

Christians didn't say, "This is My beloved Son;" God said it. My assumption is that if the voice said, "This is My...Son," then it either had to be His mother talking or His father talking. Since God is always referred to in the masculine gender as "Him" or "He," it would have to be His father speaking.

Let's look at another passage of Scripture, Matthew 27:41-43:

41   Likewise the chief priests also, mocking with the scribes and elders, said,

42   "He saved others; Himself He cannot save. If He is the King of Israel, let Him now come down from the cross, and we will believe Him.

43   "He trusted in God; let Him deliver Him now if He will have Him; for He said, 'I am the Son of God.' "

These are the people who lived in Jesus' day, and they heard Him say He was the Son of God. It wasn't Christians that said Jesus was the Son of God. Both Jesus and God said it. In Luke 9:28-35, we find this statement:

28   Now it came to pass, about eight days after these sayings, that He took Peter, John, and James and went up on the mountain to pray.

29   As He prayed, the appearance of His face was altered, and His robe became white *and* glistening.

30   And behold, two men talked with Him, who were Moses and Elijah,

31   who appeared in glory and spoke of His decease which He was about to accomplish at Jerusalem.

32   But Peter and those with Him were heavy with sleep; and when they were fully awake, they saw His glory and the two men who stood with Him.

33   Then it happened, as they were parting from Him, *that* Peter said to Jesus, "Master, it is good for us to be here; and let us make three tabernacles: one for You, one for Moses, and one for Elijah" — not knowing what he said.

34   While he was saying this, a cloud came and overshadowed them; and they were fearful as they entered the cloud.

35   And a voice came out of the cloud, saying, "This is My beloved Son. Hear Him!"

Who do you think was speaking? A Christian? Do you think that was a Christian who said that out of the cloud? There couldn't have even been any Christians then, because Jesus hadn't died yet, so no one could accept Him as personal Savior and Lord. So if He said, "My Son," again, either His mother or father is speaking, and since all the references in the Bible to God are masculine, I'd have to believe it was the Father — not Christians.

These are important observations. Whose report will you believe? There are some problems here as far as I can see. Allah or Jehovah — one of them is mixed up. Someone's confused. Jesus wasn't confused about who He was. In John 10:34-36, it says:

> **34** **Jesus answered them, "Is it not written in your law, *'I said, "You are gods"'*?**
>
> **35** **"If He called them gods, to whom the word of God came (and the Scripture cannot be broken),**
>
> **36** **"do you say of Him whom the Father sanctified and sent into the world, 'You are blaspheming,' because I said, 'I am the Son of God'?"**

It wasn't Christians who called Jesus the Son of God; we got that from the Bible. Jesus called Himself the Son of God, and the Father calls Him the Son of God. It wasn't Christians. So Mr. Muhammad is in error on that one too.

Mr. Muhammad further states that "…Christians…falsely accused Jesus of being…the Son of Allah (God) born without the agency of man, thus accusing God of an act of adultery." Remember what Mr. Muhammad has said about God, about Allah. God is not a spirit; God is a man, and men do commit adultery. That's why he could think that, because his perception of God is that God is a man and not a spirit. So if God is a man, I can understand how Mr. Muhammad could think that God committed adultery. But that's an awesome accusation against Allah, if Allah and Jehovah are one and the same. This is an awesome accusation in light of the fact that the Bible never said that God had sexual intercourse with Mary. Never! In order for God to be guilty of committing adultery with Mary, He would have to have had sexual intercourse with her. What does the Bible say about it?

In Luke 1:26-38, we find:

26   **Now in the sixth month the angel Gabriel was sent by God to a city of Galilee named Nazareth,**

27   **to a virgin betrothed to a man whose name was Joseph, of the House of David. The virgin's name *was* Mary.**

28   **And having come in, the angel said to her, "Rejoice, highly favored *one*, the Lord *is* with you; blessed *are* you among women!"**

29   **But when she saw *him*, she was troubled at his saying, and considered what manner of greeting this was.**

30   **Then the angel said to her, "Do not be afraid, Mary, for you have found favor with God.**

31   **"And behold, you will conceive in your womb and bring forth a Son, and shall call His name JESUS.**

32   **"He will be great, and will be called the Son of the Highest...."**

There it is again: Jesus is called the Son of the Highest [God], and not by Christians. The *angel* is saying that He'll be the Son of God.

32   **"...and the Lord God will give Him the throne of His father David.**

33   **"And He will reign over the house of Jacob [Israel] forever, and of His Kingdom there will be no end."**

34   **Then Mary said to the angel, "How can this be, since I do not know a man?"**

35   And the angel answered and said to her, "*The* Holy Spirit will come upon you, and the power of the Highest will overshadow you; therefore, also that Holy One who is to be born will be called the Son of God."

There it is again: Not Christians saying it; this is the angel saying it!

36   "Now indeed, Elizabeth your relative has also conceived a son in her old age; and this is now the sixth month for her who was called barren.

37   "For with God nothing will be impossible."

38   Then Mary said, "Behold, the maidservant of the Lord! Let it be to me according to your word." And the angel departed from her.

I don't see anything in there about God having intercourse with Mary. I didn't see any reference to the angel saying, "The Lord is going to come down here and go to bed with you." Do you see that in there? Go back to Verse 35, where it says, **And the angel answered and said to her, "*The* Holy Spirit will come upon you and the power of the Highest will overshadow you...."**

That word *overshadow* in the Greek is an interesting word. It means "to envelop in a haze of brilliance." In other words, I'm sure that all of us at some point in time have seen in movies, and probably in some old newsreel clips, when they used to detonate atomic bombs. You would see that great big bright flash, and then the mushroom cloud. When the bomb went off, things at ground zero were changed. Well, when the power of Almighty God envelops you, things change. There is nothing in there about adultery.

On another level, though, I don't know why people have such a hard time with this business about the virgin birth of Christ. If God in the beginning could take some dust and, without the aid of a man or a woman, make a man, then without the aid of a woman, take a rib out of the man and make a woman, then I don't see what's the difficulty in God taking a woman and without the aid of a man make another man. If God could create the universe, it looks like He could take care of bringing a baby into the world without the aid of a man. I think this business about adultery is a bit harsh. But we'll get back to this.

For now, let's look at the two books that are the foundation for Christianity and Islam. *The Holy Bible* and the *Holy Koran* [*Qur-an*]. Mr. Muhammad has some strong things to say about the Bible and the Koran. Now remember, Allah and Jehovah are supposed to be one and the same. So their books ought to say the same thing. Is that reasonable? There should be no discrepancy between the two if the author of both books is in fact the same person. They cannot contradict each other or else we're being sold a bill of goods.

Under the heading "The Bible and Holy Qur-an: True Knowledge of Bible and Holy Qur-an:" Mr. Muhammad states:

> **The Holy Qur-an Sharrieff is a revealed book (scripture) given to Muhammad, like the prophets before him....It also gives to us the perfect rule and guidance. One of its names is, "That Which Makes A Distinction," and another, "That Light" or "The Truth." It is the Book for the American so-called Negroes; and it is best that they throw the Bible in the waste pail since they cannot understand it...."[30]**

That's what the Black Muslims are following. (A complete statement of faith from the NOI appears as Appendix A, Page 349-351, "What Muslims Believe," taken from the NOI Website.) This scares me. You're talking about Allah and Jehovah being the same God? I don't think so. I don't even think they are distant acquaintances. Notice that Mr. Muhammad says, "The Holy Qur-an Sharrieff is a revealed book (Scripture) given to Muhammad, like the prophets before him." Mr. Muhammad seems to indicate

---

[30] Muhammad, 90-91.

39

(notice I said *seems*) that the Bible wasn't a revealed book given to the prophets. How does Mr. Muhammad know what or what was not given to Muhammad, the original Muhammad, the originator of Islam? Was he physically there when the Koran was revealed to Muhammad?

Obviously, Mr. Muhammad was not a born-again Christian, because if he were, he would not be a Muslim. It is impossible for him, or for that matter, anyone else who is not a born-again Christian, to be able to understand the Bible. The Bible clearly delineates who can and who cannot understand it. It is a coded book, with a coded message. You can read the Bible in your own native language, but you won't know what you're reading; you won't understand it, you won't be able to, because the Bible is not for everyone. It's only for God's people. And you have to be connected to God to have the spiritual insight to be able to understand what you are reading. You can read the words, but not know their real meaning.

For example, I can read English very well, but if I picked up a technical computer manual, for example, or an advanced textbook in biology, I can read the words, but have no idea what they mean, because I'm not clued in to the scientific or technical language they are using. Likewise, you can read the Bible in English, but if you are not a born-again Christian, if you've never made spiritual contact with God, you cannot understand the Bible. Mr. Muhammad was not born again, because if he were, he would not have made some of the statements he made.

We will now look at the Bible and see if we can determine how one can get in on the code.

There is a qualification. In John 3:1-3, we find the story of Nicodemus:

1   **There was a man of the Pharisees named Nicodemus, a ruler of the Jews.**

2   **This man came to Jesus by night and said to Him, "Rabbi, we know that You are a teacher**

> come from God; for no one can do these signs
> that You do unless God is with him."

3   Jesus answered and said to him, "Most
      assuredly, I say to you, unless one is born again,
      he cannot see the kingdom of God."

Do you know what *cannot* means? You can't do it. Look at the phrase **"he cannot see the kingdom of God."** That word *see* in the Greek is interesting in that it means "come to know." Unless a man is born again, he cannot come to know the things of the Kingdom of God. There is a similar reference to this in 1 Corinthians 2:14:

> But the natural man does not receive the things of the
> Spirit of God, for they are foolishness to him; nor can
> he know *them*, because they are spiritually discerned.

Who is this natural man? The natural man is the man who has never been born again. And the book says the natural man doesn't receive the things of the Spirit of God. In fact, he can't even know them, because they are spiritually discerned. People are trying to discern them with their intellects, with their minds. It will not compute. You'll get an error message.

Mr. Muhammad said, "...and it is best that they throw the Bible in the waste pail since they cannot understand it." That's not true. You can understand it, but only if you have been born again. What an awesome thing for one who supposedly is God's messenger to say about God's Word. Doesn't that tell you something? He's the messenger of Allah. Allah is supposed to be the same as Jehovah, and the Bible is the book of Jehovah, the book of the Christians. Why would he say, "...throw the Bible in the waste pail since they cannot understand it"? Consider this in light of 2 Timothy 3:16-17:

> 16   All Scripture *is* given by inspiration of God,
>   and *is* profitable for doctrine, for reproof, for
>   correction, for instruction in righteousness,

41

17 that the man of God may be complete, thoroughly equipped for every good work.

Right before that, in 2 Timothy 2:15, it is written **"Be diligent to present yourself approved to God, a worker who does not need to be ashamed, rightly dividing the word of truth."** In the traditional King James, it says: **"Study to shew thyself approved unto God, a workman that needeth not to be ashamed...."** Why would God tell you to study something you could not understand? You can only understand the Bible if you are hooked into God through being born from above.

Mr. Muhammad has more to say under the heading "The Bible and Holy Qu-ran: Which One is Right?" What a statement! How could God, or Allah, say, through His messenger, the Bible and the Holy Ko-ran, which one is right? *I thought they were from the same God?* They would both have to be right. If Allah and God were the same person, they would only have one book. Or, at least, if they had two books, the contents of the two books would be the same. Otherwise, you would end up confused.

At any rate, under this heading, "Which One is Right?" Mr. Muhammad writes:

> If the present Bible is the direct Word of God, why isn't God speaking rather than His Prophet Musa (Moses)? Neither does Moses tell us here in the first chapter of Genesis that it is from God. No, we do not find the name Moses mentioned in the chapter. The Bible is the graveyard of my poor people (the so-called Negroes) and I would like to dwell upon this book until I am sure that they understand that it is not quite as holy as they thought it was. I don't mean to say that there is no truth in it; certainly there is plenty of truth, if understood. Will you accept the understanding of it? The Bible charges all of its Great Prophets with evil, it makes God guilty of an act of adultery by charging Him with being the father of Mary's baby (Jesus), again it charges Noah and Lot

with drunkenness, and Lot with getting children by his daughter. What a Poison Book.[31]

And you are going to commit your life to this? I cannot visualize Almighty God calling His own Word a "poison book" under any circumstances. But that's what Mr. Muhammad says. That's strong language. He asked the question, "If the present Bible is the direct Word of God, why isn't God speaking rather than His Prophet Musa (Moses)?" My answer to that question would be the same question he asked. If the present Koran is the direct word of Allah, why isn't Allah speaking instead of the prophet Muhammad?

There are many places where it is supposedly Allah speaking through Muhammad, but there are also places where the angel Gabriel is speaking on behalf of Allah. So right there, that would discredit his argument. If there is one exception, his argument is discredited. Allah spoke through Muhammad. God spoke through Moses. What's the problem?

Continuing his discussion of "The Bible and Holy Qur-an: Which One is Right?" Mr. Muhammad writes:

> The New Testament and Holy Qur-an's teaching of a resurrection of the dead can't mean the people who have died physically and returned to the earth, but rather a mental resurrection of us, the black nation, who are mentally dead to the knowledge of truth; the truth of self, God and the arch-enemy of God and His people.[32]

It appears that Black Muslims do not believe in physical resurrection, or at least their leader did not. You are going to make a change and leave Christianity and go there? That is totally contrary to the Bible. Mr. Muhammad states "…resurrection of the dead can't mean the people who have died physically and returned to the

---

[31] Muhammad, 95.
[32] Muhammad, 97.

earth...." Black Muslims and many black people who are upset with Christianity want to dump it for a system that denies a physical resurrection? I do not see dumping it.

There is nothing wrong with Christianity because there is nothing wrong with Jesus. There may be plenty wrong with the church, and we need to fix that. The church has abused and mis-used the message of Jesus Christ, but that doesn't make anything in the message wrong, and it doesn't make Jesus wrong, and it doesn't make the Bible wrong. It means those men wrongly, sin-fully, and deliberately misinterpreted parts of the Bible for their own ends.

This resurrection issue is extremely important. Is it mental or physi-cal? Look at 1 Corinthians 15:12:

> **Now if Christ is preached that He has been raised from the dead, how do some among you say that there is no resurrection of the dead?**

Mr. Muhammad states, "...resurrection of the dead can't mean the people who have died physically and returned to the earth...." Yet in 1 Corinthians 15:42, it says:

> **So also *is* the resurrection of the dead. *The body* is sown in corruption, it is raised in incorruption.**

We know, then, that this is referring to physical resurrection, not mental resurrection. Muhammad says the resurrection is mental. So again, we have this problem. If Jehovah and Allah are the same person, He is confused. Mr. Muhammad, spokesman for Allah, says the resurrection is mental, while the Bible says it is physical.

Just consider the heading, "The Bible and Holy Qu-ran: Which One is Right?" If we stop right there, we know if one is right, the other is wrong. How could Allah, who is really Jehovah in disguise, ask "Which one is right?"

If Allah is the same God that the Christians serve, but under a different name, and if the Koran, which is the holy book of the

with drunkenness, and Lot with getting children by his
daughter. What a Poison Book.[31]

And you are going to commit your life to this? I cannot visualize
Almighty God calling His own Word a "poison book" under any
circumstances. But that's what Mr. Muhammad says. That's strong
language. He asked the question, "If the present Bible is the direct Word
of God, why isn't God speaking rather than His Prophet Musa (Moses)?"
My answer to that question would be the same question he asked. If the
present Koran is the direct word of Allah, why isn't Allah speaking instead
of the prophet Muhammad?

There are many places where it is supposedly Allah speaking through Muhammad, but there are also places where the angel
Gabriel is speaking on behalf of Allah. So right there, that would
discredit his argument. If there is one exception, his argument is
discredited. Allah spoke through Muhammad. God spoke through
Moses. What's the problem?

Continuing his discussion of "The Bible and Holy Qur-an:
Which One is Right?" Mr. Muhammad writes:

> The New Testament and Holy Qur-an's teaching of a
> resurrection of the dead can't mean the people who have
> died physically and returned to the earth, but rather a
> mental resurrection of us, the black nation, who are men-
> tally dead to the knowledge of truth; the truth of self,
> God and the arch-enemy of God and His people.[32]

It appears that Black Muslims do not believe in physical
resurrection, or at least their leader did not. You are going to make a
change and leave Christianity and go there? That is totally contrary
to the Bible. Mr. Muhammad states "...resurrection of the dead can't
mean the people who have died physically and returned to the

---

[31] Muhammad, 95.
[32] Muhammad, 97.

red people, and brown people are left out of the resurrection. The implication is that the New Testament does not have anything to say about the resurrection except in reference to black people.

We have a simple way of determining whether it is true. If we go to the New Testament, and examine every statement it makes about resurrection, then it ought to be talking about black people and should refer to something mental. Since Mr. Muhammad said that the resurrection was mental and not physical, and since Jehovah and Allah are supposedly the same God, then the New Testament should confirm this position. Of course, it does no such thing. Again, we have this statement by Paul in 1 Corinthians 15:12:

> **Now if Christ is preached that He has been raised from the dead, how do some among you say that there is no resurrection of the dead?**

It is almost as though the Holy Spirit put this in here specifically for commentators such as Mr. Muhammad. Now, in all honesty, the verse does not say "mental" or "physical," but neither does it contain any reference to Blacks in particular. However, other verses do refer to physical resurrection. Let's reread 1 Corinthians 15:42:

> **So also *is* the resurrection of the dead. *The body* [not the mind] is sown in corruption, it [referring to the "body sown in corruption"] is raised in incorruption.**

The phrase **"so also is the resurrection of the dead"** gives us a definition of the resurrection of the dead. We are going to know pretty clearly that whatever comes after that is going to tell us if the "resurrection of the dead" is mental or physical, and if it is referring to black people, red people, or pink people with purple-polka-dots. So what does Verse 42 say?

> **So also *is* the resurrection of the dead. *The body* is sown in corruption, it is raised in incorruption.**

with drunkenness, and Lot with getting children by his
daughter. What a Poison Book.[31]

And you are going to commit your life to this? I cannot visualize
Almighty God calling His own Word a "poison book" under any
circumstances. But that's what Mr. Muhammad says. That's strong
language. He asked the question, "If the present Bible is the direct Word
of God, why isn't God speaking rather than His Prophet Musa (Moses)?"
My answer to that question would be the same question he asked. If the
present Koran is the direct word of Allah, why isn't Allah speaking instead
of the prophet Muhammad?

There are many places where it is supposedly Allah speaking through Muhammad, but there are also places where the angel
Gabriel is speaking on behalf of Allah. So right there, that would
discredit his argument. If there is one exception, his argument is
discredited. Allah spoke through Muhammad. God spoke through
Moses. What's the problem?

Continuing his discussion of "The Bible and Holy Qur-an:
Which One is Right?" Mr. Muhammad writes:

> The New Testament and Holy Qur-an's teaching of a
> resurrection of the dead can't mean the people who have
> died physically and returned to the earth, but rather a
> mental resurrection of us, the black nation, who are men-
> tally dead to the knowledge of truth; the truth of self,
> God and the arch-enemy of God and His people.[32]

It appears that Black Muslims do not believe in physical
resurrection, or at least their leader did not. You are going to make a
change and leave Christianity and go there? That is totally contrary
to the Bible. Mr. Muhammad states "...resurrection of the dead can't
mean the people who have died physically and returned to the

---

[31] Muhammad, 95.
[32] Muhammad, 97.

earth...." Black Muslims and many black people who are upset with Christianity want to dump it for a system that denies a physical resurrection? I do not see dumping it.

There is nothing wrong with Christianity because there is nothing wrong with Jesus. There may be plenty wrong with the church, and we need to fix that. The church has abused and mis-used the message of Jesus Christ, but that doesn't make anything in the message wrong, and it doesn't make Jesus wrong, and it doesn't make the Bible wrong. It means those men wrongly, sin-fully, and deliberately misinterpreted parts of the Bible for their own ends.

This resurrection issue is extremely important. Is it mental or physi-cal? Look at 1 Corinthians 15:12:

> **Now if Christ is preached that He has been raised from the dead, how do some among you say that there is no resurrection of the dead?**

Mr. Muhammad states, "...resurrection of the dead can't mean the people who have died physically and returned to the earth...." Yet in 1 Corinthians 15:42, it says:

> **So also *is* the resurrection of the dead. *The body* is sown in corruption, it is raised in incorruption.**

We know, then, that this is referring to physical resurrection, not mental resurrection. Muhammad says the resurrection is mental. So again, we have this problem. If Jehovah and Allah are the same person, He is confused. Mr. Muhammad, spokesman for Allah, says the resurrection is mental, while the Bible says it is physical.

Just consider the heading, "The Bible and Holy Qu-ran: Which One is Right?" If we stop right there, we know if one is right, the other is wrong. How could Allah, who is really Jehovah in disguise, ask "Which one is right?"

If Allah is the same God that the Christians serve, but under a different name, and if the Koran, which is the holy book of the

Muslims, and the Bible, which is the holy book of the Christians, are by the same author, wouldn't they have the same thing to say about the same subjects? And wouldn't the messenger of each — Jesus Christ and Muhammad; then later, Elijah Muhammad — wouldn't they have the same respect for the holy books? Is that reasonable? But notice something else in the heading: "The Bible and the Holy Qur-an: Which one is right?" Do you see something missing in that statement? Every time the messenger of Allah refers to the Koran, it is always the "Holy Qur-an" (I use the word *Koran*, which is the Anglicized spelling. It is not a sign of disrespect, no different than using *labor* instead of the English word *labour*.) Note, though, that the phrase used by Elijah Muhammad is never the "Holy Bible," it is only "the Bible."

Now, if Allah and Jehovah were the same God, they would have the same respect for the different books — although, again, the books supposedly are by the same God and say the same thing. If Allah and God are the same, I don't understand why Allah does not have respect for Jehovah, so that when he talks about His (Jehovah's) book, he doesn't call it "the Bible" but the "Holy Bible."

Continuing with the statement in *Message to the Blackman in America*, under the heading "The Bible and Holy Qur-an: Which One is Right?" Elijah Muhammad writes:

> The New Testament and Holy Qur-an's teaching of a resurrection of the dead can't mean the people who have died physically and returned to the earth, but rather, a mental resurrection of us, the black nation, who are mentally dead to the knowledge of truth; the truth of self, God and the arch-enemy of God and His people.[33]

He is saying that when the New Testament and the Koran discuss resurrection, they are referring to a "mental resurrection" and they are *only* including black people. So Whites, yellow people,

---

[33] Muhammad, 97.

red people, and brown people are left out of the resurrection. The implication is that the New Testament does not have anything to say about the resurrection except in reference to black people.

We have a simple way of determining whether it is true. If we go to the New Testament, and examine every statement it makes about resurrection, then it ought to be talking about black people and should refer to something mental. Since Mr. Muhammad said that the resurrection was mental and not physical, and since Jehovah and Allah are supposedly the same God, then the New Testament should confirm this position. Of course, it does no such thing. Again, we have this statement by Paul in 1 Corinthians 15:12:

> **Now if Christ is preached that He has been raised from the dead, how do some among you say that there is no resurrection of the dead?**

It is almost as though the Holy Spirit put this in here specifically for commentators such as Mr. Muhammad. Now, in all honesty, the verse does not say "mental" or "physical," but neither does it contain any reference to Blacks in particular. However, other verses do refer to physical resurrection. Let's reread 1 Corinthians 15:42:

> **So also** *is* **the resurrection of the dead.** *The body* [not the mind] **is sown in corruption, it** [referring to the "body sown in corruption"] **is raised in incorruption.**

The phrase **"so also is the resurrection of the dead"** gives us a definition of the resurrection of the dead. We are going to know pretty clearly that whatever comes after that is going to tell us if the "resurrection of the dead" is mental or physical, and if it is referring to black people, red people, or pink people with purple-polka-dots. So what does Verse 42 say?

> **So also** *is* **the resurrection of the dead.** *The body* **is sown in corruption, it is raised in incorruption.**

This does not say "mind," but "body." Mr. Muhammad says "mind." Whose report will you believe?

Then in 1 Corinthians 15:51-52:

51   Behold, I tell you a mystery: We shall not all sleep, but we shall all be changed —

52   in a moment, in the twinkling of an eye, at the last trumpet. For the trumpet will sound, and the dead will be raised incorruptible, and we shall be changed.

Again, we can see that this is referring to a physical body, because the mind does not corrupt, rot, or waste away. Only the physical body rots, and while the verse does not mention the word *body*, it is plainly inferred from the word *corruption*. If the dead will be raised "incorruptible," then while they were dead they must have been corruptible. To get to incorruptible, you have to first be corrupted.

There is still more on this topic in 1 Thessalonians, 4:13-14:

13   But I do not want you to be ignorant, brethren, concerning those who have fallen asleep, lest you sorrow as others who have no hope.

14   For if we believe that Jesus died and rose again, even so God will bring with Him those who sleep in Jesus.

Here is another way you can deduce information apart from the Bible. Everyone has heard about the resurrection. It's been portrayed in movies, people wear crosses around their necks — practically everyone knows that Jesus Christ was crucified, whether people believe in Him as Savior or not. What is interesting is that people accept that it was His body that was crucified, not His mind!

47

The whole purpose of crucifixion was to kill you physically. That was the capital punishment in Roman times. If Jesus had lived in California in the late 20th Century, the state would have used the gas chamber; or in New York, the electric chair; or in England, the gallows. Those are our current methods of capital punishment. Jesus was accused of the capital crimes of blasphemy, heresy, and rebellion against the Roman Empire. So in Verse 13 again:

> **But I do not want you to be ignorant, brethren, concerning those who have fallen asleep....**

I told you previously that the Bible cannot be understood by people who are not born again. It is a coded book. You cannot hack this system. You have to be born again, literally, born from above. So when you are born again, you realize sleep refers to physical death, other than in specific instances where the context makes clear it is physical sleep under discussion. God the Father, Jehovah, is so wonderful and loves His children so much that He never sees them as dead or nonexistent. He sees them as asleep, because the resurrection is going to wake them up.

But let us get back to the resurrection discussed in 1 Thessalonians 4:13-18:

> 13 **But I do not want you to be ignorant, brethren, concerning those who have fallen asleep,** [literally, "have died"] **lest you sorrow as others who have no hope.**
>
> 14 **For if we believe that Jesus died and rose again, even so God will bring with Him those who are asleep in Jesus.**
>
> 15 **For this we say to you by the word of the Lord, that we who are alive *and* remain until the coming of the Lord will by no means precede those who are asleep** [i.e., those who have died].

16   For the Lord Himself will descend from heaven with a shout, with the voice of an archangel, and with the trumpet of God. And the dead in Christ will rise first.

17   Then we who are alive *and* remain shall be caught up together with them in the clouds to meet the Lord in the air. And thus we shall always be with the Lord.

18   Therefore comfort one another with these words.

And going back to Verse 16:

For the Lord Himself will descend from heaven with a shout, with the voice of an archangel, and with the trumpet of God. And the dead in Christ will rise first.

It didn't mention anything there about black people, and it didn't say "mind." It said those who died in Christ will be raised first. If you are a Muslim, according to Mr. Muhammad, you are not going to have a physical body resurrection. Your mind will be raised, but not your body. But the New Testament tells us — Christians, that is — that we are going to have a new body. Muslims do not have a hope of having a new body, because the resurrection is only mental. So again, we have severe disagreements between the Bible of Jehovah and the words of Mr. Muhammad, a spokesman for Allah. Are Jehovah and Allah the same person? The same God? You be the judge.

2

The Making of the Devil

 We have seen several points of disagreement between the teachings of Elijah Muhammad, messenger of Allah, and the Bible. Keep in mind that our working proposition here is that if Jehovah God and Allah God are the same person — only with different names — their message will be the same message. So far, we have not found that to be true.

This brings us to a part of the teaching in the Black Muslim movement that has utmost relevance to the series topic of *Race, Religion & Racism*, and it has to do with the devil.

Again, using *Message to the Blackman in America* as the touchstone for the writings of Mr. Elijah Muhammad, under the heading "Devil: The Making of Devil," we find the following:

> Remember the Bible's teaching of this race of devils and especially in II Thessalonians (Chapter 2:3-12), and Revelation (12:9-17, 20:10). The treatment of the so-called Negroes by the devils is sufficient proof to the so-called Negroes, that they (the white race,) are real devils.[1]

So the devil is the white man, according to Mr. Muhammad. He says, "Remember the Bible's teaching of this race of devils...."

---

[1] Muhammad, 106.

Notice he says, "the Bible's teaching," so he is telling us that the Bible teaches that the white man is the devil.[2]

In quoting from the Bible, Mr. Muhammad thus puts himself in a tough situation. If those Scriptures don't say what he says, then he brands himself a false prophet. The first scriptural reference that Mr. Muhammad gives is 2 Thessalonians 2:3-12:

> 3   **Let no one** [black or white] **deceive you by any means; for** *that Day will not come* **unless the falling away comes first, and the man of sin is revealed, the son of perdition,**

> 4   **who opposes and exalts himself above all that is called God or that is worshiped, so that he sits as God in the temple of God, showing himself that he is God.**

---

2   If this were true, it puts the Black Muslims, and Mr. Muhammad, in a rather awkward and perverse situation. According to Muhammad biographer Claude Clegg, in January 1961, with Elijah Muhammad's approval and at his instructions, Malcolm X and a local Muslim minister from Atlanta had a "secret meeting" with Georgia leaders of the Ku Klux Klan. The two groups negotiated a "non-aggression pact" whereby the Klan promised not to censure Muslim activities in the South as long as the Nation of Islam did not engage in civil rights activities there. A discussion of land sales ensued, in which the Klan offered to sell the NOI some 20,000 acres for "black separatist" activities. (Both Clegg, 152-153, and Evanzz, 226-227, using primary source documents, confirm the facts of this meeting). In other words, if Elijah Muhammad believed that white men were "devils," he did not hesitate to meet with the worst of the lot for his own purposes. But that was not the end of it. In February 1952, George Lincoln Rockwell and 20 "storm troopers" of the American Nazi Party attended a "Saviour's Day" convention at the Chicago International Amphitheater, and in the course of the meeting, Rockwell, adorned with his swastika armband, spoke to the all-black Muslim audience, praising Elijah Muhammad and saying that "When we [white supremacists]

5   Do you not remember that when I was still
        with you I told you these things?

6   And now you know what is restraining, that
        he may be revealed in his own time.

7   For the mystery of lawlessness is already at
        work; only He who now restrains *will do so*
        until He is taken out of the way.

8   And then the lawless one will be revealed,
        whom the Lord will consume with the breath
        of His mouth and destroy with the brightness
        of His coming.

9   The coming of the *lawless one* is according to
        the working of Satan, with all power, signs, and
        lying wonders,

10   and with all unrighteous deception among
        those who perish, because they did not receive
        the love of the truth, that they might be saved.

---

come to power, I promise you we will help you get what you want
[separatism]." Saying, "We don't want to integrate," Rockwell compared Elijah Muhammad to Adolf Hitler, claiming that Elijah
Muhammad "is to the so-called Negro what Adolf Hitler was to the
German people." He also said, "I believe Elijah Muhammad will solve
the race problem." (Quotations are on Page 242 of Evanzz, but the
story is reported in Clegg, 153). Biographer Evanzz is more sympa-
thetic to Mr. Muhammad, and therefore the descriptions of the reactions to the Nazis' appearance differ from those of Clegg, but both
note that Rockwell's statements were greeted with cheers (Evanzz
claims it was because Mr. Muhammad suddenly appeared). Mr.
Muhammad, while claiming not to need the Nazis' help, nevertheless approved of their position: "We want to help you keep your race
all white. We also want to keep ours all black."

11   "And for this reason God will send them strong
delusion, that they should believe the lie,

12   that they all may be condemned who did not
believe the truth but had pleasure in
unrighteousness.

These verses cited by Mr. Muhammad, the messenger of Allah, the prophet of Allah, do not contain one single reference to white people. Nothing in them in any way refers to skin color. The name *Satan* was used once, but it does not say anything about white people. Now, I'll admit that there have been some white people through time who have acted like the devil. The Klan does that on a regular basis, but this passage does not in any way indict white people as "devils."

In Mr. Muhammad's second reference, Revelation 12:9-17, we do not find anything referring to "whites," the "white race," or anything connecting white people with the devil:

9   So the great dragon was cast out, that serpent
of old, called the Devil and Satan, who deceives
the whole world; he was cast to the earth, and
his angels were cast out with him.

10   Then I heard a loud voice saying in heaven,
"Now salvation, and strength, and the kingdom
of our God, and the power of His Christ have
come, for the accuser of our brethren, who
accused them before our God day and night,
has been cast down.

11   "And they overcame him by the blood of the
Lamb and by the word of their testimony, and
they did not love their lives to the death.

12   "Therefore rejoice, O heavens, and you who
dwell in them! Woe to the inhabitants of the

earth and the sea! For the devil has come down to you, having great wrath, because he knows that he has a short time."

13   Now when the dragon saw that he had been cast to the earth, he persecuted the woman who gave birth to the male *Child*.

14   But the woman was given two wings of a great eagle, that she might fly into the wilderness to her place, where she is nourished for a time and times and half a time, from the presence of the serpent.

15   So the serpent spewed water out of his mouth like a flood after the woman, that he might cause her to be carried away by the flood.

16   But the earth helped the woman, and the earth opened its mouth and swallowed up the flood which the dragon had spewed out of his mouth.

17   And the dragon was enraged with the woman, and he went to make war with the rest of her offspring, who keep the commandments of God and have the testimony of Jesus Christ.

Note that Verse 17 does not end with "of Allah," or "of Muhammad," but **the testimony of Jesus Christ**. Again, I can't find anywhere in that passage a single reference to white people — or black people — for that matter.

Mr. Muhammad's third reference is Revelation 20:10. Just this one verse:

The devil, who deceived them, was cast into the lake of fire and brimstone where the beast and the false prophet *are*. And they will be tormented day and night forever and ever.

54

There is nothing in this verse that suggests anything about white people being devils. I think it is unfair to call white people devils when God and the Bible do not call them that. Such statements may appeal to the anger and rage and hurt of past injustices committed against black people, but to try to put it off as though all white people were responsible for slavery is both un-historical and unrighteous. Every one of the anti-slavery societies — not just for black slaves in America, but for Asian slaves in China and black slaves in the Sudan — were founded by white Christians outraged by the evils done in the name of God.[3]

In *Message to the Blackman in America*, Mr. Muhammad makes another statement that is out of this world. Under the heading "Devil: The Making of Devil," he writes:

> Again, we learn who the Bible (Genesis 1:26) is refer-
> ring to in the saying: "Let us make man." This "US"
> was fifty-nine thousand, nine hundred and ninety-nine

---

[3] Ironically, the most active of the anti-slave Christian religions in America, the Quakers, seemed to draw no benefit denominationally for their work. Even though by 1800 Quakerism had virtually severed all ties to human bondage — even in the South — and assisted freedmen financially, educationally, and otherwise, "extremely few [freedmen] joined the Society of Friends, or Quakers." (H. Shelton Smith, *In His Image, But...Racism in Southern Religion, 1780-1910* [Durham, N.C.: Duke University Press, 1972], 35.) As historian H. Shelton Smith notes, given the Quakers' record, "one would have expected the Society of Friends to reap a bountiful harvest of black members....", 34-35. The absence of former slaves in Quaker churches, he concludes, is explained by the fact that "most leaders of colonial Quakerism neither put forth any effort to make disciples of Negroe [sic] nor did they welcome them into the Society" (35). See Henry J. Cadbury, "Negro Membership in the Society of Friends," *Journal of Negro History*, Vol. 21, no. 2, April 1936, 151-213.

(59,999) black men and women; making or grafting them
into the likeness or image of the original man.[4]

That is not what the Bible says! Remember, we are reading
from a book copyrighted in 1965, which tells us that this was what
the Black Muslims believed then, and no doubt believe today,
according to Mr. Muhammad. Mr. Muhammad wants you to think
that by using Bible references, you'll be persuaded in your thinking.
He wants you to think: "This must be the same God, because after all
he's quoting the Bible."

It seems to me that if Allah is your God and the Koran is your
holy book, you would be quoting from the Koran. But the Bible is used in

---

[4]   Muhammad, 118. A full reading of the section relating to the origin
of the devil is even more bizarre. According to the section "Devil: The
Making of Devil," 110-118, "...6,600 years ago, as Allah taught me,
our nation gave birth to another God whose name was Yakub. He
started studying the life germ of man to try making a new creation
(new man).... [and Allah told Elijah Muhammad] when this man
[Yakub] is born, he will change civilization (the world), and produce a
new race of people, who would rule the original black nation for
6,000 years.... After that time, the original black nation would give
birth to one, whose wisdom, knowledge and power to rule would be
infinite.... And, that He would destroy Yakub's world and restore the
original nation...into power forever. This mighty One, is known under
many names. He has no equal.... He is referred to in the Bible as God
Almighty, and in some places as Jehovah, the God of Gods, and the
Lord of Lords. The Holy Qur-an refers to Him as Allah.... He, also, is
referred to as the Christ, the second Jesus" (110-112). Mr. Muhammad
goes on to discuss the "boyhood" of Yakub – how he "learned his
future from playing with steel." He then began to study the germ of
the black man successfully grafting the brown germ "into its last stage,
which *would be white* [emphasis mine]."

Yakub gained converts, who fell for his teaching, "100 per cent." This
caused a conflict with the king, who wanted to "work out some

---

an attempt to reach Christians who are disgruntled, upset, and disenchanted with the way the white Christian church has treated black people down through the years. But you should never move in anger when you make life decisions. Examine the evidence on all sides; then make a decision.

We are going to look now at some of the most awesome statements that you will probably ever read. You alone will have to measure their value and truth. Under the heading, "Program and Position: What Do the Muslims Want?" Mr. Muhammad states:

---

agreement" between Yakub and his followers. Yakub suggested that if the king would give them the resources to furnish them with necessities for 20 years, they would leave. Yakub took 59,999 others to an island in the Aegean Sea, which he identifies as Patmos. There, his doctors began a "grafting" of the "present white race" (112-113). Yakub's "aim was to kill and destroy the black nation. He ordered the nurses to kill all black babies that were born among his people by pricking the brains with a sharp needle as soon as the black child's head is out of the mother." [Here, he apparently did have a prophetic vision of the procedure called partial-birth abortion, except that it is used today more on white babies, proportionally, than black babies.] After 600 years, Yakub had an all-white race. Then Elijah Muhammad makes this statement: "The Yakub-made devils were really pale white, with really blue eyes...." (116). What is amazing is that there was still no explanation – let alone evidence – of what "made" these white people devils except that they were not black. We see this on Page 118, where Elijah Muhammad states, "The black people are by nature the righteous." Yet Romans 3:10 says, **"There is none righteous, no, not one [emphasis mine]."** Eventually, the devils were driven out of Paradise. Now, beyond some of the other statements here, one wonders how a nation can give birth to "another God whose name was Yakub." If man can give birth to God, that places God dependent on, or below, man. We do see, however, the assertion that God equals Jehovah equals Allah, with the rather unusual twist that they all equal Jesus Christ, the "second Jesus."

57

5.   We believe in the resurrection of the dead — not
        in physical resurrection but mental resurrection.
        We believe that the so-called Negroes are most
        in need of mental resurrection; therefore, they
        will be resurrected first.[5]

That is an awesome statement in light of Acts 24:15, which says: **"I have hope in God, which they themselves also accept, that there will be a resurrection of *the* dead, both of *the* just and *the* unjust."**

Now the thing that makes Christianity unique among all other religions is the resurrection of Jesus Christ. He is the only One about whom we have any authentic evidence of returning from the dead. Christianity stands and falls on the resurrection. All the rest of the so-called prophets died and are still dead. Muhammad is dead. Confucius is dead. Zoroaster is dead. Buddha is dead. They are all dead. In fact, Mr. Elijah Muhammad is dead. Malcolm X is dead. The only One who came back from the dead, as He prophesied, was Jesus Christ.

Mr. Muhammad says that he believes in a resurrection, but not physical resurrection. Jesus believes in physical resurrection — He did it! — and Jehovah believes in physical resurrection. Mr. Muhammad says Muslims believe in a "mental" resurrection, but if that's true, we should find something in the Bible that supports that, since he's supposed to be speaking on behalf of Allah, and Allah, under the alias of Jehovah, is the One who inspired the Bible to be written.

Another Scripture that sheds light on this resurrection issue is 1 Corinthians 15:12-21:

12   **Now if Christ is preached that He has been
        raised from the dead, how do some among you
        say that there is no resurrection of the dead?**

---

[5] This is reiterated in the statement of faith of NOI, "What Muslims Believe," Appendix A, Page 349.

13   But if there is no resurrection of the dead,
      then Christ is not risen.

14   And if Christ is not risen, then our preaching
      is empty and your faith *is* also empty.

15   Yes, and we are found false witnesses of God,
      because we have testified of God that He raised
      up Christ, whom He did not raise up — if in
      fact the dead do not rise.

16   For if *the* dead do not rise, then Christ is not
      risen.

17   And if Christ is not risen, your faith *is* futile;
      you are still in your sins!

18   Then also those who have fallen asleep in
      Christ have perished.

19   If in this life only we have hope in Christ, we
      are of all men the most pitiable.

20   But now Christ is risen from the dead, *and* has
      become the firstfruits of those who have fallen
      asleep.

21   For since by man *came* death....

What do you think the Bible means when it says, **For since by man came death?** Is this referring to mental death? When Paul said **by man,** he's referring to the first man, Adam, and Adam was the one who allowed death to come into the human race. There was no physical death until Adam disobeyed God. God told him before that if he ate of the tree in the midst of the garden that in the day he ate of it, he would surely die. God didn't say, "You're going to lose your mind," He said you are going to die.

Notice Verse 20 again:

But now Christ is risen from the dead, *and* has become the firstfruits of those who have fallen asleep.

Remember that I gave you the "sleep" definition before. In the New Testament, whenever God Jehovah talks about His people as dead, He uses the figurative language of sleep. He always refers to them as being asleep because there is presupposed in sleep an awakening. God knows that there is going to be a resurrection and you are going to wake up.

Another illustration of this death/sleep principle is found in John 11, in reference to Jesus raising Lazarus from the dead. When Jesus arrived, according to the Gospel account, He instructed the people to remove the stone from the cave or grave. The sisters said in Verse 39:

"...Lord, by this time there is a stench, for he has been *dead* four days."

Think about this: your mind doesn't begin to stink when it stops working. When people lose their mind, their mind doesn't start putting off a foul odor of decay and rottenness. Martha, the sister of Lazarus, was talking about physical death, not mental. But when Jesus referred to Lazarus in John 11:11, he said, **"Our friend Lazarus sleeps, but I go that I may wake him up."** The disciples thought He meant Lazarus was taking rest in sleep, but in Verse 14, Jesus said to them, **"Lazarus is dead."** Not asleep in the sense of resting, but dead. Again, God, calling those things that are not as though they were, sees you alive if you are a child of God.

Continuing with our discussion of 1 Corinthians 15:21-23:

21   **For since by man *came* death,** [that is, through Adam] **by Man also *came* the resurrection of the dead** [that's Jesus Christ].

22   **For as in Adam all die, even so in Christ all shall be made alive.**

23   **But each one in his own order: Christ the firstfruits, afterward those *who are* Christ's at His coming.**

Look at Verse 22 again: **For as in Adam all die....**

So I ask the question again, do you think that means mental dying or physical dying? If it means mental dying, then from where does physical death come? Why do we die? How did physical death get here if that wasn't what Adam allowed into the human race? If, as Mr. Muhammad and the Black Muslims say, the Koran is talking about mental death, then why do people physically die?

Let us look at verses 22 and 23 again:

22   **For as in Adam all die, even so in Christ all shall be made alive.**

23   **But each one in his own order: Christ the firstfruits, afterward those *who are* Christ's at His coming.**

That's talking about the resurrection, and it is not mental. Mr. Muhammad says mental; the Bible says physical. Whose report will you believe?

There are still more Scriptures that I want to consider in reference to this mental resurrection issue. In Revelation 20:4-6, it is written:

4   **And I saw thrones, and they sat on them, and judgment was committed to them. Then I *saw* the souls of those who had been beheaded for their witness to Jesus and for the word of God, who had not worshiped the beast or his image, and had not received *his* mark on their**

> **foreheads or on their hands. And they lived
> and reigned with Christ for a thousand years.**

When someone is beheaded, do you think it's mental or physical? We know from secular history that people in the beginning of Christianity were often beheaded for claiming to be Christians. They would lose their lives. They didn't have their minds cut off; their physical heads were cut off their physical bodies and they physically died.

Continuing with Verse 5:

> **But the rest of the dead did not live again until the
> thousand years were finished. This *is* the first resur-
> rection.**

Consider this. The very fact that it says "first resurrection" indicates that there has to be at least one other. You never use "first" unless there is at least a "second." I wonder which one Mr. Muhammad is referring to? Is that the mental one? If there is another one, what is it? Mr. Muhammad is only discussing one resurrection. Let's say that it is, indeed, mental. The Bible speaks about more than one, so what is the other one? In Verse 6, we see:

> **Blessed and holy *is* he who has part in the first resur-
> rection. Over such the second death has no power, but
> they shall be priests of God and of Christ, and shall
> reign with Him a thousand years.**

I ask the question again: If there is going to be more than one resurrection, which one is the mental one, and if one is mental, then what kind is the other? Mr. Muhammad continues his comments under the heading "Program and Position: What Do the Muslims Want?":

> 12.   We believe that Allah (God) appeared in the
>   Person of Master W. Fard Muhammad, July 1930

62

— the long awaited "Messiah" of the Christians
and the "Mahdi" of the Muslims.[6]

According to Mr. Muhammad, Jesus Christ is not the Messiah — Allah is the Messiah appearing in the physical form of W. Fard Muhammad in 1930. So there is no more future Messiah to look for because the Messiah came in 1930. Take note of this, black folk, people of color, because he puts his neck in a noose by saying it this way: "We believe that Allah (God) appeared in the person of Master W. Fard Muhammad, July 1930 — the long awaited Messiah of the Christians...."

If he had only stated, "the long awaited Messiah," period — that would have been one thing. But when he uses the phrase "the long awaited Messiah of the Christians," he is on our turf now. Since Mr. Muhammad in this particular statement does not give any scriptural references that we could use to validate his claims, we have a problem. So where are the Scriptures?

I'll give you Scripture! In the story of Jesus going through Samaria, having a conversation with the woman at Jacob's well (John 4:21-26), it is written:

21   Jesus said to her, "Woman, believe Me, the hour is coming when you will neither on this mountain, nor in Jerusalem, worship the Father.

22   "You worship what you do not know; we know what we worship, for salvation is of the Jews.

23   "But the hour is coming, and now is, when the true worshipers will worship the Father in spirit and truth; for the Father is seeking such to worship Him.

---

[6] Muhammad, 164.

24   "God is Spirit, and those who worship Him
       must worship in spirit and truth."

25   The woman said to Him, "I know that Messiah
       is coming" (who is called Christ). "When He
       comes, He will tell us all things."

26   Jesus said to her, "I who speak to you am *He*."

I have a problem here, because the prophet of Allah said that the long-awaited Messiah of the Christians appeared in the person of Wallace Fard Muhammad in 1930. The woman said, **"I know that Messiah is coming (who is called Christ). When He comes, He will tell us all things."** Jesus (not Wallace Fard Muhammad) said to her, **"I who speak to you am *He*."** So we have a problem: Jesus said He is the Messiah, and Elijah Muhammad said that W. Fard Muhammad was the Messiah. Whose report will you believe? There's a dinosaur-size discrepancy here. Any seeker of the truth should have a problem with this discrepancy.

Mr. Muhammad gets into a number of areas in his book, including racial harmony — or the lack thereof. In *Message to the Blackman in America*, under the heading "Economic Program: Separation! Independence!" he writes:

> IT IS FAR MORE IMPORTANT TO TEACH SEPARATION OF THE
> BLACKS AND WHITES IN AMERICA THAN PRAYER [Emphasis
> his]. Teach and train the blacks to do something for self
> in the way of uniting and seeking a home on this earth
> that they can call their own! There is no such thing as
> living in peace with white Americans.[7]

I hope you see the enormity of that statement: "It is far more important to teach separation of the Blacks and Whites in America

---

[7] Muhammad, 204.

than [to teach] prayer." The Bible says just the opposite in 1 Corinthians 1:10:

> **Now I plead with you, brethren, by the name of our Lord Jesus Christ, that you all speak the same thing, and *that* there be no divisions among you, but *that* you be perfectly joined together in the same mind and in the same judgment.**

Mr. Muhammad says we should teach separation of Blacks and Whites. He also says, "Teach and train the Blacks to do something for self...." I agree with that, but you can do that as a Christian.

"...do something for self in the way of uniting..." he says. We need to do that. We need to be united. I agree with that.

"...and seeking a home on this earth that they can call their own! There is no such thing as living in peace with white Americans," he concludes. I am home. I was born in America. This is my home! My ancestors worked, toiled, and tilled the soil and developed this land for 246 years and never had a payday! I have a right to be here! I have just as much right as any European white person has to be here. I was born here. My father was born here. Don't tell me that this is not my home. I have never lived anywhere else. I have visited Africa, but I am not from Africa — I am from America!

"...there is no such thing as living in peace with white Americans." Look at this, because this is terrible, and it's not true! The Bible tells us in Romans 12:18:

> **If it is possible, as much as depends on you, live peaceably with all men.**

God, our heavenly Father, would never admonish us to do something that we are incapable of doing. We can live in peace with white Americans, red Americans, yellow Americans, and brown Americans. Notice something even more revealing in that Scripture. It says **live peaceably with all *men*** — not all Christians, *but all men.* So it must be possible to live peaceably with all men.

Under the heading "The Persecution of the Righteous: We Seek Truth and Justice," Mr. Muhammad writes:

> **We seek truth and justice; in the past, we have been taught that God and the devil were something other than human, while the truth from Almighty God, Allah, who is now among us in Person, makes it clear that these two characters are human beings.[8]**

Again, we have an opportunity to evaluate what Mr. Muhammad says. Is God a human being? I think any Christian would challenge this comment vociferously. Let's examine that statement again, just so you see its importance: "We seek truth and justice; in the past, we have been taught that God and the devil were something other than human, while the truth from Almighty God, Allah, who is now among us in person, makes it clear that these two characters...." I want you to see that "these two characters" he refers to are "God and the devil." He goes on to say: "...that these two characters are *human beings* [emphasis mine]."

Just so we don't forget the framework within which we are examining these statements, remember that Mr. Muhammad can say anything he wants about Islam and about the Koran and about Allah as long as it isn't asserted that Allah is the same as Jehovah God. But he did say that, remember? He said that on Page 111 of his book: "This mighty One, *is known under many names*. He has no *equal*. There never was one like Him. He is referred to in the Bible as God Almighty, and *in some places as Jehovah, the God of Gods*, and *the Lord of Lords*. The Holy Quran refers to Him as *Allah*, the One God [all emphasis mine]."[9] You can't get around these comments. Allah is Jehovah is God Almighty! In fact, if you look closely, you see that Mr. Muhammad admits that He is "...God of Gods..."

---

[8] Muhammad, 210.
[9] Muhammad, 111.

Not only does Mr. Muhammad say that Jehovah God is "God of Gods," and not only does he say that God is referred to as Jehovah or as Allah, but he let something slip here: "The Holy Quran refers to Him *as Allah, the ONE GOD* [emphasis mine]." So even according to Mr. Muhammad, there is only one God, referred to by these many names, Jehovah, God, Allah. Keep that in mind because that just sealed the case against what he wrote, saying that God and the devil are "human beings." What does the Bible say? Look at John 4:21-24:

> **21** **Jesus said to her, "Woman, believe Me, the hour is coming when you will neither on this mountain, nor in Jerusalem, worship the Father.**

> **22** **"You worship what you do not know; we know what we worship, for salvation is of the Jews.** [This statement refers to the fact that salvation originated with them or through them.]

> **23** **"But the hour is coming, and now is, when the true worshipers will worship the Father in spirit and truth; for the Father is seeking such to worship Him.**

> **24** **"God *is* Spirit...."**

The New King James Version says, **"God *is* Spirit"** while the traditional King James Version says, **"God *is a* Spirit."** In either case, the capitalization of the "S" in Spirit indicates that God is the original Spirit, and Jesus made it clear that God is not a man: **"God *is* Spirit."**

If Mr. Muhammad can trace his personal origin all the way back to the beginning, with Allah, then I will be willing to consider what he has to say. But in all my research, I have not found him able to do that. On the other hand, Jesus said, **"God *is* Spirit."** How can Jesus make such an audacious statement, without giving us evidence that we can validate?

In the Gospel of John 1:1, we have our answer: **In the beginning was the Word….** The word *Word* in the original Greek is the word *Logos,* and it means "manifested word," or the Son of God that we have come to know traditionally as Jesus Christ. This was Jesus before He took upon Himself human flesh, through the Virgin Mary. So it says, **In the beginning was the Word, and the Word was with God….** If Jesus was **In the beginning…** and was **with God,** then He would know who God is and who He isn't.

In Matthew 25:31, we find another Scripture that sheds light on the issue of who God and the devil are:

> **"When the Son of Man comes in His glory, and all the holy angels with Him,…"**

At this point, I have a question. Who are angels or what are angels? In Hebrews 1:10-14, we have our answer:

10   *And: "You, Lᴏʀᴅ, in the beginning laid the foundation of the earth, and the heavens are the work of Your hands.*

11   *They will perish, but You remain; and they will all grow old like a garment;*

12   *Like a cloak You will fold them up, and they will be changed. But You are the same, and Your years will not fail."*

13   **But to which of the angels has He ever said:** *"Sit at My right hand, till I make Your enemies Your footstool"?*

14   **Are they not all ministering spirits** [human beings?] **sent forth to minister for those who will inherit salvation?**

Verse 13 mentions angels, and Verse 14 tells you exactly what they are — spirits! Can you see that? Keep in mind the Bible said it: Angels are ministering *spirits*, not human beings, but spirits. Follow this closely in Matthew 25:31-41:

31 "When the Son of Man comes in His glory, and all the holy angels with Him, then He will sit on the throne of His glory.

32 "All the nations will be gathered before Him, and He will separate them one from another, as a shepherd divides *his* sheep from the goats.

33 "And He will set the sheep on His right hand, but the goats on the left.

34 "Then the King will say to those on His right hand, 'Come, you blessed of My Father, inherit the kingdom prepared for you from the foundation of the world:

35 'for I was hungry and you gave Me food; I was thirsty and you gave Me drink; I was a stranger and you took Me in;

36 'I *was* naked and you clothed Me; I was sick and you visited Me; I was in prison and you came to Me.'

37 "Then the righteous will answer Him, saying, 'Lord, when did we see You hungry and feed *You*, or thirsty and give *You* drink?

38 'When did we see You a stranger and take *You* in, or naked and clothe *You*?

39 'Or when did we see You sick, or in prison, and come to You?'

40   "And the King will answer and say to them,
        'Assuredly, I say to you, inasmuch as you did
        it to one of the least of these My brethren, you
        did *it* to Me.'

41   "Then He will also say to those on the left hand,
        'Depart from Me, you cursed, into the
        everlasting fire prepared for the devil and his
        angels;"

Consider this: If the devil has angels, then the angels and the devil must be of the same genre. So if the angels are spirits, then the devil must be a spirit. But Mr. Muhammad said the devil is a human being. Whose report will you believe?

I have given enough evidence here to prove my point. But there are some other things Mr. Muhammad says that need to be dealt with. He states:

> I have no alternative than to tell you that there is not any life beyond the grave. There is no justice in the *sweet bye and bye* [emphasis mine]. Immortality is NOW, HERE. We are blessed of God and we must exert every means to protect ourselves.[10]

Mr. Muhammad says, "There is not any life beyond the grave." This is apparently what Allah has told Mr. Muhammad to share with the black man in America. So that means we should not find anything in the Bible that demonstrates or suggests life beyond the grave. If it does, then the Bible and Mr. Muhammad would be in conflict with each other.

Look at the text again: "...I have no alternative than to tell you that there is not any life beyond the grave. There is no justice in the sweet bye and bye. Immortality is NOW, HERE." That's plain. No life beyond the grave! Now Muslims may believe that, or if they

---

[10] Muhammad, 219.

don't believe that and they're a part of the Nation of Islam, then they don't believe what their founder believed. But the Bible tells me something different.[11] For instance, Luke 16:19-31:

> **19** **"There was a certain rich man who was clothed in purple and fine linen and fared sumptuously every day.**
>
> **20** **"But there was a certain beggar named Lazarus, full of sores, who was laid at his gate,**
>
> **21** **"desiring to be fed with the crumbs which fell from the rich man's table. Moreover the dogs came and licked his sores.**
>
> **22** **"So it was that the beggar died, and was carried by the angels to Abraham's bosom. The rich man also died and was buried.**

Well, you know when you die and there is no life beyond the grave, then that is the end. It's over! So we shouldn't find anything else, right? However, let's read on:

> **23** **"And....**

Oh, oh. "And" means there's something else that is to come, correct?

> **"...being in torments in Hades...."**

In the traditional King James Version, it says "hell." But the actual Greek word is *Hades*, and Hades is the place of the departed spirits of the dead. It says, **"and being in torments in**

---

[11] Even the Old Testament, which is viewed as a "holy book" to the Muslims, confirms there is life after death: Proverbs 23:18 says, **For surely there is a hereafter, and your hope will not be cut off.**

Hades...." If there's no life beyond the grave — and prophet Elijah Muhammad says there isn't — then you cannot be tormented beyond the grave.

> 23   **"And being in torments in Hades, he lifted up his eyes and saw Abraham afar off, and Lazarus in his bosom.**
>
> 24   **"Then he cried....**

If he had a voice, and cried, then he must have been alive and conscious.

> 23   **"And being in torments in Hades, he lifted up his eyes and saw Abraham afar off, and Lazarus in his bosom.**
>
> 24   **"Then he cried and said, 'Father Abraham, have mercy on me, and send Lazarus that he may dip the tip of his finger in water and cool my tongue; for I am tormented in this flame.'**
>
> 25   **"But Abraham said, 'Son, remember that in your lifetime you received your good things, and likewise Lazarus evil things; but now he is comforted and you are tormented.**
>
> 26   **'And besides all this, between us and you there is a great gulf fixed, so that those who want to pass from here to you cannot, nor can those from there pass to us.'**
>
> 27   **"Then he said, 'I beg you therefore, father, that you would send him to my father's house,**
>
> 28   **'for I have five brothers....' "**

What would be the point of sending Lazarus to his father's house? Because he was concerned about his brothers. Which is exactly why I've written this book, because I'm concerned about my brothers.

> **...that he may testify to them, lest they also come to this place of torment.'**

Here we have a dead man. The people had a funeral for him, and buried him. They put the brother away, but he was still conscious after what we call "death." Yet Mr. Muhammad says "...I have to tell you that there is no life beyond the grave...." This story tells us there is life beyond the grave.

> **29   "Abraham said to him, 'They have Moses and the prophets; let them hear them.'**
>
> **30   "And he said, 'No, father Abraham; but if one goes to them from the dead, they will repent.'**
>
> **31   "But he said to him, 'If they do not hear Moses and the prophets, neither will they be persuaded though one rise from the dead.' "**

I know what some Muslims are going to say: "This was only a parable." Oh no! If you read and study every parable that Jesus taught, which I have done, you will find an interesting fact, namely that it is unique among all other parables. Jesus was a consistent person, and we have no reason to believe that He would suddenly change His teaching methods. He is unchanging: Hebrews 13:8 says, **Jesus Christ *is* the same yesterday, today, and forever.**

So there is evidence that this particular incident was not a parable but in fact referred to real, living people. Jesus used names in this teaching, unlike any parable in the New Testament. For example, He said in one parable that a woman lost a coin, and swept her house and found it, whereupon she rejoiced and told her neighbors. Why didn't He tell us that Mary lost the coin, or Esmerelda lost the coin, or Latisha lost the coin? He said a "woman," because the issue in the story was the principle, not the people. In another,

He said, "A farmer went forth to sow…." He also told the parable of the rich man with so much wealth that he built more barns, and then died. At no time did He name names. Yet all of a sudden He used specific names, "Lazarus" and "Abraham." What difference does it make if it's just a story to illustrate a principle?

I believe this is an actual story about people who really lived, and that Jesus used names because the people to whom He was speaking would relate to those people easily. He could have said a "beggar" died, but I believe that many of the people in His audience actually knew, or had seen, both Lazarus and this rich man, and they all knew Abraham. Jesus could have just said that the man called out to heaven (at that time it was "paradise," but it still was separated from hell). But the believing Jews knew that Abraham was alive in the after world.

Think about this: If God, Jehovah, is a fair God, then He has to show us both sides of the ledger, as it were. In other words, He would have to show us the outcome of the righteous and the unrighteous. We hear a lot about heaven and we can go to the Book of Revelation and read about all the good stuff. But it's not fair to tell us about the good stuff and not about the bad, because I might decide that while the good stuff is good, how bad can the bad stuff be? I may just want to do my own thing here and take my chances on the other side. God is required by His own fairness to give us the basis upon which to make a choice.

Joshua said, **"…choose for yourselves this day whom you will serve…. But as for me and my house, we will serve the LORD"** (Joshua 24:15). Elijah stood single-handedly against 450 prophets of Baal and the 400 prophets of the groves on top of Mount Carmel, and asked them, **"How long will you falter between two opinions? If the LORD *is* God, follow Him; but if Baal, follow him."** (1 Kings 18:21). Everywhere you find choices. You cannot have a genuine choice if there are not at least two options available.

Remember also that you are not what I see, nor am I what you see. All we see is the earthly house that we each live in —

our earth suit, the way astronauts have a spacesuit. They have to take their environment with them. When I go scuba diving, I have to take my environment. I can't breathe air through water the way fish can, because I don't have a gill system to extract oxygen from water. So in order to live in this three-dimensional world, you have to have a house, a body. Your body is your earth suit, but it is not you.

Do you recall the movie *Independence Day?* The evil alien creatures looked like these big, squid-like monsters, but when the scientists looked at them, they realized those were their spacesuits. Your body is not you; it is your earth suit.

There is another world, the spirit world, that produced this physical world. That world is more real than this one, and this world is only a mirror image of that one. In John 4:24, remember, Jesus said **God** *is* **a Spirit,** so as a Spirit, God must live in a spirit world. We, too, are spirits, but spirits created to live specifically in this three-dimensional world. To do so, we need a house — our bodies. That is why evil spirits try to get hold of people's minds and ultimately their spirits. (If you keep listening to the psychics, you open yourself up to the possibility of demon possession. The demonic spirits who operate through those psychics want to come into this physical three-dimensional world, but they cannot do it without a channel. They need a physical body so they can do their greatest degree of damage.)

We were originally from God's realm, the spirit world, but we were put in physical bodies on the earth. When you die physically, your body goes back into the ground from which it was made. The Bible says that God created Adam out of the dust. Therefore all of us were created from dust, and the Bible says we will all return to dust. (This is exactly what happens to a body that completely decomposes. It goes back to dust.) But the real you vacates the premises and goes back to the spirit world.

In the book of Ecclesiastes, we find a revelation of this principle. Ecclesiastes 12:6-7 says:

6   *Remember your Creator* **before the silver cord is loosed, or the golden bowl is broken, or the pitcher shattered at the fountain, or the wheel broken at the well.**

7   **Then the dust will return to the earth as it was, and the spirit will return to God who gave it.**

You are a spirit, you have a soul, and you live in a body.

Now, back to the story in Luke's Gospel, Chapter 16. It says the rich man died and in hell (or Hades), he lifted up his eyes. Beyond this life, you are still conscious, and still have a spirit body or substance. That is why one spirit can recognize another spirit. Spirits have shape and substance.

Mr. Muhammad said, "...I have no alternative than to tell you that there is not any life beyond the grave...." In the book of Revelation 1:1 we find further evidence that invalidates Mr. Muhammad's assertions.

> **The Revelation of Jesus Christ, which God gave Him to show His servants — things which must shortly take place. And He sent and signified *it* by His angel to His servant John.**

This makes clear that this revelation was given to John. Let's continue with Revelation 4:1-2:

1   **After these things I looked...**

Who do you think "I" refers to? That's right: John.

1   **...and behold, a door *standing* open in heaven. And the first voice which I heard *was* like a trumpet speaking with me, saying, "Come up here, and I will show you things which must take place after this."**

2   **Immediately I was in the Spirit....**

Understand that physical death is not the end of conscious existence. Physical death is simply the separation of the spirit and the soul from the body. God can allow, since He is the Creator, our spirits and our souls to leave our bodies for His specific purpose and our bodies can still live without our spirits and souls in them. Since He created the body, He can keep it alive while the spirit and soul leave for a while. John said, **I was in the Spirit.** That meant that his spirit, the real John, left his body and went into the other realm, which is the spirit world.

The passage we are going to read is of paramount importance to us because it affects deeply Mr. Elijah Muhammad's contention that "There is not any life beyond the grave." We have to find out if that is true, because if we're going to follow the Muslims, we need to know if what they believe is true. And if it isn't true, then we need to know if there are other assertions Mr. Muhammad has made that are not true. So in Revelation 6:9:

> **When He opened the fifth seal, I saw under the altar the souls of those who had been slain....**

Etymologically, the word *slain* means "killed," right? When you are killed, you die. If you die, you are not conscious and cannot talk, right? Notice carefully what the ninth verse *does not say*. It does not say, "When he opened the fifth seal I saw under the altar *those who had been slain.*" He said, **I saw the souls of those who had been slain.** That means that "souls" and "those" are separate. "Souls" belong to "those." But, "souls" are not "those!" "Souls" *belong* to "those."

> **When He opened the fifth seal, I saw under the altar the souls of those who had been slain....**

Do you see what I mean? It doesn't say, "I saw *those who had been slain*," but **the souls of those who had been slain.** He saw the souls of physically dead people, yet Mr. Muhammad says, "There is not any life beyond the grave."

Returning to Revelation 6:9-11, we see:

9   ...I saw under the altar the souls of those
         who had been slain for the word of God and
         for the testimony which they held.

10   And they cried with a loud voice....

If they cried, there had to be life there. Dead people do not
cry. Those "souls" cried out with a loud voice — yet they were the
souls that John saw under the altar in heaven, in the spirit world.
Their bodies were still in the cemetery. But they were still alive,
conscious, and could talk. They were crying out with a loud voice.
Verse 10 says:

> And they cried with a loud voice, saying, "How long,
> O Lord, holy and true, until You judge and avenge
> our blood on those who dwell on the earth?"

Apparently, those souls were not on the earth when they cried,
because you wouldn't say **avenge our blood on those who dwell on
the earth** if you were on the earth at the time!

In Verse 11 it says:

> Then a white robe was given to each of them; and it
> was said to them that they should rest a little while
> longer, until both *the number of* their fellow servants
> and their brethren, who would be killed as they *were*,
> was completed.

Notice that "robes" were given to "them," and "them" refers
to "souls." The souls of people who had been slain. Really, it is
referring here to the spirits, and every spirit has a soul. But spirits
have shape and substance — spirits are not like "Casper the Friendly
Ghost," or a puff of intangible nothingness, but substance. There is
a spiritual composition to that substance for it to exist in the spirit

realm, although it is different from the physical matter we have on earth. Spirits have as much shape and substance as you do physically, or there would be no point in giving them robes.

Later in Revelation 20:4, in fact, referring to the saints, John says, **And I saw thrones, and they sat on them….** That must mean that the saints (which "they" is referring to) have some sort of material substance to place on the thrones — "they" must have "seats" on which to sit! Indeed, throughout Revelation John keeps saying **And I *saw*.** Isn't it interesting that he doesn't just say "and it *was*," nor does he use phraseology indicating that he "just knew," or "God just told him," but that he "saw?" For you to see anything there has to be something there to see. Seeing is a sense, and clearly John's vision, even in the spirit world, was registering images, which have some materiality.

God Himself has substance. Referring to God, John said in Revelation 20:11-12:

11   **Then I saw a great white throne and Him who sat on it, from whose face the earth and the heaven fled away. And there was found no place for them.**

12   **And I saw the dead, small and great, standing before God….**

The One John saw had to have had substance, or John wouldn't know if He was standing, sitting, or lying down. But He was seated on the throne, and in Revelation 5:1, it says **And I saw in the right *hand* of Him who sat on the throne.** That tells you that God has two hands, otherwise why distinguish right from left?

Our spirit bodies probably resemble our physical bodies — actually, to say that our physical bodies somehow resemble our spirit bodies is more appropriate. Since each spirit is separate and unique, each spirit is identifiable and has a distinct personality. In the story of the rich man and Lazarus the beggar, how did the rich man know it was

Abraham? Obviously, the spirit forms of Lazarus and Abraham looked enough like the physical forms they had on earth to be recognized. Had the rich man ever met Abraham? No, because he lived later, but they had art and pictures in that time. Since Abraham was the fountainhead out of which the nation of Israel came, I am sure they passed pictures down through time. So the rich man and Lazarus alike had probably seen images of Abraham.

The point of all of this is that Mr. Muhammad is telling me, a black man in America, something that I cannot validate or support by the Bible. Yet he wants me to believe that Allah and Jehovah are one and the same. He wants black people to think that if they go to Islam and serve Allah, it is the same as if they served Jehovah. But that isn't the case. I have to conclude that Jehovah and Allah are not related at all, because they have completely different messages in their holy books.

There is still more evidence on the separation of you (your spirit) and your body (as Paul calls it, your "earthly house"). In 2 Corinthians 5:1, Paul writes: **"For we know that if our earthly house...."** Now, right there, if you didn't see anything else, it should imply something. If you have an "earthly house," then at the very least this indicates that you also have at least one other house. If there were only one, you would say "your house." The term *earthly* distinguishes this house from a "heavenly" or "spiritual" house.

> 1   **For we know that if our earthly house, *this* tent, is destroyed, we have a building from God, a house not made with hands, eternal in the heavens.**

I have no idea what that house, which your spirit man gets clothed with, is. I'm just going by what it says. If it says **house eternal in the heavens**, it must be there. Somehow, that house will overshadow our spirit and soul. When we continue with Verses 2 to 6, we see **For in this....** Even though the word *house* isn't mentioned in Verse 2, Verse 1 discusses our house, so it is clear that *house* is still the subject in the first part of the second verse. We could read it this way:

2   **For in this [house] we groan, earnestly desiring to be clothed with our habitation** [or house] **which is from heaven,**

3   **if indeed, having been clothed, we shall not be found naked.**

4   **For we who are in *this* tent [house] groan, being burdened, not because we want to be unclothed, but further clothed, that mortality may be swallowed up by life.**

5   **Now He who has prepared us for this very thing *is* God, who also has given us the Spirit as a guarantee.**

The word *guarantee* in the Greek carries the idea of a down payment, so if you have a down payment, that means something else is coming. Follow this now:

6   **So *we are* always confident, knowing that while we are at home in the body we are absent from the Lord.**

Again, notice the words *at home in the body*. Your body is your earthly house, and here it is stated again. Reiterating Verse 6:

6   **So *we are* always confident, knowing that while we are at *home*...**[emphasis mine].

See, that *we* and *home* are separate: **So *we are* always confident, knowing that while we are at home in the body....** It does not say, "with" the body, but "in" it. The spirit and soul dwell in the physical body while we are alive on earth, because we need this body, this house, to live on this planet. Paul says, **...while we are at home in the**

body...we are absent.... As long as I'm in my body, I'm absent from the Lord. What does **absent from** mean? It means that if you want to go be with the Lord, you have to *leave home.*

This is repeated in 2 Corinthians 5:8:

> **We are confident, yes, well pleased rather to be absent**
> **from the body and to be present with the Lord.**

If you want to be present with the Lord, you have to leave your body. Put another way, if you are with the Lord, you are somewhere other than where your body is, because you are not your body and your body is not you.

Now back to Mr. Muhammad's statement that "I have no alternative than to tell you that there is not any life beyond the grave." It seems pretty clear to me that there is life beyond the grave, and that tells me that Mr. Muhammad's message is in error. He continues by saying, "There is no justice in the sweet bye and bye." What does justice mean? In order to have justice, there has to be judgment. Well, in 2 Corinthians 5:10-11 we see:

> 10   **For we must all appear before the judgment**
>   **seat of Christ....**

Mr. Muhammad says there is no justice after the grave, yet Jehovah says, **For we must all appear....** Moreover, remember that the letter to the church at Corinth was written to Christians — not to sinners. So when it says "us," it's referring to Christians. When it says "we," it is referring to Christians. Paul, speaking for Jehovah God, says, **For we must all...,** and that means all of us Christians. Also, it is interesting that it did not say we were going to appear before the "seat of Christ," but **the judgment seat of Christ.** Obviously, there will be judgment going on there, and that, in turn, means justice. To continue:

> 10   **For we must all appear before the judgment**
>   **seat of Christ, that each one may receive the**

things *done* in the body, according to what he
has done, whether good or bad.

11   Knowing, therefore, the terror of the Lord,
we persuade men; but we are well known to
God, and I also trust are well known in your
consciences.

It appears to me that there will be judgment dispensed, or
Paul would not refer to "the terror of the Lord." Otherwise, who
cares about "persuading men?"

There is more evidence on this issue of justice and judgment. In Romans 14:10-12, Paul, under the influence of the Holy
Spirit, writes:

10   But why do you judge your brother? Or why
do you show contempt for your brother? For
we shall all [there it is again!] stand before the
judgment seat of Christ.

11   For it is written: *"As I live, says the Lord, every
knee shall bow to Me, and every tongue shall
confess to God."*

12   So then each of us shall give account of himself
to God.

I have news for you. If you claim to be a Christian, Judgment
Day is coming. You will have to give account of your works as a
child of God. But if you are not a Christian, you will have to appear
before another judgment seat — and you won't be in front of Jesus,
discussing your rewards! You will be in front of the Father at the
Great White Throne. And you don't want to come up in front of that
seat! Time and space doesn't allow us to deal with that here, but
suffice it to say, if you come before the Great White Throne, there
won't be any rewards involved. You will stand accused, your deeds

and words will convict you, and all you will be able to say at the end will be "I have no defense." And you *won't* have any.

Look at Verse 12 again: **So then each of us shall give account of himself to God.** I am so glad that this is true. I would hate to think of following a religion that is supposed to represent God and think that there is never going to be a Judgment Day. Thank God Judgment Day is coming. God would be unjust if He doesn't mete out judgment for some of these rascals who have been living like dogs all their lives, right in the face of God. But Judgment Day *is coming!*

That's another reason for the popularity of the Muslim message. It's just what people want: a religion that doesn't call them into question for their deeds. But there will be a settling up one day. Someone has to pay for all this stuff that has been done, whether to black people in America, or to those Protestant martyrs in Europe, or to the missionaries to China. A holy and just God demands an accounting. We see further revelation on this in Matthew 25:31-46, where Jesus says:

31   **"When the Son of Man comes in His glory, and all the holy angels with Him, then He will sit on the throne of His glory.**

32   **"All the nations will be gathered before Him, and He will separate them one from another, as a shepherd divides *his* sheep from the goats.**

33   **"And He will set the sheep on His right hand, but the goats on the left.**

34   **"Then the King will say to those on His right hand, 'Come, you blessed of My Father, inherit the kingdom prepared for you from the foundation of the world:**

35   **'for I was hungry and you gave Me food; I was thirsty and you gave Me drink; I was a stranger and you took Me in;**

36   'I was naked and you clothed Me; I was sick and you visited Me; I was in prison and you came to Me.'

37   "Then the righteous will answer Him, saying, 'Lord, when did we see You hungry and feed *You*, or thirsty and give *You* drink?

38   'When did we see You a stranger and take *You* in, or naked and clothe *You*?

39   'Or when did we see You sick, or in prison, and come to You?'

40   "And the King will answer and say to them, 'Assuredly, I say to you, inasmuch as you did *it* to one of the least of these My brethren, you did *it* to Me.'

41   "Then He will also say to those on the left hand, 'Depart from Me, you cursed, into the everlasting fire prepared for the devil and his angels;

42   'for I was hungry and you gave Me no food; I was thirsty and you gave Me no drink;

43   'I was a stranger and you did not take Me in, naked and you did not clothe Me, sick and in prison and you did not visit Me.'

44   "Then they also will answer Him, saying, 'Lord, when did we see You hungry or thirsty or a stranger or naked or sick or in prison, and did not minister to You?'

45   "Then He will answer them, saying, 'Assuredly, I say to you, inasmuch as you did not do *it* to one of the least of these, you did not do *it* to Me.'

46   **"And these will go away into everlasting punishment, but the righteous into eternal life."**

Don't tell me there's not going to be any judgment in the sweet bye and bye! There *is* a Judgment Day, and if you're following something that tells you there is none, you're going to be in serious trouble. I'm a black man, I'm in America, and I reject that message. That's not for me.

There is still more. In *Message to the Blackman in America*, Mr. Muhammad states, under the heading "Land of Our Own and Qualifications: The Unity of 22 Million":

> There is no hope for us in Christianity; it is a religion organized by the enemies (the white race) of the Black Nation to enslave us to the white race's rule.[12]

That is a strong statement. If Allah and Jehovah God are the same, and this man, Elijah Muhammad, was the spokesman for Allah, then he must speak on behalf of Allah! So I don't know how Allah and Jehovah could be the same God if Allah tells the messenger of Allah, Mr. Muhammad, to say something like this: "There is no hope for us in Christianity...."

He told me this message was for me, but I have a problem with it. I have researched both Christianity and Islam and I have to tell you that if there's no hope in Christianity, there's no hope at all for us. I use the word *us* to include all humanity, not just Blacks and Whites.

Mr. Muhammad stated that "There is no hope for us in Christianity; it is a religion *organized* [emphasis mine] by the enemies (the white race) of the Black Nation...." There is no other way to put it: That statement is grossly untrue. The white man did not start Christianity. Oh, he has perverted it — I'll give him that. (Again,

---

[12] Muhammad, 221.

reader, don't take any of this personally. I'm not talking about you, but these are historical facts that you may not know.)

White America has perverted Christianity and made people think it was the "white man's religion," but it is not. More important, the white race is not my problem. White people are not my enemy. Some Blacks get upset if the white folks categorize them as a race in which every black person is portrayed as a mugger, rapist, and doper. They get upset about that, but they don't mind making every white person into a racist. That's not true, so let's be fair about it.

Mr. Muhammad continues under the heading, "Land of Our Own Qualifications: We Must Have Some Earth and Soon!":

> Believe it or not, we have been serving and worshiping the REAL DEVILS! STOP preaching that old lie that God loves all human beings. He most certainly DOES NOT love the devils (the white race) [emphasis his].[13]

If you didn't know anything more about the Bible than John 3:16, and you heard this, you would know that this one statement completely disproves the notion that Allah and Jehovah are the same God. Mr. Muhammad says, "STOP preaching that old lie that God loves all human beings." Lie? John 3:16 says, **"For God so loved the world that He gave His only begotten Son...."** Who is in the world? Are white people in the world? Yes. Black people — are they in the world? Yes.

This is so powerful, because it would be enough if just the Bible said this. If one of the prophets, such as Habakkuk, or Joel, said this, then that alone would serve to disqualify Mr. Muhammad's remark. But this was the Son of God — the Person who knew the Father better than anyone — and He said of His own Father that **God so loved the world**. Not, "God so loved black people. Not, "God so loved white people." No — the world!

---

[13] Muhammad, 228.

Now you may rightly say, "Well, that's the Bible and I don't accept that, since I don't believe the Bible." Fine. But you cannot any longer continue under the false impression that God and Allah are the same person, the same God. We have shown that to be totally and completely untrue. You do not have to accept Jesus; you do not have to accept Jehovah God. You can accept Allah, or any of his messengers. But when you do, you can no longer pretend that you are worshipping Jehovah God "under another name."

3

What Does Islam Say?

 We have examined Elijah Muhammad's *Message to the Blackman in America* as a way to begin this part of the series on religion, simply because it was specifically addressed to black Americans. I want to reiterate, though, that there are several denominations or variations of black Muslims in the United States alone, and certainly Elijah Muhammad does not speak for all of them. Moreover, Islam is much more than the Muslim movement in America, and of course there are large divisions in Islam, just as there are in Christianity. You have the *Sunni* Muslims and the *Shiite* Muslims, but, again, there are subdivisions of Islam just as there are subdivisions of Christianity.

Whereas Jesus is the centerpiece of Christianity, and spoke on behalf of God, in Islam, Muhammad said the Koran was divinely given to him by Allah. Muhammad, therefore, claimed to be Allah's messenger. Well, any black person who is seriously considering becoming a Muslim should examine carefully the facts I am about to present. I will give you irrefutable documented evidence to support every word I say. Again, let me repeat my disclaimer: I'm not trying to tell anyone not to become a Muslim. That decision is yours. I believe, however, that if you leave Christianity to become a Muslim, especially as a black person, you should have all the facts that pertain to you as a black person.

First, we need to define some terms. The Muslim scholar Dr. Muhammad Hamidullah, in his book *Introduction to Islam*, states that "The custodian and repository of the original teachings of Islam" are found "above all in the Quran and the Hadith."[1] Hamidullah goes on to argue that for all intents and purposes, to a Muslim, the Quran and the Hadith are to have the same legal authority. Most people have heard of Islam, and many people know of the Koran, but how many have ever heard of the Hadith? Probably not many. Yet according to Dr. Hamidullah, Muslims revere the Hadith as well as the Koran because the Hadith is as divinely inspired as the Koran itself! He writes: "The teachings of Islam are based primarily on the Quran and Hadith, and, as we shall presently see, both are based on divine inspiration."[2]

We are using the translation of the Hadith made by Dr. Muhammad Muhsin Kahn, Islamic University, Medina Al-Munawwara, entitled *The Translation of the Meaning of Sahih Al-Bukhari (Arabic-English)*.[3] In this nine-volume set there are 4,705 pages. I have read and studied every one of them. So I'm saying to every Muslim, every Christian, and every whatever you may be, don't come to me with any rebuttal to what I have written until you have read and studied all 4,705 pages. Unless you have studied you don't qualify to discourse with me about it.

The Koran, of course, is the Bible of Islam. Christianity has the *Holy Bible*, and Islam has the *Holy Koran*, which is the holy book of the Muslims. The Hadith, on the other hand, consists of the oral traditions of the prophet Muhammad, made by the people who lived with him, slept in his bed, ate with him, went to war with him, bathed with him, heard him teach, and went to the mosque with him.

---

[1] Muhammad Hamidullah, *Introduction to Islam*, 5th edition (Chicago: Kazi Publications, 1981), 163.

[2] Hamidullah, 18.

[3] Muhammad Muhsin Kahn, *The Translation of the Meaning of Sahih Al-Bukhari (Arabic-English)* (New Delhi: Kitab Bhavan, 1984).

These were people who saw him on a daily basis and observed his actions. They weren't people who heard about him later — they walked with the man every day. I am dedicating some discussion to this because there is information in here that you need to know. This particular translation is recommended and approved by all Muslim authorities, including the spiritual heads of Mecca and Medina, Islam's two holy sites.

In the Hadith, Volume 7, #93, Chapter 32, #571 (1), Page 427, it says:

> Some Islamic sects such as Mutazila and others, believe that the Quran is created, but Bukhari and the Muslims of the first three centuries of Islam believe that the Quran is a quality of Allah (like seeing, hearing, knowing) and not created. So Bukhari refuted the dogma of Mutazila and others.

I point this out to show you that all Muslims do not believe the same thing the same way. They differ much in the way there are denominational differences in the Christian church. But be that as it may, I want to contrast the Koran, the Bible, and the Hadith. The Bible uses chapters and verses. The Koran uses "surahs," or "suras," (which literally means "rows") and verses. So instead of chapter, it would say Sura 9, verse so-and-so. We want to see what the Bible, the Koran, and the Hadith have to say, for instance, about Jesus, about God, about Muhammad, about women, and about slaves. You are going to be surprised, I guarantee it.

I will be using two versions of the Koran. The first is *The Koran*, translated with notes by N.J. Dawood; the second, *The Meaning of the Glorious Quran*, by Abdullah Yusuf Ali. Let's start by examining what the Koran has to say about women. In *The Koran*, by Dawood,[4] Sura 2:228 says:

---

[4] N. J. Dawood, *The Koran* (London: Penguin, 1999 [1916]).

Women shall with justice have rights similar to those ex-
ercised against them, although men have a status above
women. God is mighty and wise.[5]

In the Hadith, Volume 3, Chapter 12, The Witness of Women
and the Statement of Allah, #826: Page 502, it is stated:

Narrated Abu Sa 'id Al-Khudri: The Prophet said....

Just by way of passing, remember these are the recollections
of those who lived and worked with Muhammad the prophet, so
these usually begin with "Narrated...."

...The Prophet said, "Isn't the witness of a woman equal
to half of that of a man?" The woman said, "Yes." He
[the Prophet] said, "This is because of the deficiency of a
woman's mind."

So you women didn't know you were deficient. How do you
like that, ladies? Here is what the Bible has to say about it, in Galatians
3:28:

**There is neither Jew nor Greek, there is neither slave
nor free, there is neither male nor female; for you are
all one in Christ Jesus.**

Apparently, Allah told Muhammad that the female creature
whom Allah had created is deficient mentally, compared to a man.

I have a question for you. Did you know that Muhammad
was white? Not European white, obviously. He wouldn't be
Scandinavian white. But he wasn't black, he was white, according
to the Hadith! I'm only going to use the words that are in the book,
because I never met the man. But this is what the Muslims say in the
Hadith. Now, if white is of the devil — and I want you Black Muslims

---

[5] Dawood, 33.

to pick up on this — as Elijah Muhammad stated in his book where he calls white men devils, why would a black person want to leave a supposedly white Jesus to follow a white Muhammad? But don't take my word for it. Let's look at some evidence stating that the Prophet was white.

In the Hadith, Volume 1, Chapter 7, #63, Page 54:

> Narrated Anas bin Malik: While we were sitting with the Prophet in the mosque, a man came riding on a camel. He made his camel kneel down in the mosque, tied its foreleg and then said: "Who amongst you is Muhammad?" At that time the Prophet was sitting amongst us (his companions) leaning on his arm. We replied, "This white man reclining on his arm." The man then addressed him, "O Son of Abdul Muttalib."

Then, we see in the Hadith, Volume 1, Chapter 27, #385(B), Page 234:

> Narrated Abdullah bin Malik Ibn Buhaina, "When the Prophet prayed prostrated, he used to separate his arms from his body so widely that the whiteness of his armpits was visible."

We also find in the Hadith, Volume 1, Chapter 12, #367, Page 224:

> Narrated Abdul-Aziz: Anas said, "When Allah's Messenger invaded Khaibar, we offered the Fajr prayer there (early in the morning) when it was still dark. The Prophet rode and Abu Talha rode too and I was riding behind Abu Talha. The Prophet passed through the lane of Khaibar quickly and my knee was touching the thigh of the Prophet. He uncovered his thigh and I saw the whiteness of the thigh of the Prophet.

There is still more evidence that Muhammad was white. In the Hadith, Volume 2, Chapter 3A, #122, Page 65:

> Narrated Abdullah bin Dinar: My father said, "I heard
> Ibn Umar reciting the poetic verses of Abu Talib: And a
> white (person) (i.e. the Prophet) who is requested to pray
> for rain and who takes care of the orphans and is the
> guardian of widows."

Generally speaking, you do not call someone who is black a white person. We have four separate references by the people who lived with Muhammad that state categorically that he was white. He had white armpits and a white thigh, and twice people referred to him as a "white person" or this "white man." But there is more in the Hadith, Volume 9, Chapter 7, #342, Pages 258-259:

> Narrated Al-Bara bin Azib: The Prophet was carrying
> earth with us on the day of the battle of Al-Ahzab (con-
> federates) and I saw that the dust was covering the white-
> ness of his abdomen, and he (the Prophet) was saying,
> "(O Allah)! Without You, we would not have been guided,
> nor would we have given in charity, nor would we have
> prayed."

It seems from these passages in the Hadith that Muhammad was definitely not black. It further seems to me that we are right back at the starting blocks — a so-called white Jesus or a so-called white Muhammad. Interesting, don't you think?

What does Islam say about marriage and wives? How many wives should one have? The Koran says — and remember, the Koran is the holy book of the Muslim religion — in Sura 4:2,3:

> Give orphans the property which belongs to them. Do not
> exchange their valuables for worthless things or cheat
> them of their possessions; for this would surely be a
> grievous sin. If you fear that you cannot treat orphan
> [orphan girls] with fairness, then you may marry other
> women who seem good to you: two, three, or four of them.[6]

---

[6] Dawood, 60.

94

What Does Islam Say?

The Hadith goes on to tell us of the many (emphasis on *many*) wives of Muhammad. In Hadith, Volume 1, Chapter 13, #268, Page 165:

> Narrated Qatada: Anas bin Malik said, "The Prophet used to visit all his wives in a round, during the day and night and they were eleven in number." I asked Anas, "Had the Prophet the strength for it?" Anas replied, "We used to say that the Prophet was given the strength of thirty (men)." And Sa'id said on the authority of Qatada that Anas had told him about nine wives only (not eleven).

Did you know that the Prophet had between nine and eleven wives? This is confirmed further in the Hadith, Volume 3, Chapter 8, #755, Page 454:

> Narrated Urwa from Aisha: [Aisha was one of Muhammad's many wives.] The wives of Allah's Messenger were in two groups. One group consisted of Aisha, Hafsa, Safiyya, and Sauda; and the other group consisted of Um Salama and the other wives of Allah's Messenger.

From these references, it appears that Muslims can have more than one wife. Again, in the Hadith, Volume 4, Chapter 33, The Salary of the Administrator of an Endowment, #37, Page 29:

> Narrated Abu Huraira: Allah's Messenger said, "My heirs will not inherit a Dinar or a Dirham [i.e. money], for whatever I leave (excluding the adequate support of my wives and the wages of my employees) is to be given in charity."

We see again that Muhammad had more than one wife, and as many as eleven according to one of these reports. This is different indeed from what the Bible says about marriage, but we will save that for the time being. Again, in the Hadith, Volume 4, Chapter 7, #476, Page 310:

> Narrated Abu Huraira: The Prophet said, "The first batch (of people) who will enter Paradise will be (glittering) like the full moon, and the batch next to them will be (glittering) like the most brilliant star in the sky. Their hearts will be as if the heart of a single man, for they will have neither enmity nor jealousy amongst themselves; everyone will have two wives from the houris, (who will be so beautiful, pure and transparent that) the marrow of the bones of their legs will be seen through the bones and the flesh."

Not only did Muhammad have many wives, but he started on them early, as we see in Hadith, Volume 5, Chapter 43, #234, Page 152:

> Narrated Aisha: The Prophet engaged me when I was a girl of six (years). We went to Medina and stayed at the home of Bani-al-Harith bin Khazraj. Then I got ill and my hair fell down. Later on my hair grew (again) and my mother, Um Ruman, came to me while I was playing in a swing with some of my girl friends. She called me, and I went to her, not knowing what she wanted to do to me. She caught me by the hand and made me stand at the door of the house. I was breathless then, and when my breathing became alright, she took some water and rubbed my face and head with it. Then she took me into the house. There in the house, I saw some Ansari women who said, "Best wishes and Allah's Blessing and a good luck." Then she entrusted me to them and they prepared me (for the marriage). Unexpectedly Allah's Messenger came to me in the forenoon and my mother handed me over to him, and at that time I was a girl of nine years of age.

Another reference to Muhammad having multiple wives appears in the Hadith, Volume 7, Chapter 4, #5, Page 4:

> Narrated Ata: We attended along with Ibn 'Abbas at the funeral procession of Maimuna at a place called Sarif. Ibn 'Abbas said, "This is the wife of the Prophet, so when

you lift her bier, do not jerk it or shake it much, but walk smoothly because the Prophet had nine wives and he used to observe the night turns with eight of them, and for one of them there was no night turn."

Still another reference to multiple wives is found in the Hadith, Volume 7, Chapter 4, #6, Page 5:

Narrated Anas: The Prophet used to go round (have sexual relations with) all his wives in one night, and he had nine wives.

We will look at one more reference to Muhammad before we examine what the Bible has to say about the number of wives a man may have. In the Hadith, Volume 7, Chapter 39, #64, Page 50:

Narrated Aisha that the Prophet wrote the marriage contract with her when she was six years old and he consummated his marriage when she was nine years old, and then she remained with him for nine years(i.e. till his death).

It may seem that I have belabored the issue of Muhammad's wives, but I wanted to give you a full spectrum of references both from the Koran and the Hadith. In that regard, let's look at what the Bible has to say about having multiple wives. We find in 1 Corinthians 7:1-2:

1   Now concerning the things of which you wrote to me: *It is* good for a man not to touch a woman.

2   Nevertheless, because of sexual immorality, let each man have his own wife, and let each woman have her own husband.

That sounds like monogamy to me. In Ephesians 5:22-33, we see these illuminating words:

22   Wives, submit to your own husbands, as to the Lord.

23   For the husband is head of the wife [not wives], as also Christ is head of the church; and He is the Savior of the body.

24   Therefore, just as the church is subject to Christ, so *let* the wives *be* to their own husbands in everything.

25   Husbands, love your wives, just as Christ also loved the church and gave Himself for her,

26   that He might sanctify and cleanse her with the washing of water by the word,

27   that He might present her to Himself a glorious church, not having spot or wrinkle or any such thing, but that she should be holy and without blemish.

28   So husbands ought to love their own wives as their own bodies; he who loves his wife [not wives] loves himself.

29   For no one ever hated his own flesh, but nourishes and cherishes it, just as the Lord *does* the church.

30   For we are members of His body, of His flesh and of His bones.

31   *"For this reason a man shall leave his father and mother and be joined to his wife,* [not wives] *and the two* [not nine, or ten] *shall become one flesh."*

What Does Islam Say?

That again is monogamy, which means marriage to one person at a time. The statement in Verse 31 is a quotation from the first book in the Bible, so it goes all the way back to the beginning:

"For this reason a man shall leave his father and mother and be joined to his wife, and the two shall become one flesh."

Again, it doesn't say that "the seven shall become one flesh," or "the ten shall become one flesh," but the two — one woman and one man — shall become one flesh. This continues:

32 **This is a great mystery, but I speak concerning Christ and the church.**

33 **Nevertheless let each one of you in particular so love his own wife** [not wives] **as himself, and let the wife** [not wives] *see* **that she respects** *her* **husband.**

These verses attest again that the Bible and the Koran could not possibly have been written by the same author. The Bible has more to say on this matter, though, in 1 Timothy 3:1-2:

1 **This is a faithful saying: If a man desires the position of bishop, he desires a good work.**

2 **A bishop then must be blameless, the husband of one wife, temperate, sober-minded, of good behavior, hospitable, able to teach....**

Titus 1:1-6 is similar to 1 Timothy:

1 **Paul, a bondservant of God and an apostle of Jesus Christ, according to the faith of God's elect and the acknowledgment of the truth which accords with godliness,**

2   in *the* hope of eternal life which God, who cannot
        lie, promised before time began,

3   but has in due time manifested His word through
        preaching, which was committed to me according
        to the commandment of God our Savior;

4   To Titus, a true son in *our* common faith: Grace,
        mercy, *and* peace from God the Father and the
        Lord Jesus Christ our Savior.

5   For this reason I left you in Crete, that you should
        set in order the things that are lacking, and appoint
        elders in every city as I commanded you —

6   if a man is blameless, the husband of [how many
        wives?] one wife...

So if you're going to be an elder, you have to have one wife at a time.

Remember, Muhammad said that in paradise everyone would have two wives. Paradise means after death — the future. Then, of course, there is the phrase that we read in Elijah Muhammad's book, *Message to the Blackman in America*, where he said: "I have no alternative than to tell you that there is not any life beyond the grave." Remember that one? Now, we just read that Muhammad said that in Paradise everyone would have two wives.

The Bible has a different slant on it. Look at Matthew 22: 23-30:

23   The same day the Sadducees, who say there is no
        resurrection, came to Him and asked Him,

24   saying: "Teacher, Moses said that if a man dies,
        having no children, his brother shall marry his
        wife and raise up offspring for his brother.

25   "Now there were with us seven brothers. The
        first died after he had married, and having no
        offspring, left his wife to his brother.

26   "Likewise the second also, and the third, even
        to the seventh.

27   "Last of all the woman died also.

28   "Therefore, in the resurrection, whose wife of
        the seven will she be? For they all had her."

29   Jesus answered and said to them, "You are
        mistaken, not knowing the Scriptures nor the
        power of God.

30   "For in the resurrection they neither marry
        nor are given in marriage, but are like angels
        of God in heaven."

Muhammad said you will have two wives in paradise, yet Jesus said you are not married or given in marriage in the resurrection.

From our knowledge of the Bible, God doesn't have a wife and it looks like He's getting along pretty well. My point is that the sole purpose of marriage is to produce more humans. In that context, there are a lot of personal benefits that both the male and female get as a result of marriage. But the primary purpose is to perpetuate the human race. As a Christian, when you are resurrected and receive your glorified body, you'll never die again, so there is no need to perpetuate yourself. You will be you forever.

Now to another matter: Did you know that the Hadith reveals the fact that Muhammad *was not* sinless while the Bible reveals that Jesus *was* sinless. I think that's a significant point. In the Hadith, Volume 7, LXII, The Book of Nikah (Wedlock), Chapter 1, #1, Page 1:

> Narrated Anas bin Malik: A group of three men came to the houses of the wives of the Prophet asking how the Prophet worshipped (Allah), and when they were informed about that, they considered their worship insufficient and said, "Where are we from the Prophet as his past and future sins have been forgiven."

Excuse me? "...his [Muhammad's] past and future sins have been forgiven..."? So Muhammad sinned prior to becoming the Prophet, and apparently sinned afterward as well. Maybe this is some odd example that can be explained away — except it's not the only instance. We see also in the Hadith, Volume 8, Chapter 3, The Asking of the Prophet for Forgiveness From Allah by Daytime and at Night, #319, Page 213:

> Narrated Abu Huraira: I heard Allah's Messenger saying. "By Allah! I ask for forgiveness from Allah and turn to Him in repentance more than seventy times a day."

That is quite a bit of repentance, wouldn't you say? Muhammad even spelled out his sins in the Hadith, Volume 8, Chapter 40, To Seek Refuge With Allah From All Kinds of Sins and From Being in Debt, #379, Page 252:

> Narrated Aisha: The Prophet used to say, "O Allah! I seek refuge with You from laziness and geriatric old age, from all kinds of sins and from being in debt; from the affliction of the Fire and from the punishment of the Fire and from the evil of the affliction of wealth; and I seek refuge with You from the affliction of poverty, and I seek refuge with You from the affliction of Al-Masih Ad-Dajjal. *O Allah! Wash away my sins* [emphasis mine] with the water of snow and hail, and cleanse my heart from all the sins as a white garment is cleansed from the filth, and let there be a long distance between me and my sins, as You made East and West far from each other."

There is still more evidence that the Prophet sinned. Muhammad said, on another occasion, as documented in the Hadith, Volume 8, Chapter 62, The Statement of the Prophet: "O Allah! Forgive My Past and Future Sins," #407 (1), Page 271, we find:

> (1) O my Lord! Forgive my sins and my ignorance and my exceeding the limits (boundaries) of righteousness in all my deeds and what you know better than I. O Allah! Forgive my mistakes, those done intentionally or out of my ignorance or (without) or with seriousness, and I confess that all such mistakes are done by me. O Allah! Forgive my sins of the past and of the future which I did openly or secretly. You are the One Who makes the things go before, and You are the One Who delays them, and You are the Omnipotent.

We are reading what the Prophet said out of his own mouth, as recorded by those around him. There is more. In the Hadith, Volume 8, Chapter 63, To Invoke Allah, (1), Page 272, we find this statement:

> (1) "O Allah! Forgive my mistakes and my ignorance and my exceeding the limit (boundaries) of righteousness in my deeds; and forgive whatever You know better than I. O Allah! Forgive the wrong I have done jokingly or seriously, and forgive my accidental and intentional errors, all that is present in me."

This is quite a revelation and quite a confession, don't you think? What does the Bible have to say about Jesus Christ and His sin, or about His need to seek forgiveness from God? In Hebrews 4:14-15 it is written:

> **14**   **Seeing then that we have a great High Priest who has passed through the heavens, Jesus the Son of God, let us hold fast *our* confession.**

**15   For we do not have a High Priest who cannot
         sympathize with our weaknesses, but was in
         all *points* tempted as *we are*, *yet* without sin.**

That's what I need. I need someone who can understand what
I'm going through. I don't need someone who has never gone through
or been subjected to what I have gone through. No, I need someone
who has won. I need someone who has overcome the temptations,
not given in to them. I can give in to temptations without any help
from anyone else, whether it is Muhammad or another "savior." I
need someone to whom I can appeal, whom I can look up to with
respect, knowing that he has walked through what I have walked
through, but has overcome it. **...tempted as *we are*, YET WITHOUT
SIN.** That last part is the kicker! That's what makes Jesus special. He
did not sin. He could have. He had the opportunity, but he didn't.

Look at 2 Corinthians 5:17-21:

**17   Therefore, if anyone *is* in Christ, *he is* a new
         creation; old things have passed away; behold,
         all things have become new.**

**18   Now all things *are* of God, who has reconciled
         us to Himself through Jesus Christ, and has
         given us the ministry of reconciliation,**

**19   that is, that God was in Christ reconciling the
         world to Himself, not imputing their trespasses
         to them, and has committed to us the word of
         reconciliation.**

**20   Now then, we are ambassadors for Christ, as
         though God were pleading through us: we
         implore *you* on Christ's behalf, be reconciled
         to God**

**21   [Now comes the punch line:] For He [that is, God]
         made Him [that is, Christ] who *knew no sin***

[emphasis mine] *to be* **sin for us, that we might become the righteousness of God in Him.**

That's entirely different than what we just read about Muhammad. But we are not finished yet. We want to find out about Jesus and compare, so that you will have information upon which to make a decision. John 8:25-29 says:

25   **Then they said to Him, "Who are you?" And Jesus said to them, "Just what I have been saying to you from the beginning.**

26   **"I have many things to say and to judge concerning you, but He who sent Me is true; and I speak to the world those things which I heard from Him."**

One thing is certain: Muhammad and Jesus could not possibly be from the same source, because they have different and opposing messages. In John, the story continues:

27   **They did not understand that He spoke to them of the Father.**

28   **Then Jesus said to them, "When you lift up [crucify] the Son of Man, then you will know that I am *He*, and *that* I do nothing of Myself; but as My Father taught Me, I speak these things.**

29   **"And He who sent Me is with Me. The Father has not left Me alone, for I always do those things that please Him."**

Now, what Jesus says here is a little subtle, so you have to think about it: We know that sin does not please God. So this is an awesome statement that let's us know that Jesus doesn't sin, because

He says, **"…for I always do those things that please Him."** He doesn't say, "For I sometimes…" or, "For I occasionally…" or even, "For I try to do those things that please Him…." No, He said he *always* pleased the Father. That would mean that Jesus was righteous, and that He was always righteous.

In 1 Peter 2:21-22, we find Peter writing:

> **21** **For to this you were called, because Christ also suffered for us, leaving us an example, that you should follow in His steps:**

> **22** ***"Who committed no sin, nor was deceit found in His mouth";***

Jesus **committed no sin**. Based on what we read about Muhammad and Jesus, there is a gigantic difference between the two. Does the Koran or the Hadith say anything about Jesus? Look at Sura 4:171, in the Koran:

> The Messiah, Jesus the son of Mary, was no more than God's apostle and His Word which He cast to Mary: a spirit from Him. So believe in God and His apostles and do not say: "Three." Forbear, and it shall be better for you. God is but one God. God forbid that He should have a son![7]

So, based on this, Muslims do not believe that Jesus is the Son of God. They do not believe that God has a Son. The Koran says Jesus was no more than an apostle, so He could not be the Savior, the Redeemer, or the King of Kings. The phrase *no more than* indicates that He is only an apostle, and no more. This is more evidence that Jehovah and Allah could not possibly be the same God! "God forbid that He should have a son!" Remember that statement, because we will come back to it shortly.

---

[7] **Dawood, 78.**

What Does Islam Say?

In the Koran, Sura 5:75, Page 88, it says:

> The Messiah, the son of Mary, was no more than an apostle: other apostles passed away before him. His mother was a saintly woman. They both ate earthly food.[8]

Let me point out in passing that the way the Koran is written, it will say something the same way perhaps four or five times with only a few different words. You will notice that this statement is almost the same as the earlier reference to Jesus being only an apostle.

To continue, in the Koran, Sura 19:88, it says:

> Those who say: "The Lord of Mercy has begotten a son," preach a monstrous falsehood, at which the very heavens might crack, the earth break asunder, and the mountains crumble to dust. That they should ascribe a son to the Merciful, when it does not become the Lord of Mercy to beget one!"[9]

The Koran says it doesn't "become" God to beget a son. The Bible says that God so loved the world that He gave His only begotten Son (John 3:16). Allah and Jehovah cannot possibly know each other. No way!

Continuing with John 3:16-18, it is written:

16   "For God so loved the world that He gave His only *begotten Son* [emphasis mine], that whoever believes in Him should not perish but have everlasting life."

17   "For God did not send His *Son* [emphasis mine] into the world to condemn the world, but that the world through Him might be saved.

---

8 Dawood, 88.
9 Dawood, 219.

18   **"He who believes in Him is not condemned; but He who does not believe is condemned already, because he has not believed in the name of the only *begotten Son* of God** [emphasis mine].

Now, whose report will you believe? There is diametrical opposition between what the Bible and the Koran state. The Koran said that God could not have a son and that Jesus was not the Son of God, and we just read from the Bible that God gave His Son. The choice is yours.

The Koran also says, in Sura 19:88, Page 219, "Those who say: 'The Lord of Mercy has begotten a son' preach a monstrous falsehood...." In essence, this says that we Christians preach a lie. It is more serious than that, though. This means that the Koran is saying that God Almighty Jehovah preaches a "monstrous falsehood" because He's the One who called Jesus His Son.

What does the Bible say? In Luke 3:21-22, we find Jesus getting baptized:

21   **When all the people were baptized, it came to pass that Jesus also was baptized; and while He prayed, the heaven was opened.**

22   **And the Holy Spirit descended in bodily form like a dove upon Him, and a voice came from heaven which said, *"You are My beloved Son; in You I am well pleased."* [emphasis mine]**

So the Koran said that God preaches a "monstrous falsehood." But, as you read, the voice from heaven said, **"You are My beloved Son."** If the voice says, **"You are My Son,"** doesn't that mean that it is a parent speaking? And everywhere we read God referred to as the male gender, and He is always mentioned as the "Father." So this is Jehovah God speaking. But whether it is intentional or not, the Koran has just accused Jehovah of a "monstrous falsehood."

There is more on this subject in the Hadith, Volume 7, #63, The Book of Divorce, Chapter 18, The Statement of Allah, #209, Pages 155-156:

> Narrated Nafi: Whenever Ibn Umar was asked about marrying a Christian lady or a Jewess, he would say: "Allah has made it unlawful for the believers to marry ladies who ascribe partners in worship to Allah, and I do not know of a greater thing, as regards to ascribing partners in worship, etc., to Allah, than that a lady should say that Jesus is her Lord although he is just one of Allah's slaves."

Here we have in the Hadith, out of the mouth of Ibn Umar, that Jesus is "just one of Allah's slaves." But in Matthew 16:15-16 it says:

> 15   He [Jesus] said to them, "But who do you say that I am?"
>
> 16   Simon Peter answered and said, "You are the Christ, the *Son* of the living God." [emphasis mine]

He didn't say, the "slave" of the living God, but the **"Son of the living God."** Ibn Umar said Jesus was a slave; Peter said Jesus was the Son of God. Do you see a difference between "son" and "slave?"

We find another interesting statement in Luke 4:40-41:

> 40   When the sun was setting, all those who had any that were sick with various diseases brought them to Him [Jesus]; and He laid His hands on every one of them and healed them.
>
> 41   And demons also came out of many, crying out and saying, "You are the Christ, the Son of God!" And He, rebuking *them,* did not allow

them to speak, for they knew that He was
the Christ.

The Hadith said that Jesus is just one of Allah's slaves. But even
the demons knew better than that. They weren't speculating about it,
they weren't discussing it among themselves — they knew it, because the
demons came from the spirit world and that is where Jesus came from.
They recognized Him. Ibn Umar, in the Hadith, said that Jesus was just
one of Allah's slaves. Now who is right?

How about Luke 8:26-28?

26   Then they sailed to the country of the
        Gadarenes, which is opposite Galilee.

27   And when He [again, Jesus] stepped out on the
        land, there met Him a certain man from the
        city who had demons for a long time. And he
        wore no clothes, nor did he live in a house but
        in the tombs.

28   When he saw Jesus, he cried out, fell down
        before Him, and with a loud voice said, "What
        have I to do with You, Jesus, Son of the Most
        High God? I beg You, do not torment me!"

Here it is again — a demon attesting to Jesus' origin and
acknowledging the fact that He is the Son of God. But Allah's
messenger said that Jesus is just one of Allah's slaves.

In John 4:24-26, which we have already read in another context, Jesus, speaking with the woman at the well in Samaria, said:

24   "God *is* Spirit, and those who worship Him
        must worship in spirit and truth."

25   The woman said to Him, "I know that Messiah
        is coming" (who is called Christ). "When He
        comes, He will tell us all things."

110

26   **Jesus said to her, "I who speak to you am *He*."**

Jesus said of Himself: "I am Messiah; that one that you just referred to — the Messiah that you have waited for." Jesus stated who He was; Peter, James, John, Andrew, and hundreds if not thousands of other people knew who He was; the demons knew who He was; and God stated who He was. But we're not finished.

In John 6:66-69:

66   **From that *time* many of His disciples went back and walked with Him no more.**

67   **Then Jesus said to the twelve, "Do you also want to go away?"**

68   **But Simon Peter answered Him, "Lord, to whom shall we go? You have the words of eternal life.**

69   **"Also we have come to believe and know that You are the Christ, the Son of the living God."**

This is how it works. You believe first, then you know. The believing causes the knowing. Notice the progression. Peter said, in essence, "We started out believing You were the Son of God, and that's why we followed You in the beginning. But after following You, now we know You are the Son of the living God."

It is important for people flirting with Islam to know who Jesus is. The Muslims are telling their followers that Jesus is just a slave of Allah. But why not go to the source, where Jesus is most readily presented? The Koran and the Hadith both have passages about Jesus, but Jesus Himself is never quoted in either the Koran or the Hadith. If they did that, they would find in John 10:34-36, that Jesus spoke for Himself:

34   **Jesus answered them, "Is it not written in your law, '*I said, You are gods*' "?**

111

35 "**If He** [God the Father] **called them gods, to whom the word of God came (and the Scripture cannot be broken),**

36 "**do you say of Him whom the Father sanctified and sent into the world, 'You are blaspheming,' because I said, 'I am the Son of God'?"**

This is not someone else's opinion of who Jesus was. This is Jesus stating who He is. We see in John 17:1-5 that **Jesus spoke these words, lifted up His eyes to heaven, and said: "Father...."** You don't call someone "Father" unless you are a son or daughter. Isn't that true?

1 **Jesus spoke these words, lifted up His eyes to heaven, and said: "Father, the hour has come. Glorify Your Son, that Your Son also may glorify You,**

2 "**as You have given Him authority over all flesh, that He should give eternal life to as many as You have given Him."**

I have not found anywhere in my research where Muhammad ever offered anyone eternal life. Don't get upset about it. I'm just giving you the facts. Let's read Verse 2 again, because it is important:

2 "**as You have given Him authority over all flesh, that He should give eternal life to as many as You have given Him.**

3 "**And this is eternal life, that they may know You, the only true God, and Jesus Christ whom You have sent.**

4 "**I have glorified You on the earth. I have finished the work which You have given Me to do.**

> 5   "And now, O Father, glorify Me together with
>   Yourself, with the glory which I had with You
>   before the world was."

That is a remarkable statement — that Jesus was with God **"before the world was."** Remember our working text here from the Hadith, Volume 7, #63, Chapter 18, #209, on Page 155-156: "...Allah has made it unlawful for the believers to marry ladies who ascribe partners in worship to Allah, and I do not know of a greater thing, as regards to ascribing partners in worship, etc. to Allah, than that a lady should say that Jesus is her Lord although he is just one of Allah's slaves." This says "Allah has made it unlawful...." I am not a law enforcement officer, and I'm not a lawyer and not a judge. But I understand that when something is unlawful, that means it is against the law. This is an awesome statement: "Allah has made it unlawful...." Islam says through the Hadith in these writings that if you call Jesus "Lord," that is an affront to Allah and it is unlawful. Yet look at Romans 10:8-9:

> 8   But what does it say? *"The word is near you, in
>   your mouth and in your heart"* (that is, the word
>   of faith which we preach):
>
> 9   that if you confess with your mouth the Lord
>   Jesus and believe in your heart that God has
>   raised Him from the dead, you will be saved.

That is how you get saved in Christianity: You make an oral confession that Jesus is Lord. These verses from the Bible establish beyond any question that Jesus Christ was and is more than an apostle, more than a slave. If Jesus is "no more than an apostle," as the Muslims say, then He cannot be savior. Yet the Bible says that He is the Savior.

There are more passages in the Hadith that we want to investigate relative to Jesus and Muhammad. In Hadith, Volume 9, Chapter 10, #97, Pages 79-80, we find:

> Narrated Um Salama: The Prophet said, "I am only a human being, and you people have disputes. May be some one amongst you can present his case in a more eloquent and convincing manner than the other, and I give my judgment in his favor according to what I hear. Beware! If ever I give (by error) somebody something of his brother's right then he should not take it as I have only given him a piece of Fire."

The first sentence is the one that concerns us: "The Prophet said, 'I am only...'." *Only* means that there is nothing else beyond that — it's the end of the road. You are that and nothing else. Jesus said He was the Son of God. God said Jesus was His Son. The demons said Jesus was the Son of God. But Allah said Jesus is a slave. Now, the Prophet says that he, Muhammad, is "only a human being." If you are "only a human being," you might be a fine person, but you cannot do anything about my sin, or my eternal life. We need someone unlike us, yet like us — but above and beyond us, who is able to do something for us. Muhammad's statement that he is "only a human being" means that he came into this world through a natural birth, while Jesus Christ came into this world through a supernatural birth. Look at Luke 1:26-35:

26   Now in the sixth month the angel Gabriel was sent by God to a city of Galilee named Nazareth,

27   to a virgin betrothed to a man whose name was Joseph, of the House of David. The virgin's name *was* Mary.

28   And having come in, the angel said to her, "Rejoice, highly favored *one*, the Lord *is* with you; blessed *are* you among women!"

29   But when she saw *him*, she was troubled at his saying, and considered what manner of greeting this was.

114

30   Then the angel said to her, "Do not be afraid, Mary, for you have found favor with God.

31   "And behold, you will conceive in your womb and bring forth a Son, and shall call His name JESUS.

32   "He will be great, and will be called the Son of the Highest; and the Lord God will give Him the throne of His father David.

33   "And He will reign over the house of Jacob forever, and of His kingdom there will be no end."

34   Then Mary said to the angel, "How can this be, since I do not know a man?"

35   And the angel answered and said to her, "The Holy Spirit will come upon you, and the power of the Highest will overshadow you; therefore, also, that Holy One who is to be born will be called the Son of God."

Muhammad said of himself, "I am only a human being...."
The angel said Jesus "will be called the Son of God."
Now let's look at Matthew 1:18-23:

18   Now the birth of Jesus Christ was as follows: After His mother Mary was betrothed to Joseph, before they came together, she was found with child of the Holy Spirit.

19   Then Joseph her husband, being a just *man*, and not wanting to make her a public example, was minded to put her away secretly.

20   But while he thought about these things, behold, an angel of the Lord appeared to him

in a dream, saying, "Joseph, son of David, do not be afraid to take to you Mary your wife, for that which is conceived in her is of the Holy Spirit.

21   "And she will bring forth a Son, and you shall call His name JESUS, for He will save His people from their sins."

22   So all this was done that it might be fulfilled which was spoken by the Lord through the prophet, saying:

23   *"Behold, the virgin shall be with child, and bear a Son, and they shall call His name Immanuel,"* which is translated, "God with us."

If Jesus is going to save His people from their sins, then that would make Him a Savior. To save the human race from its sin, you have to be more than a man. You have to be God, or the Son of God. Muhammad, by his own admission, is "only a human being." Jesus Christ is the Son of the Living God. I think there is a difference. What do you think?

4

Consumer Reports: Islam and Christianity

 We cannot just ignore Islam because that's exactly what the devil wants. He's a liar and he'll try to keep us from addressing the claims of Islam through a variety of lies. We have already seen — and refuted — one lie, which is that Islam and Christianity worship the same God, only under different names. But if you are planning to become a Muslim, even if you do not follow the Nation of Islam, and you think you are simply going to follow the Koran and the holy books of Islam, you better know what they say.

In that regard, another lie is that it isn't respectful to examine another person's religion. Jesus challenged people's religion all the time. In John 4:22, He told the Samaritan woman at the well, **"You worship what you do not know; we know what we worship, for salvation is of the Jews."** That is pretty direct.

People need to know what it is they worship. It's interesting that when we talk about Christians — churchgoers — we know for a fact that many of them don't know what's in the Word. That doesn't surprise us. That's why teaching ministries like mine have grown so much over the years, because people are hungry for the Word. When we see people of other faiths, such as Muslims, we somehow assume that they are super-spiritual people who know all about their religion. But in fact, many, if not most, of them are just like Christians who were raised in the church, grew up in the church, yet never took the time or had the instruction in what their "faith" really meant. Many Muslims who have been brought up in Islam have never taken the time to read their holy book. They are going by what a mother or father or some relative told them.

For our part, if we, the Christian church, are going to have an impact on these people, we need to know what their holy books say. We especially need to know if these holy books say what God says.

Let's continue our investigation of the differences in Islam and Christianity by examining what the Hadith has to say about salvation. After all, if we, as Christians, accept that the only route to salvation is through Jesus Christ, wouldn't it be logical to assume that Islam would say that all salvation must go through Muhammad the Prophet? But that isn't the case. Look at the Hadith, Volume 8, Chapter 18, #470, Page 313:

> Narrated Abu Huraira: Allah's Messenger said, "The deeds of anyone of you will not save you [from the (Hell) Fire]." They said, "Even you (will not be saved by your deeds), O' Allah's Messenger?" He said, "No, even I (will not be saved) unless and until Allah bestows His Mercy upon me. Therefore, do good deeds properly, sincerely and moderately, and worship Allah in the forenoon and in the afternoon and during a part of the night, and always adopt a middle, moderate, regular course whereby you will reach your target (Paradise)."

This is an awesome statement, because it indicates that Muhammad was in need of salvation himself. Jesus Christ did not need to be saved, because He is the One commissioned by God to be the Savior. Look at that again: "They said, 'Even you (will not be saved by your deeds), O' Allah's Messenger?' He said, 'No, even I (will not be saved) unless and until Allah bestows His Mercy upon me.'" Compare that with Jesus' statement in Luke, 19:10, that **"...the Son of Man has come to seek and to save that which was lost."**

118

It would appear from these statements that Muhammad admitted that he needed to be saved, and Jesus is just the Savior to save him! How can a "savior" who himself needs saving save us?

The Prophet Muhammad says that through a "middle, moderate, regular course...you will reach your target (Paradise)." Well, what do the Koran, the Hadith, and the Bible have to say about which spiritual path is right? In the Koran, Sura 3:19, it reads: "The only true faith in God's sight is Islam."

Yet the Bible, in Ephesians 4:1-6, we find the Apostle Paul saying:

1   **I, [the Apostle Paul] therefore, the prisoner of the Lord, beseech you to walk worthy of the calling with which you were called,**

2   **with all lowliness and gentleness, with longsuffering, bearing with one another in love,**

3   **endeavoring to keep the unity of the Spirit in the bond of peace.**

4   ***There is* one body and one Spirit, just as you were called in one hope of your calling;**

5   **one Lord, one faith, one baptism;**

6   **one God and Father of all, who is above all, and through all, and in you all.**

The words *one Lord* is referring to Jesus Christ.

The Koran also says in Sura 3:85, "He that chooses a religion other than Islam, it will not be accepted from him and in the world to come he will surely be among the losers." The Bible says it differently. Acts 4:8-12 says:

8   **Then Peter, filled with the Holy Spirit, said to them, "Rulers of the people and elders of Israel:**

119

9   "If we this day are judged for a good deed *done* to a helpless man, by what means he has been made well,

10   "let it be known to you all, and to all the people of Israel, that by the name of Jesus Christ of Nazareth, whom you crucified, whom God raised from the dead, by Him this man stands here before you whole.

11   "This is the *'stone which was rejected by you builders, which has become the chief cornerstone.'*

12   "Nor is there salvation in any other, for there is no other name under heaven given among men by which we must be saved."

Again, the Koran says, "He that chooses a religion other than Islam, it will not be accepted from him and in the world to come he will surely be among the losers." And, again, the Bible says, **"Nor is there salvation in any other, for there is no other name under heaven given among men by which we must be saved."**

Remember, going back to verses 10 and 11, they're talking about Jesus the Christ. And then, in Verse 12, it says, **"Nor is there salvation in any other...."** Any other who? Any other than Jesus the Christ, **"...for there is no other name** [than Jesus the Christ] **under heaven given among men by which we must be saved."**

Notice the difference between these two, if you are spiritual enough to see it. In the Koran, it says "He that chooses a religion other than Islam...." But Jesus never came to bring us religion — He came to bring us *salvation*! That's an awesome difference.

There is something else in this statement from the Koran: "He that chooses a religion other than Islam...." You don't choose Christianity, because Christianity is not offered to you. Whenever we give an invitation, we don't offer Christianity. We're offering you Jesus Christ! There's the big difference. Islam is a religion — the Koran says so. But religion can't do anything but confuse you. The Bible says, **"Nor is there salvation...."** I don't need a religion; I need salvation.

Think about this. If religion was the key, I could just make my own religion. But the Bible says, **"Nor is there salvation in any other, for there is no other name under heaven given among men by which we must be saved"** — not "by which we must have religion," but "by which we must be saved." There it is. You make your own decision, but you need to be very careful.

The Hadith gives us some glimpses of Muhammad's attitude toward those who embrace Islam and then turn from it. It shows us a side of Muhammad that, to say the least, does not appear compassionate or loving. But I'll let you be the judge. The Hadith, Volume 4, Chapter 149, One Should Not Punish (Anybody) With Allah's Punishment, #260, Pages 160-161, states:

> **Narrated Ikrima: Ali burnt some people and this news reached Ibn Abbas, who said, "Had I been in his place I would not have burnt them, as the Prophet said, 'Don't punish (anybody) with Allah's Punishment.' No doubt, I would have killed them, for the Prophet said, 'If somebody (a muslim) discards his religion, kill him.'"**

It is pretty clear here that they were burning people because they had discarded their religion. That's strong indeed! The Hadith goes on to say in Volume 1, Chapter 70, #234, Page 148:

> **Narrated Abu Qilaba: Anas said, "Some people of Ukl or Uraina tribe came to Medina and its climate did not suit them. So the Prophet ordered them to go to the herd of (milch) camels and to drink their milk and urine (as a medicine). So they went as directed and after they became healthy, they killed the shepherd of the Prophet and drove away all the camels. The news reached the Prophet early in the morning and he sent (men) in their pursuit and they were captured and brought at noon.**

He then ordered to cut their hands and feet (and it was done), and their eyes were branded with heated pieces of iron. They were put in Al-Harra and when they asked for water, no water was given to them."

That does not appear to me to show much love or compassion, does it? Then we have this passage in the Hadith, Volume 3, Chapter 18, #72, Page 44:

Narrated Anas bin Malik: Allah's Messenger entered Mecca in the year of its Conquest wearing an Arabian helmet on his head (1) and when the Prophet took it off, a person came and said, "Ibn Khatal is holding the covering of the Kaba (taking refuge in the Kaba)." The Prophet said, "Kill him." (2)

Now, I've read the New Testament many times and I have never found a place where Jesus ever said go kill someone. In the Hadith, Volume 3, #45, Chapter 3, Mortgaging the Arms, #687, Page 415:

Narrated Jabir bin Abdullah: Allah's Messenger said, "Who would kill Kab bin Al-Ashraf as he has harmed Allah and His Messenger?" Muhammad bin Maslama (got up and) said, "I will kill him." So, Muhammad bin Maslama went to Kab and said, "I want a loan of one or two Wasqs of foodgrains." Kab said, "Mortgage your women to me." Muhammad bin Maslama said, "How can we mortgage our women, and you are the most handsome among the Arabs?" He said, "Then mortgage your sons to me." Muhammad said, "How can we mortgage our sons, as the people will abuse them for being mortgaged for one or two Wasqs of foodgrains? It is shameful for us. But we will mortgage our arms to you." So, Muhammad bin Maslama promised him that he would come to him next time. They (Muhammad bin Maslama and his companions) came to him as promised and murdered him. Then they went to the Prophet and told him about it.

It appears from this that Muhammad condones murder, doesn't it? Let's go on. In the Hadith, Volume 3, #48, Chapter 8, #816, Page 496:

> Narrated Urwa bin Az-Zubair: A woman committed theft in the Ghazwa of the Conquest (of Mecca) and she was taken to the Prophet who ordered her hand to be cut off. Aisha said, "Her repentance was perfect and she was married (later) and used to come to me (after that) and I would present her needs to Allah's Messenger."

Muhammad ordered her hand to be cut off. That doesn't appear to show much compassion or forgiveness, does it? Let's look at Jesus in a similar situation and examine His response.

In John 8:1-11, it says:

1   **But Jesus went to the Mount of Olives.**

2   **Now early in the morning He came again into the temple, and all the people came to Him; and He sat down and taught them.**

3   **Then the scribes and Pharisees brought to Him a woman caught in adultery. And when they had set her in the midst,**

4   **they said to Him, "Teacher, this woman was caught in adultery, in the very act.**

5   **"Now Moses, in the law, commanded us that such should be stoned. But what do You say?"**

6   **This they said, testing Him, that they might have *something* of which to accuse Him. But Jesus stooped down and wrote on the ground with *His* finger, as though He did not hear.**

7   **So when they continued asking Him, He raised Himself up and said to them, "He who is**

without sin among you, let him throw a stone at her first."

8 And again He stooped down and wrote on the ground.

9 Then those who heard *it*, being convicted by *their* conscience, went out one by one, beginning with the oldest, *even* to the last. And Jesus was left alone, and the woman standing in the midst.

10 When Jesus had raised Himself up and saw no one but the woman, He said to her, "Woman, where are those accusers of yours? Has no one condemned you?"

11 She said, "No one, Lord." And Jesus said to her, "Neither do I condemn you; go and sin no more."

Given these two situations — the woman thief in the marketplace, and the woman taken in adultery — I would rather go before Jesus than Muhammad. Now, understand that Jesus did not condone her sin. She was wrong and the Law said she should be stoned. The Law was made for man, not man for the Law, so that you have order. But Law without mercy is tyranny.

In our law today there are different degrees of punishment for different crimes. You kill someone in one situation, it might not be first-degree murder but manslaughter. The judge might even rule that a crime which may be punishable by death, can be judged with leniency if there were extenuating circumstances. That is, in the case of the law, a version of mercy.

Muhammad had the woman's hand cut off. In contrast, Jesus confirmed that she sinned, that she committed adultery. But then He said, "Where are your accusers? Has no man condemned you?" She said, "No man…." He said, "Neither do I. Go, but sin no more."

Now that is mercy. It is quite a contrast from the treatment by Muhammad, don't you think?

In another quote from the Hadith, Volume 4, Chapter 107, Bidding Farewell, Pages 127-128, we find:

> Narrated Abu Huraira: Allah's Messenger sent us on a military expedition telling us, "If you find such and such persons (he named two men from Quraish), burn them with fire." Then we came to bid him farewell, when we wanted to set out, he said, "Previously I ordered you to burn so-and-so and so-and-so with fire, but as punishment with fire is done by none except Allah, if you capture them, kill them, (instead)."

Still again, in the Hadith, Volume 4, Chapter 152, If a Pagan Burns a Muslim Should He Be Burnt (in Retaliation)?, #261 (A), Pages 161-162:

> Narrated Anas Bin Malik: A group of eight men from the tribe of Ukil came to the Prophet and then they found the climate of Medina unsuitable for them...."

Let me stop here and point out that in the Hadith, you will often find the same story told two or three times, but every time with a difference, almost as though there is an addendum to it. You will find information not in the previous accounts of the same story. So even though we read this story before, there is a difference that will be readily seen by the astute observer:

> Narrated Anas Bin Malik: A group of eight men from the tribe of Ukil came to the Prophet and then they found the climate of Medina unsuitable for them. So, they said, "O, Allah's Messenger! Provide us with some milk." Allah's Messenger said, "I recommend that you should join the herd of camels." So they went and drank the urine and the milk of the camels (as a medicine) till they became healthy and fat. Then they killed the shepherd and drove away the camels, and they became

unbelievers after they were Muslims. When the Prophet was informed by a shouter for help, he sent some men in their pursuit, and before the sun rose high, they were brought, and he had their hands and feet cut off. Then he ordered for nails which were heated and passed over their eyes, and they were left in the Harra (i.e. rocky land in Medina). They asked for water and no body provided them with water till they died. (Abu Qilaba, a sub-narrator said, "They committed murder and theft and fought against Allah and His Messenger and spread evil in the land.")

That's rather drastic, I would say. Nowhere in the life of Jesus have I found an instance where He told His followers to kill someone, even if they departed from the faith. Quite the contrary. In the garden, when the men came to arrest him, Peter took a sword and sliced off the ear of one of Jesus' attackers and Jesus said (Matthew 26:52) **"Put your sword in its place, for all who take the sword will perish by the sword."** And then, according to Luke 22:51, Jesus **touched his ear** [the man whom Peter struck] **and *healed him*** [emphasis added]. Jesus not only did not tell His followers to kill his enemies, but He healed them!

Let's examine the contrast further. In the Hadith, Volume 4, Chapter 173, If an Infidel Warrior Comes in an Islamic Territory Without Having the Assurance of Protection (Is It Permissible to Kill Him?), #286, Pages 181-182, it is written:

Narrated Salama bin Al-Akwa "An infidel spy came to the Prophet while he was on a journey. The spy sat with the companions of the Prophet and started talking and then went away. The Prophet said (to his companions), 'Chase and kill him.' So, I killed him." The Prophet then gave him the belongings of the killed spy (in addition to his share of the war booty).

Now, you might say that Judas was a spy of sorts. Certainly he was a traitor and actually betrayed Jesus for thirty pieces of silver.

But even though Jesus knew by the Holy Spirit that Judas was a traitor, He didn't send His disciples after him with instructions to kill him, even though He knew Judas had "sold Him out" for thirty pieces of silver.

In the Hadith, Volume 5, Chapter 14, The Killing of Kab Bin Al-Ashraf, #369, Pages 248 and 250, there is another telling incident:

> Narrated Jabir bin Abdullah: Allah's Messenger said, "Who is willing to kill Kab bin Al-Ashraf who has hurt Allah and His Apostle?" Thereupon Muhammad bin Maslama got up saying, "O Allah's Messenger! Would you like that I kill him?" The Prophet said, "Yes." Muhammad bin Maslama said, "Then allow me to say a (false) thing (i.e. to deceive Kab.) The Prophet said, "You may say it...."

(Not only is Muhammad instructing his follower to kill the man, he's saying that it's okay to trick him and to lie to him.)

> ...Muhammad bin Maslama requested Kab "Will you allow me to smell your head?" Kab said, "Yes." Muhammad smelt it and made his companions smell it as well. Then he requested Kab again, "Will you let me (smell your head)?" Kab said, "Yes." When Muhammad got a strong hold of him, he said (to his companions), "Get at him!" So they killed him and went to the Prophet and informed him.

It appears that Muhammad is condoning both murder and deception. Based on this, I sure would not want to be a follower of Muhammad!

We will now look at other specific references in the Hadith to the consequences of turning from Islam. This is one of the things that black folk, in particular, need to be aware of, because, as I've said, racism in the church has created a pull for Blacks to leave Christianity. "Come to Islam," black people are told. "It's the religion of the black man." I'm not telling you not to do that, but I do want to inform you of the consequences you *may* have to endure if you later decide to leave that religion. You should know this going into it.

Let's begin with the Hadith, Volume 8, Chapter 1, The Statement of Allah, #794, Pages 519-520:

> Narrated Anas: Some People from the tribe of Ukl came to the Prophet and embraced Islam. The climate of Medina did not suit them, so the Prophet ordered them to go to the (herd of Milch) camels of charity and to drink their milk and urine (as a medicine). They did so, and after they had recovered from their ailment (became healthy) they turned renegades (reverted from Islam) and killed the shepherd of the camels and took the camels away. The Prophet sent (some people) in their pursuit and so they were (caught and) brought, and the Prophet ordered that their hands and legs should be cut off and that their eyes should be branded with heated pieces of iron, and that their cut hands and legs should not be cauterised, till they die.

Again, there is not much mercy shown here! In the Hadith, Volume 8, Chapter 2, Page 520:

> The Prophet did not cauterise (the amputated limbs of) those who fought (against Allah and His Messenger) and of those who were renegades (reverted from Islam) (therefore they bled) till they died.

This doesn't sound like compassion to me! Still again, in the Hadith, Volume 9, Chapter 2: #57, Page 45:

> Narrated Ikrima: Some Zanadiqa (atheists) were brought to Ali; and he burnt them. The news of this event, reached Ibn Abbas who said, "If I had been in his place, I would not have burnt them, as Allah's Messenger forbade it, saying, 'Do not punish anybody with Allah's punishment (fire).' I would have killed them according to the statement of Allah's Messenger, 'Whoever changed his Islamic religion, then kill him.'"

If you become a Muslim, then decide to leave, according to what the Prophet told his people, you should be killed! You see, Muslims — I'm talking about real Muslims — don't play games with Islam.

During the time I taught *Race, Religion & Racism* as a series at the FaithDome, I received a letter from an ex-Muslim that shows the reality in our day of the consequences of turning from Islam:

Dear Pastor,

First of all, I'd like to commend you on your obedience to God to fulfill an awesome assignment. There aren't many in the body of Christ who God can trust to deliver a baby that has been in labor too long. I have observed the outcome of the responses of the Christian leaders, and all I can say is that it certainly has exposed the heart of the problem. Pastor, there are many that said God has chosen them and anointed them to preach the good news. But when you actually boiled down to it, only a few stood with the truth God wanted to reveal.

I was raised a Muslim with the Nation of Islam. My sister and I attended the Muslim schools and my father sold bean pies and the *Mohammad Speaks* [sic] newspaper that is now called the *Final Call*. We were taught to fear Allah, in a sense, that if we didn't act properly, He, Allah, would punish us. My parents separated as a result of the teachings that were instilled in my father. You know the teaching about the women being inferior to the man. And the man being able to have affairs with women while the wife stayed home with the children with little or no opinion about her husband's actions. My father eventually became a minister and served the Muslim religion for many years. As I listened to you teach about the only way out of the religion is through death, I thought about the time when my dad got out of the religion. They actually came to his home in the middle of the night and attempted to murder him. They were unsuccessful.

Pastor, I do not want to call names of a particular group that was responsible nor do I want to say what city they were from. However, I wanted to let you and the congregation know that you are not making this up.

....I personally was set free from some prejudice in my heart, as a result of this series, "Race, Religion & Racism." I received Jesus the Christ as my Lord and Savior in 1986 and assurance of salvation in 1991. I am filled with the Holy Spirit and I am called and chosen, handpicked, to the ministry in the office of evangelist....

Pastor, don't take it lightly when I tell you I am on a mission. My family, as well as many others, need to be called out of deception, Mohammad [sic], into the Truth, the Way and the Light, Jesus. It's time, the time is now....

Sincerely,

(Name withheld)

I wanted to use this letter simply to validate, based on someone's personal experience, what we read in the Hadith about the seriousness of changing from Islam. And that's from someone who lived it! Compare Islam's approach to keeping people "in the faith" with what Christianity has to say about such things. In 2 Timothy 2:11-13, it says:

11   *This is* a faithful saying: For if we died with *Him*, we shall also live with *Him*.

12   If we endure, we shall also reign with *Him*. If we deny *Him*, He also will deny us.

13   If we are faithless, He remains faithful; He cannot deny Himself.

Look at Verse 12 again: **If we endure, we shall also reign with Him. If we deny *Him*, He also will deny us.** Jesus is not going to have a contract put out on you, instructing someone to kill you. If you deny Him, He will deny you. That seems simple enough. Why would you kill someone on this earth because that person turned and walked the other way? I would think you would want people to do things voluntarily. You would want a people to be a part of something because they wanted to, not out of fear that if they leave they will be killed.

Let's look at one more reference to changing religion. In the Hadith, Volume 9, Chapter 2, #58, Pages 45-46:

> The Prophet then sent Muadh bin Jabal after him and when Muadh reached him, he spread out a cushion for him and requested him to get down (and sit on the cushion). Behold: There was a fettered man beside Abu Musa. Muadh asked, "Who is this (man)?" Abu Musa said, "He was a Jew and became a Muslim and then reverted back to Judaism." Then Abu Musa requested Muadh to sit down but Muadh said, "I will not sit down till he has been killed. This is the judgment of Allah and His Messenger (for such cases) and repeated it thrice. Then Abu Musa ordered that the man be killed, and he was killed. Abu Musa added, "Then we discussed the night prayers and one of us said, 'I pray and sleep, and I hope that Allah will reward me for my sleep as well as for my prayers'."

The penalty for leaving Islam is steep, and you should know that going in.

In addition to the treatment of people who leave the faith, there are other important differences between the way Jehovah God of the Bible treats people in general and the way Allah treats people. For example, what does the Hadith say about Muhammad, Allah, and sickness? We will begin with the Hadith, Volume 7, Chapter 1, #548, Page 373:

> Narrated Abu Huraira: Allah's Messenger said, "If Al-lah wants to do good to somebody, He afflicts him with trials."

Thank God the Bible has something different to say about afflictions. In 2 Timothy 3:10-12, we find:

10   But you have carefully followed my doctrine, manner of life, purpose, faith, longsuffering, love, perseverance,

11   persecutions, afflictions, which happened to me at Antioch, at Iconium, at Lystra — what persecutions I endured. And out of *them* all the Lord delivered me.

12   Yes, and all who desire to live godly in Christ Jesus will suffer [or put up with] **persecution.**

Obviously, if God Jehovah delivers from afflictions and persecutions, then He must not be the One putting afflictions and persecutions on you. If His reason for putting them on you is to teach you something, and then He delivers you from it, it didn't do any good to put them on you in the first place, did it? What was the purpose? More important, though, we know as Christians from our study of the Bible that God does not put afflictions on people. He will *allow* them, because He has no choice if we allow them. God gave us free wills, and based on His promise and His Word, He must allow you to exercise your free will. So if you allow afflictions, He'll allow them. But if you want out, Timothy says God will deliver you.

We see this with the "Hall of Fame of the Heroes of Faith" in Hebrews 11:35, where Paul, listing all the persecutions that befell early believers, said this: **Women received their dead raised to life again. Others were tortured, not accepting deliverance, that they might obtain a better resurrection.** Did you see that phrase — **not accepting deliverance**? Apparently God was ready to deliver them from torture. Indeed, if God provided a "deliverance," isn't it reasonable to conclude that He must have *wanted* them delivered. Now, I have no idea what the "better resurrection" is. I can't see how it can get much better than the one that we are told about in the Bible. But obviously these people thought that it was good enough to pass on God's deliverance.

The point is that God had made available to them a way to be delivered out of the pain and suffering. Muhammad said, "…if Allah wants to do good to somebody, He afflicts them with trials." You have to make a judgment. Which would you rather be, afflicted with the trial or delivered from the trial?[1]

We find another example of sickness and suffering in the Hadith, Volume 7, Chapter 2, The Severity of Disease, #549, Page 373:

Narrated Aisha: "I never saw anybody suffering so much from sickness as Allah's Messenger."

It is interesting to realize who is doing the narrating here. Aisha was one of Muhammad's several wives, and she ought to know what she was talking about. Aisha says that she "never saw anybody suffering so much from *sickness* [emphasis mine] as Allah's Messenger." That would be Muhammad, who was Allah's messenger — he's the one suffering so much from sickness. Yet Jesus Christ was never sick. In fact, according to the biblical accounts, He spent most of His time during His earthly ministry healing people who were sick. But in the Hadith, Volume 7, LXXI, The Book of Medicine, Chapter 1, #582, Page 395, it says: "Narrated Abu Huraira: The Prophet said, 'There is no disease that Allah has created, except that He also has created its treatment.'" This tells me that sickness and disease is "sent down," or created, by Allah.

---

[1] When it comes to afflictions, people always want to raise the story of Job. "Wasn't Job afflicted by God?" they ask. No. In Job 1:12, God says to Satan, **"Behold, all that he has *is in your* power . . . .** [emphasis mine]"** Job's friends blamed God, but Satan, not God, was afflicting Job.

Remember that Muhammad stands between Allah and man-kind. Where did Muhammad get his information? Either Allah told him this, or he made it up. If he made it up, that's a tragedy, because he would be guilty of misrepresenting Allah. If he heard it straight from Allah, we would have to agree, then, that disease was created by Allah.

What does the Bible say? In Acts 10:34-38:

34   Then Peter opened *his* mouth and said: "In truth I perceive that God shows no partiality.

35   "But in every nation whoever fears [reverences] **Him and works righteousness is accepted by Him.**

36   "The word which *God* sent to the children of Israel, preaching peace through Jesus Christ — He is Lord of all —

37   "that word you know, which was proclaimed throughout all Judea, and began from Galilee after the baptism which John preached:

38   "how God anointed Jesus of Nazareth with the Holy Spirit and with power, who went about doing good and healing all who were oppressed by the devil, for God was with Him."

Look at that last verse: **"...God anointed Jesus of Nazareth with the Holy Spirit and with power, who went about doing good and healing...."** Even if we stopped right there, we know that healing is good. So whatever is at the other extreme of healing must be bad. Since the only people who need healing are sick people, then sickness must be bad and healing must be good.

But there is more to the passage: "...how God anointed Jesus of Nazareth with the Holy Spirit and with power, who went about doing good and healing all who were oppressed by the devil, for

God was with Him." This tells me that sickness and disease are satanic oppression — it is not brought by Jehovah God.

Yet Muhammad said "…there is no disease that Allah has created, except that He also has created its treatment." Contrast that with God who **"…anointed Jesus of Nazareth with the Holy Spirit and with power, who went about doing good and healing all who were oppressed by the devil, for God was with Him."** So if God was with Him while he was healing people, then God couldn't have been the author or the creator of the sickness and disease because if He did create sickness and disease, He must have had a reason for it. And if He has a reason for it, and He heals someone who is sick, then the reason for putting the sickness on them has been nullified by the healing.

I'll be the first to admit that in traditional Christianity we have been told in some churches that God does, in fact, afflict people with sickness and disease, but that's not biblically true! Remember, I told you before, Christianity is not Christians and it certainly is not preachers. Christianity is Jesus Christ.

If I have to compare the compassion, mercy, and love expressed by Jehovah God through Jesus the Christ to the rigid rules and vengeance displayed by Allah through His messenger, Muhammad, it's no contest. On the one hand, I have a Savior who tells a harlot caught in the act, **"…neither do I condemn you…,"** and commands her to **"go and sin no more."** On the other hand, I have a Muhammad who routinely orders people who cross him to be killed. I have a Jesus anointed by God who goes about **"healing all,"** and then, I have an Allah who puts sickness and disease on his followers. If we were doing a "Consumer Reports" comparison of Jesus and Muhammad, Jehovah and Allah, which "product" would you choose?

On the one hand we have Allah, who uses sickness and disease to instruct people. On the other hand we have James 1:17, which says, **Every good gift and every perfect gift is from above, and comes down from the Father of lights, with whom there is no variation or**

shadow of turning. Sickness and disease, no matter how you cut it, are not "good and perfect" gifts. So when we do a comparison of Jesus Christ and Allah, Jesus wins, hands down.

5

Slavery, Islam and Christianity

 We have been doing a comparison of Islam and Christianity in a number of key areas, such as how Jesus and Muhammad treated people under a number of circumstances, and how God gives healing, but Allah places suffering on his followers. Now we will deal with a touchy subject, the subject of slavery. But this isn't the kind of slavery you think.

I bring this subject up because many Blacks, particularly black Muslims, perceive Christianity as the "white man's religion" designed to enslave the black race. What we're going to look at now is going to shock and astound most black Muslims, and Blacks and Whites alike. It has been said that the Bible has been used as a justification for enslaving black people down through history, especially in the United States. You will be surprised when we read what the Koran and the Hadith have to say about slavery and about Muhammad himself owning slaves. You can be sure of one thing; Jesus had no slaves!

Let's begin in the Koran, Sura 4:2-3:

Give orphans the property that belongs to them. Do not exchange their valuables for worthless things or cheat them of their possessions; for this would surely be a grievous sin. If you fear that you cannot treat orphan girls with fairness, then you marry other women who seem

137

good to you: two, three, or four of them. But if you fear that you cannot maintain equality among them, marry one only or any slave-girls you may own. This will make it easier for you to avoid injustice.[1]

Did you notice that last part? Remember Allah is speaking through his Prophet, Muhammad. So Allah is dealing with slavery, letting us know that to own slaves is acceptable:

"...then marry one only or any slave-girls you may own...."

Interesting, don't you think?
But there is more. In Sura 4:36, it says:

Serve God and associate none with Him. Show kindness to parents and kindred, to orphans and to the destitute, to near and distant neighbors, to those that keep company with you, to the traveller [sic] in need, and to the slaves you own.[2]

Now, you might say, "Well, Dr. Price, Christians in America owned slaves. They justified it with the Bible." That is absolutely true, and they were absolutely wrong. Those who founded America — the people who arrived at Jamestown, followed by generations of colonists — kidnapped, stole, and took into slavery millions of black Africans. There was a concerted, deliberate, purposeful effort on the part of the Founding Fathers, who were Christians, to keep black people ignorant of the Bible. Some slave owners gave their slaves just enough of the Bible to keep them quiet and prevent rebellion. But this was done orally; they never let the slaves read the Word for themselves! The goal was to get slaves to think, "As bad as it is now, don't worry about it. Over there, on the other side, you can see the Pearly Gates. Things will get better in the sweet bye-and -bye."

---

[1] Dawood, 60.
[2] Dawood, 64-65.

So for 246 years, slave owners and non-slave-owning Whites who supported them kept slaves ignorant. Thank God some broke away and learned to read despite the rules.

Under these conditions, you can see how it was easy for the people who claimed to be Christians to distort the Bible and to use it to support slavery. Since the people couldn't check it out for themselves, they had to take what was told to them. But if they had read the Bible, this is what it says about slavery, in I Corinthians 7:23:

> **You were bought at a price; do not become slaves of men.**

There will be those so-called scholars who will point out that under the Old Testament, the Lord allowed the children of Israel to have slaves.[3] That is correct. However, those Israelites did not go to Africa and kidnap people, destroying their villages, chaining up

---

[3] Exodus, Chapter 21, contains the laws related to the Hebrew practice of slavery. In Jewish law, a man who was in financial trouble could sell himself to another for a period of seven years. At the end of that seven-year period, the slave had to be offered freedom. But (21:5) **"...if the servant plainly says, 'I love my master, my wife, and my children; I will not go out free,'..."** then the servant had to (21:6) **"...serve him forever."** Clearly this is a different practice than what occurred with African slaves in the United States. Moreover, the nature of the Middle Eastern economy was such that people, especially if not in their own tribe, could have a hard time making a living. In reality, this was a means of support for people who would otherwise be destitute. On the other hand, note that in Exodus 21:16, it is written: **"He who kidnaps a man** [not a Hebrew, so apparently this applied to any man] **and sells him . . . [he] shall surely be put to death."** Moreover, in the 49th year, Hebrews were to release slaves and even "hired servants" who were Hebrews. They were permitted to buy **"male and female slaves"** (Leviticus 25:44), and buy **"the children of the strangers who dwell among you . . . ."** (Leviticus 25:45). But these slaves were always to be available to relatives purchasing them (Leviticus 25:47-

people to bring them on boats to Israel. Those slaves in Israel were people taken in the process of war — which was a common practice of the day — and such slaves were to be offered their freedom, after seven years, at the time of Jubilee.

First, it is obvious that the term *Old Testament* indicates that it is not the final word on things — that there is a New Testament. Any time you have a new will and testament, it supersedes the old. It makes the old will passé. The instruction that we just read, **do not become slaves of men,** supersedes all laws of slavery in Israel.

Second, remember that Christianity is not Christians, but Christ. People can claim to be Christians and do all sorts of sinful things. Just because a lot of so-called Christians did a lot of ugly things doesn't mean that God did them, nor does it mean He approved of them. So you have to be careful, or risk throwing the baby out with the bathwater. But let's further examine the contrast between Islam and Christianity on this issue of slavery.

In the Koran, Sura 23:1-5 says:

> Blessed are the believers, who are humble in their prayers; who avoid profane talk, and give alms to the destitute; who restrain their carnal desires (except with their wives and *slave-girls* [emphasis mine], for these are lawful to them: transgressors are those who lust after other than these); who are true to their trusts and promises, and diligent in their prayers. These are the heirs of Paradise; they shall abide in it for ever.[4]

---

55), and if not redeemed, even these "strangers" were to be freed during the Jubilee year! This is a world of difference from the type of slavery practiced in Latin America, the West Indies, and in the United States, which was perpetual, with no hope of escape, and with no Jubilee year. It is also worth noting that the Lord allowed the children of Israel to *become* slaves, to know how it felt, which at the very least broadened their view of how to treat their own slaves.

4 Dawood, 240-241.

And in Sura 24:30 it is written:

Enjoin believing women to turn their eyes away from
temptation and to preserve their chastity; not to display
their adornments (except such as are normally revealed);
to draw their veils over their bosoms and not display
their finery except to their husbands, their fathers, their
husbands' fathers, their sons, their step-sons, their brothers, their brothers' sons, their sisters' sons, their women-
servants, and their slave-girls; male attendants lacking
in natural vigour, and children who have no carnal
knowledge of women. And let them not stamp their feet
when walking, so as to reveal their hidden trinkets.[5]

Allah apparently condones slavery, based on these verses from
the Koran.

The Bible has a different view. In Colossians 3:11 we find
this interesting statement: **...where there is neither Greek nor Jew,
circumcised nor uncircumcised, barbarian, Scythian, slave *nor* free,
but Christ *is* all and in all**. In Christ there are to be no slaves.

However, in the Koran, Sura 24:32, it says:

Take in marriage those among you who are single and
those of your male and female slaves who are honest. If
they are poor, God will enrich them from His own bounty.
God is munificent and all-knowing.[6]

Compare that with Galatians 4:7: **Therefore you are no longer
a slave but a son, and if a son, then an heir of God through Christ.**
Obviously, this verse shows how wrong America has been! This
was the expressed will of God 2,000 years ago when it was written.
Some may ask, "Yeah, well, how come God let it happen then? How
come He let all those people drag us out of Africa and bring us over
here and make slaves out of us?" He allowed it because *we* allowed

---

[5] Dawood, 248.
[6] Dawood, 248-249.

it. The European settlers didn't make slaves out of the American Indians. Oh, they tried, but the Indians revolted — they wouldn't have it.[7] And then some of our own black brothers sold other Blacks to the slave traders in the first place, for money.

But none of this has to do with the Christ of the Bible. Under the influence of the Holy Spirit, Paul said in Galatians 4:7, again, **you are no longer a slave but a son.** That's good enough for me. That tells me that God, the Jehovah God of the Bible, does not favor slavery. But there is nothing He can do about it unless I do something about it. If I choose not to do anything about it, He cannot help me because He has guaranteed that I have free will. Of course, He is God and from a pure power standpoint He can do whatever He wants. But He has committed Himself, in dealings with man, to His word. God is not a man, that He should lie (Numbers 23:19). So to honor His Word, which requires Him to honor our free will, God cannot do something on your behalf if you do not will that it be done.

The Bible says, **you are no longer a slave but a son.** There is a big difference between slave and son. It seems consistent and logical that if God doesn't want me to be a slave, He certainly would not want me to make a slave out of you. Again, though, how does the Koran see things? In Sura 24:33 it says:

> Let those who cannot afford to marry live in continence until God shall enrich them from His own bounty. As for those of your slaves who wish to buy their liberty, free

---

[7] It is also worth noting that the Indians had the advantage of being on their home turf, knowing the ground, and having a common language. The slave traders, beginning with the Spanish and Portuguese, learned from their experience with the Indians and deliberately mixed up African tribes during transport and sale so as to make communication more difficult. Then, the Africans were stuck in a land as foreign to them as the Arctic. Thus escape and rebellion, while certainly not impossible, were made far more difficult than with the Indians, and the first slave revolts did not occur for decades.

them if you find in them any promise and bestow on them a part of the riches which God has given you.

You shall not force your slave-girls into prostitution in order that you may enrich yourselves, if they wish to preserve their chastity. If anyone compels them, God will be forgiving and merciful to them.[8]

Note this passage, "...as for those of your slaves...." Allah doesn't tell them to get rid of their slaves; He just tells them how to treat their slaves. Allah doesn't say, "You shall not have slaves." That concerns me. Black Americans just got out of that slavery situation and sure don't need to go back!

In Galatians 3:28, the Bible says it this way: **There is neither Jew nor Greek, there is neither slave nor free, there is neither male nor female; for you are all one in Christ Jesus.**

The so-called visible Church tried for decades in the American colonial period to avoid discussions of slavery. Then the mainstream churches split over whether slavery was biblical or not, with the Southern churches invoking the "curse of Ham," which we disproved in Volume 2.[9]

When Galatians says, **There is neither Jew nor Greek, there is neither slave nor free...,** then it is clear there are no slaves in Jesus. That is part of the reason this nation is reaping the whirlwind today in the form of drugs, violence, teen pregnancy, and all the rest, because we as a so-called Christian nation have not played the game right. We've been lying about God, lying about the Bible and lying about Jesus, and now we are paying the price. The Bible says, **"all liars shall have their part in the lake which burns with fire"** (Revelation 21:8) and our nation is burning for its sin.

And the deception was not an "honest mistake." The (mostly) Southern preachers and ministers who condoned slavery, who wrote

---

[8] Dawood, 249.
[9] See Race, Religion & Racism, Vol. 2, 189-205.

defenses of slavery supposedly based on the Bible, knew what they were doing.[9] One historian has pointed out that prior to the Declaration of Independence, there was little disagreement over the fact that black people were people.[10] There was slavery, but most people pretty well understood that they were enslaving fellow humans. Only after Thomas Jefferson wrote that "all men are created equal" did a political problem appear, because if all men were equal, why weren't black slaves equal? And if they were equal, why were they still slaves? The answer, according to the book *The End of Racism*, is that the only way they could justify slavery any more was to make black people "subhuman." So they started writing all this junk about how black people weren't really people, but some lower species.

---

[9] Interestingly, then, as now, few of these preachers used or even attempted to use any genuine scriptural evidence to support their racist claims. Generally, their anti-black tirades were based on generalities, or occasionally invoking the "curse of Ham" with virtually no analysis or explanation. See Smith, 129-165.

[10] Dinesh D'Souza, *The End of Racism: Principles for a Multiracial Society* (New York: Free Press, 1995). D'Souza finds an abrupt change in the descriptions of slaves from the period prior to the Revolution and the decades immediately after the Revolution. Southern apologists for slavery, such as George Fitzhugh and John C. Calhoun, all emphasized the "subhuman" characteristics of slaves (i.e., black people) and apparently were never challenged or contradicted by leading Southern Christian pastors or preachers. See George Fitzhugh, *Cannibals All! Or, Slaves Without Masters*, ed., C. Vann Woodward (Cambridge: Belknap Press, 1960 [1857]); John C. Calhoun, *A Disquisition on Government* (New York: The Liberal Arts Press, 1953). Lincoln, despite never viewing Blacks as social equals, always maintained their essential humanness, and thought all people capable of equal political participation after the proper education and acculturation. Some historians see the dehumanization process starting somewhat earlier, but the key point remains that not all (or even most) Whites ever accepted that Blacks were not people. See, for example, William M. Wiecek, *The Sources of Antislavery Constitutionalism in America, 1760-1848* (Ithaca: Cornell University Press, 1977), 120-125.

Slavery, Islam and Christianity

But the point is, American writers — Christian writers and preachers — *knew* enslaving people of any color was wrong, but due to their greed they didn't want to give it up. So they concocted this whole notion that Blacks weren't "real people" in the way white Europeans were. But thank God even a slave owner like Thomas Jefferson put it in writing that "all men are created equal," even if he never intended that it apply to black men and women.[11] The fact is you can play games for only so long before you have to deal with the reality that men are men are men, and women are women are women, no matter what color. And once it's "on paper," once it's "in the document," then it's only a matter of time before people claim what's theirs.[12]

---

[11] Jefferson is far less innocent of racism that most biographers claim. The general picture presented is that Jefferson was "personally opposed" to slavery but did not think a political solution was realistic. Legal historian Paul Finkelman, however, in his book, *Slavery and the Founders*, presents a methodical indictment of Jefferson, indicating that in fact he had no moral qualms at all about enslaving Blacks, even those he likely knew were his own relations. Jefferson freed only a handful of slaves in his life, compared to George Washington and Benjamin Franklin, and, more important, he opposed various plans to manumit slaves in Virginia, blocking such plans as governor and, in general, arguing against them. Liberty came to black people through the Declaration of Independence, it could be argued, in spite of Jefferson rather than because of him. See Paul Finkelman, *Slavery and the Founders: Race and Liberty in the Age of Jefferson* (Armonk, New York: M. E. Sharpe, 2001). On the other hand, his construction of the Ordinance of 1784 was a model for emancipated society, and, as Wiecek and others point out, it was Jefferson's ambiguity over slavery (as well as other Founders' inconsistencies) that allowed many elements of the Jefferson Constitution to be used to eliminate slavery later. See Wiecek, *passim*. So the controversy remains, and like most men, Jefferson was personally complicated and inconsistent.

[12] Forrest G. Wood's *The Arrogance of Faith* makes a sharp indictment of Christianity as a religion for its part in slavery. Instead of seeing slavery as a sinful departure from God's plan, Wood maintains that

There is quite a difference in what the Bible and the Koran have to say about slavery. Even today, while you are reading this book, Arab Muslims are the biggest slave traders in the world. I'll discuss this at length in another chapter in this book, but not only do Arab Muslims trade in slaves today, but they trade in black slaves. That is their primary target — black people. Again, this is not to call names, but to give you information. You can do with that information whatever you please, but I have kept my charge from God in presenting that information to you. Yes, even today, Arab Muslims are capturing Blacks and selling them into slavery. You can say whatever you want about Christianity as far as the past is concerned, but at least in America, today, we are not physically being sold as slaves. We have problems, but slavery isn't one of them. So that has to be an improvement.

We have looked at what the Koran has had to say about Muslims owning slaves. So let's turn now to the Hadith — keeping in mind that this is the other holy book of Islam that holds doctrine that is just as

---

the evangelical nature of Christianity requires it to "demonize" all non-Christian people, and therefore slavery occurred *because of* Christianity, not in spite of it. Or, as he says, "English North Americans embraced slavery *because* they were Christians, not in spite of it," 38. This link, he claims, was only strengthened by notions that to "save" the Africans, Europeans had to "enslave them" first. Wood not only misreads the Bible, and thus excuses others who do so, but he also brushes away centuries of slavery by virtually every other civilization on the earth, going so far as to find an odd honor in Islamic Mameluke slavery. He also dismisses without evidence the fact that other non-Christian religions, especially Islam (but also most animistic primitive North American Indian or Far Eastern cults), practiced and endorsed slavery as a way of life. It was *only* the Christians who struggled intellectually with the problem to the point that they eventually ended the practice. See Wood, *The Arrogance of Faith: Christianity and Race in America From the Colonial Era to the Twentieth Century* (New York: Alfred A. Knopf, 1990), 4-38.

sacred as the Koran. In the Hadith, Volume 2, Chapter 44, No Zakat [obligatory charity] Is Imposed on the Horse of a Muslim, #542, Page 314, it says:

> Narrated Abu Huraira: Allah's Messenger said, "There is no Zakat either on a horse or a slave belonging to a Muslim."

And, in the Hadith, Volume 2, Chapter 60, Page 331, we find:

> May the freed slave-girls of the wives of the Prophet accept things given in charity?

Still again, in the Hadith, Volume 2, Chapter 2, Sadaqat-Ul-Fitr is Compulsory on the Free or the Slave Muslims, #580, Page 339, we find:

> Narrated Ibn Umar: Allah's Messenger made it incumbent on all the slave or free Muslims, male or female, to pay one Sa of dates or barley as Zakat-ul-Fitr.

In the Hadith, Volume 3, Chapter 112, #435, Page 238:

> Narrated Zaid bin Khalid and Abu Huraira that Allah's Messenger was asked about an unmarried slave-girl who committed illegal sexual intercourse. They heard him saying, "Flog (1) her, and if she commits illegal sexual intercourse after that, flog her again, and on the third (or the fourth) offense, sell her." (2)

Now, that is the Prophet Muhammad himself, saying it's not only all right to have slaves, but to beat them. And, again, this is in stark contrast to what Jesus did in the case of the woman caught in the act of illegal sexual intercourse. We find that story in John 8:1-11:

1   But Jesus went to the Mount of Olives.

2 Now early in the morning He came again into the temple, and all the people came to Him; and He sat down and taught them.

3 Then the scribes and Pharisees brought to Him a woman caught in adultery. And when they had set her in the midst,

4 they said to Him, "Teacher, this woman was caught in adultery, in the very act.

5 "Now Moses, in the law, commanded us that such should be stoned. But what do You say?"

6 This they said, testing Him, that they might have *something* of which to accuse Him. But Jesus stooped down and wrote on the ground with *His* finger, as though He did not hear.

7 So when they continued asking Him, He raised Himself up and said to them, "He who is without sin among you, let him throw a stone at her first."

8 And again He stooped down and wrote on the ground.

9 Then those who heard *it*, being convicted by *their* conscience, went out one by one, beginning with the oldest *even* to the last. And Jesus was left alone, and the woman standing in the midst.

10 When Jesus had raised Himself up and saw no one but the woman, He said to her, "Woman, where are those accusers of yours? Has no

one condemned you?"

11 **She said, "No one, Lord." And Jesus said to her, "Neither do I condemn you; go and sin no more."**

I'll ask a simple question: Whose hands would you rather have fallen into? I mean, Jesus didn't say "beat her, flog her." He sure didn't say "sell her." He forgave her and told her not to sin anymore. I think that is classified as mercy, but I don't see much mercy with Muhammad.

There is much more on slavery in Islamic teachings. In the Hadith, Volume 3, Chapter 113, Page 239, it says:

> One can travel with a slave-girl without knowing whether she is pregnant or not? Al-Hasan found no harm in her master's kissing or fondling with her.

> Ibn Umar said, "If a slave girl who is suitable to have sexual relations is given to somebody as a gift, or sold or manumitted, her master should not have sexual intercourse with her before she gets one menstruation so as to be sure of absence of pregnancy, and there is no such necessity for a virgin."

So not only did the Muslims have slaves, but they had sexual intercourse with them whenever they wanted to. And, of course, they did that in this country, too. But the difference is, it wasn't condoned in the Bible. So-called Christians did it in spite of the instructions from their religious book, not because of it.

I think these references from the Hadith and the Koran show that the Muslims condone slavery. The New Testament does not teach this, nor do we find any evidence that Jesus Christ condoned it. Now let's look at what Muhammad himself had to say about having slaves and about slavery. In the Hadith, Volume 3, Chapter 26, #648, Page 389, it says:

...So I went to the upper room where the Prophet was and requested to a black slave of his: "Will you get the permission of (Allah's Messenger) for Umar (to enter)?" The slave went in, talked to the Prophet about it and came out saying, 'I mentioned you to him but he did not reply.' So, I went and sat with the people who were sitting by the pulpit, but I could not bear the situation, so I went to the slave again and said: "Will you get the permission for Umar?" He went in and brought the same reply as before. When I was leaving, behold, the slave called me saying, "Allah's Messenger has granted you permission."

This seems to indicate that Muhammad had more than one slave because of the words *black slave* — if all the slaves were black, you wouldn't mention the color of a slave. Apparently the term "black slave" distinguished this slave from others who weren't black.

Now as a black person, are you going to accept the notion that Islam is the "black man's religion" when Muhammad enslaved black people? Here we see the very leader of Islam having a black slave, yet Jesus did not have any slaves, of any color! But let's be fair: The Bible says, "in the mouths of two or three witnesses." Even though we are not required to apply biblical standards to Islam — only Islamic standards — I'm going to give you another witness that Muhammad had a black slave. In the Hadith, Volume 6, Chapter 316, #435, Page 407, we find:

...[Umar said] "Has the king of Ghassan come?" He [Umar's Ansari friend] said, 'No, but something worse; Allah's Messenger has isolated himself from his wives." I said, "Let the nose of Aisha and Hafsa be stuck to dust (i.e. humiliated)!" Then I put on my clothes and went to Allah's Messenger's residence, and behold, he was staying in an upper room of his to which he ascended by a ladder, and a black slave of Allah's Messenger was (sitting) at the first ladder-step.

So this may have been the same "black slave of Allah's messenger" we read about before, but clearly Muhammad had a black slave. There are more references to Muhammad condoning slavery. Look at the Hadith, Volume 7, Chapter 36, #346, Page 254:

> Narrated Anas: I was a young boy when I once was walking with Allah's Messenger. Allah's Messenger entered the house of his slave tailor and the latter brought a dish filled with food covered with pieces of gourd. Allah's Messenger started picking and eating the gourd. When I saw that, I started collecting and placing the gourd before him. Then the slave returned to his work. Anas added: I have kept on loving gourd since I saw Allah's Messenger doing what he was doing.

Now, someone may say, "What's so different about Allah's messenger, Muhammad, having a slave when the white so-called ministers and preachers down through the years enslaved people?" God never condoned that. People have their own agendas, and God has to allow it if the Christians allow it, because we have free will.

Because this is such a difficult subject for some people to understand, let me give you an example that will make this business of free will abundantly clear. As you read this book, do you have on clothes, or are you naked? I will assume that you have on some type of clothing. Question: Are the clothes that you have on the only clothes you own? If you are like most people, the answer to that is probably no. Could you have worn other clothes today? I am certain your answer would be yes. Well, what made you put on the clothes you chose to wear? Did you hear the voice of God speaking to you, saying, "Thou shalt put on thy brown jacket with thy tan slacks?" Or, "Thou shalt select thy purple dress with the gold earrings?" No! You have on what you have on because you made a choice — you permitted it. You willed to wear what you are wearing.

God will let you be enslaved if you allow yourself to be enslaved. You have a free will, and you could do something about it.

"Oh no I couldn't," you say. Oh yes you could! It may cost you something. But you do have another choice. You could have said, "Kill me. I'm not going to be a slave." That option was available. It might not be the one you were willing to pay the price for, but it was most definitely an option. To suggest otherwise would demean the efforts of all those runaways who managed to escape and find the Underground Railroad, or would trivialize the slave rebellions that took place in the South.

Many of those people paid with their lives, but they made a choice not to be slaves. Others made similar decisions. The Jewish Zealots at Masada all chose suicide rather than to become Roman slaves or be crucified. God has to allow whatever we allow because He designed the system that way. Again, I'm not speaking from a pure power standpoint, because, of course, in terms of raw power, God can do anything He chooses. In His dealings with man, however, God established the ground rules, and since He is not a man, He cannot lie.

The psalmist says of God, **...For You have magnified Your word above all Your name** (Psalm 138:2). For God not to honor His Word, for Him to interfere with our free will, would make Him no more than a man.

Our model is not American slave owners, but God's Son, Jesus. You don't find Him having any slaves. But the Hadith, given under divine inspiration, records that Muhammad had slaves. Let me give you a third witness that Muhammad had slaves. The Hadith, Volume 8, Chapter 95, #182, Page 117, contains this passage:

> Narrated Anas bin Malik: Allah's Messenger was on a journey and he had a black slave called Anjasha, and he was driving the camels (very fast, and there were women riding on those camels). Allah's Messenger said, "Waihaka (May Allah be merciful to you), O Anjasha! Drive slowly (the camels) with the glass vessels (women)!"

Was this another black slave or was this the slave tailor mentioned in Volume 7 on Page 151? We don't know. But there is still another reference in the Hadith, Volume 9, Chapter 4, To Listen to and Obey One's Ruler as Long as His Orders Involve Not One in Disobedience (to Allah), #256, Page 192:

> **Narrated Anas Bin Malik: Allah's Messenger said,** [We are quoting the Prophet Muhammad himself here!] **"You should listen to and obey, your ruler even if he was an Ethiopian (black) slave whose head looks like a raisin."**

It appears to me that Muhammad is calling Blacks "raisin heads." I said it "appears." Jesus Christ never did that. I want to reiterate that Jesus never had slaves nor did He ever endorse having any.

It is also clear that Muhammad had several female slaves who apparently were distinct from his wives. We find this in the Hadith, Volume 9, Chapter 49, #321, Page 244:

> **Narrated Aisha: The Prophet used to take the Pledge of allegiance from the women by words only after reciting this Holy Verse: — (60:12)** [This apparently is a reference to the Koran, Sura 60, Verse 12]
> **(1) "...that they will not associate anything in worship with Allah." (60:12) And the hand of Allah's Messenger did not touch any woman's hand except the hand of that woman his right hand possessed (i.e. his captives or his lady slaves).**

Apparently, Muhammad was quite a slaver! But let's look at yet one more reference in the Hadith, Volume 9, Chapter 3, #368, Page 275, where we find:

> **Narrated Umar: I came and behold, Allah's Messenger was staying on a Mashroba (attic room) and a black slave of Allah's Messenger was at the top if its stairs. I said to him, "(Tell the Prophet) that here is Umar bin Al-Khattab (asking for permission to enter)." Then he admitted me.**

So here is yet another reference to a black slave.

This black slave thing really bothers me. I personally don't want anything to do with a religion that espouses slavery, and Islam seems to do that. Remember, we are reading about the founder of Islam, Muhammad himself. Remember also that the Hadith records the oral traditions of the Prophet Muhammad by those who actually saw him, lived with him, fought beside him in battle, and were married to him.

It could be argued that the Koran and the Hadith are rather ancient documents, and some might be tempted to say, "That was a long time ago." With that in mind, what do we know about Islamic slavery in modern times? In *Slavery and Human Progress*, by David Brion Davis, this specialist in the area of historical slavery notes:

> Given the scarcity and unreliability of quantitative evidence, the magnitude of the Islamic slave trade cannot be measured with any precision. We know that after the Islamic conquest of Egypt and Tripoli, the Nilotic and central Sudanese states regularly delivered slaves to the north as part of a commercial pact or as a form of tribute. Muslim domination of the long Red Sea coast ensured a continuous shipment of *black* [italics mine] slaves to Yemen, Arabia, Iraq, Iran, and eventually Muslim India.[13]

Members of the Nation of Islam, Blacks, Whites — did you know this? I doubt it. Bernard Lewis, a student of slavery in the Middle East, points out that "an African jurist, Ahmad Baba of Timbuktu…reaffirms the classical Islamic position. Muslims, and also non-Muslims living under Muslim rule and protection, may in no circumstances be enslaved. Idolaters captured in a holy war may lawfully be enslaved, and their slave status is not ended by any subsequent conversion to Islam."[14]

---

[13] David Brion Davis, *Slavery and Human Progress* (New York: Oxford, 1984), 45-46.

[14] Bernard Lewis, *Race and Slavery in the Middle East* (Oxford: Oxford University Press, 1990), 57-58.

Nobel Prize-winning economist Robert Fogel points out that "the last great victory of the British abolitionists was the suppression of the Islamic slave trade.... [which] originated in the early Middle Ages. According to recent estimates, the cumulated trade to Islamic countries in northern Africa and the Near East probably exceeded 4 million persons before the New World was even discovered."[15] That trade doubled by 1800, and "although the Atlantic trade went into decline after 1830, the trade to the Islamic regions continued to expand. The total for the 19th Century appears to have been about three million."[16]

What about our own time? The 1800s may be ancient history as far as some are concerned, but what about the 1990s? In an article in the October 17, 1993, edition of the *Washington Post*, "Where Slavery Isn't History, in War-ravaged Sudan, a Still Bustling Trade in Human Chattel," the reporter wrote:

> Slavery still lives in Sudan. The U.S. State Department, as well as international organizations including the British Anti-Slavery Society, the International Labor Organization and Africa Watch, have documented how Arabs have enslaved the African people of southern Sudan, especially in the Nuba mountains....[17]

The article goes on to describe how "traditional slavery...survives in modern-day Sudan [and] seems to be on the increase." In 1990, Africa Watch concluded that there "was evidence [of] kidnapping, hostage-taking and other monetary transactions involving human beings 'on a sufficiently serious scale as to represent a resurgence of slavery.'"[18] A declassified report from the U.S.

---

[15] Robert William Fogel, *Without Consent or Contract: the Rise and Fall of American Slavery* (New York: W. W. Norton, 1989), 236.

[16] Fogel, 236.

[17] "Where Slavery Isn't History, in War-ravaged Sudan, a Still Bustling Trade in Human Chattel," *Washington Post*, October 17, 1993, section C-3.

[18] Africa Watch quoted in "Where Slavery Isn't History."

Embassy in Khartoum, Sudan, released by Congressman Frank Wolf (R-Va.), documented that government troops and armed Arab militias were kidnapping and transporting African Sudanese to Libya, and the *Post* article concluded that "There are credible reports of contemporary slavery from other countries, including Saudi Arabia, Mauritania and Sierra Leone, but the case of Sudan is especially clear-cut."[19] Now, this is awesome and terrifying. We are talking about the 1990s! Cell phones. Microwave ovens. Satellite television. Slavery!!

The same article goes on to say:

> ...In 1987, investigators for the Anti-Slavery Society, a British organization...estimated that in 1987 alone, Arabs enslaved 7,000 African women and children.... The second element of slavery, the denial of all forms of human rights and freedoms, is made possible by the current Sudanese civil war. The conflict has sent millions of African civilians fleeing for their lives to the northern part of the country, which is predominantly *Arab* [italics mine — this would indicate, would it not, "predominantly Islamic?"]. Refugees in their own country, they are forced to live in camps in the desert. Most importantly, they are subjects of an Arab-dominated government which seeks to make the *Koran* the law of the land [italics mine].

This isn't intended to come against the Arabs. Instead, we are trying to see what the Koran teaches on slavery, and who practices slavery. The so-called western world eliminated slavery. British Christians led the movement in the early 1800s that banned it in the British Empire. In America, we had to fight a war over it, but praise God we did get rid of it here. Yet slavery still exists in the 1990s — in countries directed by the Koran. Countries that worship Allah. Countries that call Muhammad their Prophet. Don't take my word for it — the *Washington Post* article continues:

---

[19] "Where Slavery Isn't History."

> The use of violence is perhaps the most crucial charac-
> teristic that distinguishes slavery from other forms of
> forced labor. Ferocious raids by government forces and
> militias on African communities have resulted in the en-
> slavement of a large number of black Africans, accord-
> ing to "Slavery and Abolition."[20]

The last statement in the article, though, puts the icing on the
cake. It says:

> While denying human rights abuses, the government of
> Sudan defends its policies of Islamization as [a] legiti-
> mate means of building the Sudanese nation. Gen. Omar
> Hassan El Beshir, the country's current military leader,
> maintains that 'Arabism without Islam will degenerate
> into tribalism.'

According to the *Washington Post* article, quoting *New
African Magazine,* Gen. El Beshir himself "is reputed to have a
number of Dinka and Nuer slaves in his own home, from the time he
was military commander in Muglad, southwest Sudan."[21]

Now, I have an important question for everyone, but
particularly Blacks in America, because here, Islam draws
disgruntled, disheartened, disenfranchised Blacks away from
Christianity. The Nation of Islam, as I said, is the most familiar of
these groups, but not the only one. Here is my question: If the religion
you intend to adopt condones enslaving your black relatives in Africa,
are you sure you want to become a Muslim?

And although we will get to Minister Louis Farrakhan in the
following chapters, it is worth noting here that there is plenty of
evidence that he not only has been aware of this slavery in the Sudan
— slavery of Blacks! — but has so far refused to condemn it. In
April 1997, journalist Jeff Jacoby reported that there were two

---

[20] "Where Slavery Isn't History."
[21] "Where Slavery Isn't History."

meetings between Mr. Farrakhan and the leaders of the Sudanese resistance in 1994, and one of the two men stated flatly that Farrakhan knew about the slave camps.[22] Moreover, in the July 23, 1996, issue of *The Final Call*, the NOI's weekly newsletter, Mr. Farrakhan questions the motives of anyone who criticized black slavery in the Sudan.[23] Responding to reports in the *Baltimore Sun* about Sudanese (black) slavery, Mr. Farrakhan dismissed such claims as "propaganda against Sudan" by a "Zionist Jewish daily."[24] On another occasion, Mr. Farrakhan simply denied that slavery existed in the Sudan, and, writing in *The Final Call* on April 26, 1995, alleged that the reports of slavery in the Sudan were "propaganda...to divert attention from the role Jews played in the slave trade...."[25] Again, on April 12, 1995, in *The Final Call*, he called the evidence of slavery a Big Lie being circulated by the American Anti-Slavery Group...."[26]

And Mr. Farrakhan is not the only representative of the American Muslim community holding those views. The *Daily Challenge*, a New York black community daily paper, reported on May 30, 1995, that Abdul Akbar Muhammad, the International representative of NOI, said that slavery allegations against the Sudanese government were part of a "Jewish conspiracy" to divide the black community.[27]

---

[22] Jeff Jacoby's article in the *Boston Globe*, April 1, 1997, cited by the Anti-Defamation League on its Website: 206.3.178.10/issue_nation_of_islam/farrakhan_and_slavery_in_sudan.html.

[23] *The Final Call* cited on the Anti-Defamation League Website.

[24] Mr. Farrakhan's statements of July 16, 1996, cited on the Anti-Defamation League Website.

[25] Mr. Farrakhan's statements on *The Final Call,* April 26, 1995, cited on the Anti-Defamation League Website.

[26] Mr. Farrakhan's statements on *The Final Call*, April 12, 1995, cited on the Anti-Defamation League Website.

[27] Mr. Muhammad's comments in *The Daily Challenge*, May 30, 1995, appear on the Anti-Defamation League website.

Although Muhammad noted that Charles Jacobs, the cofounder of the American Anti-Slavery Group, was Jewish, he did not mention that the other cofounder, Mohamed Athie, was a former Mauritanian diplomat.[28]

Right now, in *this* world, not only are Muslim nations still enslaving black people, but the Nation of Islam — at least some of its

---

[28] While the focus of this section is not on Islamic attitudes toward Jews, or of NOI's positions in general, it is worth noting some of the statements made by Mr. Farrakhan's associates on Jews. For example, the late Khalid Abdul Muhammad, former national spokesman of NOI, in a speech at San Francisco State University in May 1997, claimed that there was "no proof . . . absolutely no evidence to substantiate, to prove that six million so-called Jews lost their lives in Nazi Germany . . . ." He claimed that rabbis sucked the blood of male babies during circumcision, but that he personally couldn't be an anti-Semite, because Jews were not true Semites. But, he continued, "If you say you're White [expletive deleted], I'm against you. If you're a Jew, I'm against you. Whatever the hell you want to call yourself, I'm against you." (Interview in the publication *XXL*, Volume 1, number 1, September 1997). This and all other quotations appear on the Anti-Defamation League Website, "ADL Backgrounder," www.adl.org/presrele/asus_12/3221_12a.html. Mr. Farrakhan, after a speech at Kean College in 1994, dismissed Mr. Muhammad but said that he (Farrakhan) agreed with the content.

It is useful to compare these attitudes ("I'm against you") to the words of Christ in Luke 4:18-19: **"The Spirit of the Lord is upon Me, because He has anointed Me to preach the gospel to the poor; He has sent Me to heal the brokenhearted, to proclaim liberty to the captives and recovery of sight to the blind, to set at liberty those who are oppressed; to proclaim the acceptable year of the Lord."** Or Luke 6:45: **"A good man out of the good treasure of his heart brings forth good; and an evil man out of the evil treasure of his heart brings forth evil. For out of the abundance of the heart his mouth speaks."** What have you heard from the mouth of Mr. Muhammad?

main spokesmen — not only do not condemn these practices but even deny that slavery exists. For me, as a black man, that presents a huge problem, and makes the differences between Christianity and Islam all the more clear.

6

Whose Report Will You Believe?

Racism in the Christian Church has permitted the inroads made by Islam into the black community, but we have seen that many perceptions of Islam may in fact be wrong. We have examined some of the works of Elijah Muhammad, and investigated what the Koran and Hadith say about slaves, salvation, and other topics. Perceptions count, and to confront those perceptions about who Jesus is and what Christianity is requires that we deal with some of the groups that are challenging Christianity in the black community, most especially the influential Muslim sect in America called the Nation of Islam, or NOI.

Having looked at the founder of the NOI in America, Elijah Muhammad, we are ready to check out the claims of the NOI that are made today regarding Jesus Christ. In particular, we are going to look at the statements and comments about Jesus and Christianity made by the well-known leader of the NOI, Mr. Louis Farrakhan.[1] We want to know — no, we *need to know* — what does he say about Jesus? What claims does he make, and what claims does the Bible make? For black people thinking about joining the NOI and

---

[1] For a recent biography of Louis Farrakhan, see Florence H. Levinsohn, *Looking for Farrakhan* (Chicago: Ivan R. Dee, 1997).

becoming Black Muslims, it is important to know whether the claims that are made regarding Jesus are true. Ultimately, if there are competing claims, and if there are competing reports, "Whose report will you believe?"

Let me state categorically at the outset that I have never met the Honorable Louis Farrakhan. He has never done anything to me. I've read nothing that he has said or written about me, so he is not my enemy. I have nothing against the man personally. However, he is a leader — a vocal leader of the Nation of Islam — and he makes statements that, as a minister of the Gospel and as a Christian of more than 40 years, are disturbing to me. Whatever he has to say about Muhammad, whatever he has to say about Allah, whatever he has to say about Islam, is not relevant to me. *But*, when a non-Christian says things about the Bible and about Jesus Christ, my antennae go up! Let me again remind the reader that unless you are a born-again child of God through Jesus Christ, if you have not accepted and confessed Jesus Christ as your personal Savior and Lord, you *cannot* possibly understand the Bible. So when a person makes categorical statements that contradict God's Word, the Holy Bible, even though that may not be that person's intent, I have to speak up. I speak up against what is being proclaimed — not against a person.

Several years ago, I went to a "Muslim Awareness Conference." At the time, I was in the midst of compiling research for this book. The Lord had been dealing with me about Islam, and about Muhammad, and about the NOI. I thought this conference would be a good place to begin to gather information, because I wanted to be informed. At this conference, I watched an excerpt from a five-part television series called *Farrakhan: Charismatic Beacon or Cult Leader?* The sponsor of this conference, Glenn R. Plummer, provided me with a copy of this video.

In watching this series, I heard some things from the lips of the Honorable Louis Farrakhan that were disturbing to me in reference to the Jesus of the Bible. I think in light of our current study, we should examine some of the things Mr. Farrakhan says about

Jesus. Mr. Farrakhan, after all, is an outstanding leader of the NOI, and there are many people who look up to him. I certainly wouldn't want to defame this man, but when he claims to discuss things that are from the Bible or in the Bible, then I need to check that out. If you are contemplating becoming a member of the NOI, or are one now, there are some things you should know about it, and about the Christianity of the Bible. Again, I have to separate the Christianity of the Bible from the Christianity of man, because men do all sorts of ungodly and unscriptural things. So we need to know what the Bible says about Jesus Christ, and compare that with what Mr. Farrakhan says about Him.

It will be best to start this discussion with the following passage from Galatians 1:1-10:

1   **Paul, an apostle (not from men nor through man, but through Jesus Christ and God the Father who raised Him from the dead),**

2   **and all the brethren who are with me, to the churches of Galatia:**

3   **Grace to you and peace from God the Father and our Lord Jesus Christ,**

4   **who gave Himself for our sins, that He might deliver us from this present evil age, according to the will of our God and Father,**

5   **to whom *be* glory forever and ever. Amen.**

6   **I marvel that you are turning away so soon from Him who called you in the grace of Christ, to a different gospel,**

7   **which is not another; but there are some who trouble you and want to pervert the gospel of Christ.**

8   **But even if we, or an angel from heaven, preach any other gospel to you than what we have preached to you, let him be accursed.**

9   **As we have said before, so now I say again, if anyone preaches any other gospel to you than what you have received, let him be accursed.**

10   **For do I now persuade men, of God? Or do I seek to please men? For if I still pleased men, I would not be a bondservant of Christ.**

In light of that phrase, **preaches any other gospel to you than what you have received,** consider what we see in 1 John 4:1-3:

1   **Beloved, do not believe every spirit, but test the spirits, whether they are of God; because many false prophets have gone out into the world.**

2   **By this you know the Spirit of God: Every spirit that confesses that Jesus Christ has come in the flesh is of God,**

3   **and every spirit that does not confess that Jesus Christ has come in the flesh is not of God. And this is the *spirit* of the Antichrist, which you have heard was coming, and is now already in the world.**

So they had antichrists back then — 2,000 years ago. Look at Verses 2 and 3 again:

2   **By this you know the Spirit of God: Every spirit that confesses that Jesus Christ has come in the flesh is of God,**

3   **and every spirit that does not confess that Jesus Christ has come in the flesh is not of God. And**

164

> **this is the *spirit* of the Antichrist, which you**
> **have heard was coming, and is now already**
> **in the world.**

When the Bible says that **...Jesus Christ has come in the flesh...**, it's talking about Jesus the Anointed of God. "Christ" means the "Anointed One" and it also means "Messiah." (*Christ* is the Greek word for the Hebrew word *Messiah* — both of them mean "Anointed of God" or "Anointed One.") Anyone can agree with the statement that a man named Jesus came in the flesh, because we have historical records outside of the Bible. But that is not the same as saying that Jesus *Christ* the Anointed of God has come in the flesh. You must make that distinction.

With that in mind, let's examine some statements by leaders of the NOI. First, in the process of introducing Mr. Farrakhan at a mosque, a Muslim minister makes the following comment (the transcript of Mr. Farrakhan's comments appears in Appendix B):

> ...we would be remiss and considered ungrateful if we did not thank Allah for raising from the midst of us not one, but two messiahs. The most honorable Elijah Muhammad and the honorable Louis Farrakhan. It is in their names and in the name of righteous men and women everywhere, those that are living and those who have already become ancestors and even in the names of those who are yet to be born onto the earth. We offer the greetings of peace we say in Arabic "Asalam Alaycom" [peace be upon you]. I have something that I'm sure some of you have seen; it's a copy of *Newsweek* magazine. It has a picture of someone that they say is Jesus, but I would respectfully say, he doesn't look like the Jesus that we know. They had a picture of the Jesus that we know a few weeks ago on the cover of *Time* magazine. All praises due to Allah, but everybody is excited about Jesus. They want you to look backwards 2,000 years to a Jesus that is no longer here. That's so that you will be turned 180 degrees in the wrong direction and miss the

Jesus that is in your midst. All praises due to Allah! A lot of people don't know that the Muslims believe in Jesus just like the Christians. That's why we wonder what is wrong with your thinking when you go out on Easter weekend and you spend all of your money with merchants who don't even believe in Jesus, and you accept them better as your friends than the Muslims who believe in Jesus and who are waiting on Jesus just like you're waiting on Jesus. The Holy Koran teaches us about Jesus.

The Holy Koran teaches us that, and I quote, "We made Jesus and His mother Mary as a sign." We have been taught that a sign of something is not the same [as the thing] itself. This is to let us know that the Bible and Koran contain a prophetic reference to someone called Jesus, but that is just a sign. You have to wait until the fulfillment of the sign.... And so that's what we're waiting on in a few minutes, the fulfillment of the sign of Jesus will be in our presence in just a few minutes.[2]

These statements make it look like there's really no difference between Christians and Muslims. Sure, Muslims say they believe in Jesus. But what does that really mean? I *believe* there was a man named Columbus who came here with the Nina, the Pinta, and the Santa Maria, but I don't believe in Columbus as my Savior and Lord. There is a difference between *believing in* or *accepting the historical fact* of someone living and accepting that a person is your Savior and Lord. This provides enough of a gray area that people who were raised in the Christian Church, and put up with some of the racism that the white church perpetuated against people of color, felt like they were safe in going to Islam, because, after all, Muslims "believe in Jesus too." And they think

---

[2] Transcript from the video, *Farrakhan: Charismatic Beacon or Cult Leader?*, copyright 1996, Christian Television Network.

they will be welcomed by Islam because of similar skin color. But you have to be extremely careful.

James 2:19 gives us an illuminating insight: **You believe that there is one God. You do well. Even the demons believe — and tremble!** Also, in Mark 1:23-24, we find this statement:

> **23** **Now there was a man in their synagogue with an unclean spirit. And he cried out,**

> **24** **saying, "Let *us* alone! What have we to do with You, Jesus of Nazareth? Did You come to destroy us? I know who You are — the Holy One of God!"**

So we see that the demons believe in God and Jesus. They believe that He lived, but they don't accept Him as their Savior and Lord, but they *do believe* in Jesus. The minister in the mosque, introducing Mr. Farrakhan, gave an indication about what the Koran says about Jesus: he said "we made Mary and her baby Jesus as a sign." What they don't say is that the Koran also says that Jesus was no more than an apostle. He was not the Son of God. In fact, the Koran goes so far as to say that God could not have a son. Believe in Jesus? Believe what about Jesus?

Now let's see what the Honorable Louis Farrakhan himself says. Mr. Farrakhan, after being introduced:[3]

> ...Even the prophets of God are not the best examples. They are good examples, good examples, but the best example of what man is and of what man and woman can become is in the personage of Jesus Christ. "What? I didn't expect to hear that in a Muslim Mosque. I thought that you people were Muhammadans!" [This is a derogatory term for Muslims, akin to "Christers."] When you

---

[3] *Farrakhan: Charismatic Beacon or Cult Leader*, Appendix B, Pages 352-356.

look at Muhammad, the Muslims are making the same mistake that the Christians are making. The Muslims are saying Muhammad of 1,400 years ago is the seal of the prophets. Yes, a billion Muslims believe that. Well, the question is, is your belief true? You are just like the Christians. They are looking back 2,000 years ago for the real man, and missing the man who comes today. Muslims [are] looking 1,400 years ago to the Prophet Muhammad, and missing the real man [who] he prefigured.

Now, listen, if the scholars of Islam and the scholars of Christianity are honest men, and honest women, then we will have to admit that both the Jesus of 2,000 years ago and the Muhammad of 1,400 years ago did not fulfill all the signs of the one they prefigured. Jesus, 2,000 years ago, was overcome by the powers of wickedness, and his community has been turned upside down. So it is with the Muslims. If Jesus of 2,000 ago and the Muhammad of 1,400 years ago fulfilled the scriptures that are given to the fulfiller, when you seal something, you approve it or you close it. If you approve it, that means that the life of Jesus and Muhammad would fulfill in every aspect what the prophet assigns...that the last one gave us in their lives. The fulfiller doesn't look like the prophet. The fulfiller verifies the prophet as prophet. You call the prophets liars if the fufiller does not come to do what the prophets said he would do. If you think that your man, 1,400 years ago as an orthodox Muslim, or 2,000 years [ago] as a Christian, fulfilled it all, then there is no need for us to be here today. Because the work of the fulfiller would have ushered in a brand-new world and civilization. It has not happened yet; it's coming now — to seal up the book.

Keep in mind that if you are not born again, if you haven't been re-created in your human spirit, then you can't understand the spiritual significance of the Bible. You'll simply read it as a historical document and miss out on what it's really saying.

What is Mr. Farrakhan really saying? He is saying that the Jesus that came 2,000 years ago did not fulfill the prophecies. Mr. Farrakhan makes some mistakes because he's thinking about the "end times" and the end of everything — the end of this age, in other words. Mr. Farrakhan later claims that the Jews did not accept Jesus, because He wasn't the fulfiller. The Jews were expecting a conquering king to come — someone who could throw the Roman yoke off their backs right away.

But the Jews were not born again, and apparently, because Mr. Farrakhan is not born again, neither of them knows about the redemptive work of Messiah. They are only looking at the end of everything and thinking that because He didn't change everything and usher in the glorious kingdom of God that was prophesied, then He must not be the one. But they didn't understand that there had to be the cross before the crown.

To continue with Minister Farrakhan's comments:

> ...you're the people that Jesus is going to be raised among. He's not a white man, believe it or not. He's one of your own brothers. Now I'm going to prove it and I'm going home, and happy Easter to you too! He wasn't born in Bethlehem of Judea, he was born in Sandersville, Georgia.... The book says, can any good come out of Nazareth? It ain't likely that something good is going to come out of black folks, that's why the scriptures says, can any good come out of Nazareth? He's a man; you didn't understand him, we didn't either. Little humble, meek man, walked among us for 40 years laying a foundation. The Bible closes in the Old Testament, "Behold, before the great and dreadful day of the Lord, I will send you (who?) Elijah."

> What does Elijah mean?...It means God. Some say God is with us, Emmanuel means, "God is with us." Elijah means God. Eli! When Jesus was on the cross, they said he said "Eli, Eli, Lama Sabacthani." My God! So you got God, God. Jah, Jah, Jah is the name of God, so when

you have Eli-Jah, you have "God, my God! My God, God!"
Elijah the Prophet, now the Bible says, Elijah would turn
the hearts of the children to their fathers, and the father's
hearts to the children. When you close the Old Testament, you open the New Testament with the genealogy
of Jesus. But the Old Testament closes saying Elijah is
coming. God, my God is coming! Then you open up with
the genealogy of Jesus. So who is Jesus, who is Elijah?
Jesus and Elijah, one and the same!

Jesus and Elijah are one and the same? Now I have a problem
with this. This is Mr. Farrakhan's version of who Elijah is. Mr.
Farrakhan is a Muslim and speaks for God (Allah) based upon the
teachings of the Koran, the holy book of the Muslims. Don't you
think it fair that we let Jesus speak for God (Jehovah) based upon
the teachings of the Bible, the holy book of the Christians? If anyone
ought to know who Jesus and Elijah are, it ought to be the one God
(Jehovah) sent with His own message.

Any of you Christians thinking about making a move to Islam? — You better read this carefully. Mr. Farrakhan asked two questions, "Who is Jesus?" and "Who is Elijah?" Jesus and Elijah are
one and the same, he says. If they're one and the same, then Jesus is
Elijah and Elijah is Jesus. Fred Price didn't say it — the honorable
Louis Farrakhan said it.

What does the Bible say? Are they the same?

In John 8:18, we see the words of Jesus Himself:

**"I am One who bears witness of Myself, and the Fa-
ther who sent Me bears witness of Me."**

Then, in John 16:25-27, Jesus tells His disciples:

**25   "These things I have spoken to you in figurative
         language; but the time is coming when I will
         no longer speak to you in figurative language,
         but I will tell you plainly about the Father.**

26   **"In that day you will ask in My name, and I
do not say to you that I shall pray the Father
for you;"**

27   **for the Father Himself loves you, because you
have loved Me, and have believed that I came
forth from God.**

In both these passages, we see that Jesus came from God.
Now go to the last book of the Old Testament, Malachi 4:5-6:

5   **"Behold, I will send you Elijah the prophet
before the coming of the great and dreadful
day of the LORD.**

6   **"And he will turn the hearts of the fathers to
the children, and the hearts of the children to
their fathers, lest I come and strike the earth
with a curse."**

The Honorable Louis Farrakhan quoted that. Now I have a
question for you. Did this mean that God was going to send the physical
Elijah the prophet, who used to live on earth, to us? To determine this,
we need to examine the last time we heard anything about Elijah the
prophet, because at that time, something else occurred.

We find it in 2 Kings 2:11:

**Then it happened, as they continued on and talked,
that suddenly a chariot of fire *appeared* with horses of
fire, and separated the two of them; and Elijah went
up by a whirlwind into heaven.**

Elijah, the prophet, went up into heaven, alive. So does that
mean that God was going to send back Elijah physically, the one
who went up in a chariot?

In general, the Bible will interpret itself if you let it. When it
makes a statement like this, and you take the statement literally with-

out reservation, it has to mean that Elijah — the one who went up in the chariot — is coming back. But is that, in fact, what it means? Let's see what Jesus says about it.

We get some insight on this issue in John 3:22-36:

22   After these things Jesus and His disciples came into the land of Judea, and there He remained with them and baptized.

23   Now John also was baptizing in Aenon near Salim, because there was much water there. And they came and were baptized.

24   For John had not yet been thrown into prison.

25   Then there arose a dispute between *some* of John's disciples and the Jews about purification.

26   And they came to John and said to him, "Rabbi, He who was with you beyond the Jordan, to whom you have testified — behold, He is baptizing, and all are coming to Him!"

27   John answered and said, "A man can receive nothing unless it has been given to him from heaven.

28   "You yourselves bear me witness, that I said, 'I am not the Christ,' but, 'I have been sent before Him.'

29   "He who has the bride is the bridegroom; but the friend of the bridegroom, who stands and hears him, rejoices greatly because of the bridegroom's voice. Therefore this joy of mine is fulfilled.

30   "He must increase, but I *must* decrease.

31   "He who comes from above is above all; he who
        is of the earth is earthly and speaks of the earth.
        He who comes from heaven is above all.

32   "And what He has seen and heard, that He
        testifies; and no one receives His testimony.

33   "He who has received His testimony has
        certified that God is true.

34   "For He whom God has sent speaks the words
        of God, for God does not give the Spirit by
        measure.

35   "The Father loves the Son, and has given all
        things into His hand.

36   "He who believes in the Son has everlasting life;
        and he who does not believe the Son shall not
        see life, but the wrath of God abides on him."

The person whom God has sent speaks the words of God —
that is, Jehovah God, Creator God. Everyone whom God has sent
will have the same thing to say about the same subject. There can be
no deviation in their message, because if so, then God is confused.
So if Jehovah God, whom the Muslims say is Allah, sent the
Honorable Louis Farrakhan to tell us that Jesus and Elijah are one
and the same, then Jesus will also say that He and Elijah are one and
the same. Are you following my reasoning?

John the Baptist said that Jesus speaks the words of God.
Whatever Jesus says about this Elijah, whom God said He would
send, must in fact be the words of God, correct? Well, what did
Jesus say about Elijah?

We will have to believe what Jesus says about Elijah in order
to believe what God says about Elijah. Let's look at Matthew 11:11-
14, where Jesus is speaking:

11   "Assuredly, I say to you, among those born of
        women there has not risen one greater than

173

> John the Baptist; but he who is least in the kingdom of heaven is greater than he.
>
> 12   "And from the days of John the Baptist until now the kingdom of heaven suffers violence, and the violent take it by force.
>
> 13   "For all the prophets and the law prophesied until John.
>
> 14   "And if you are willing to receive *it*, he is Elijah who is to come."

Jesus clearly says that *John the Baptist* is Elijah! Not Jesus, John the Baptist. But Mr. Farrakhan said that Elijah and Jesus are one and the same.

There is more on this. In Luke 1:5-17:

> 5   There was in the days of Herod, the king of Judea, a certain priest named Zacharias, of the division of Abijah. His wife *was* of the daughters of Aaron, and her name *was* Elizabeth.
>
> 6   And they were both righteous before God, walking in all the commandments and ordinances of the Lord blameless.
>
> 7   But they had no child, because Elizabeth was barren, and they were both well advanced in years.
>
> 8   So it was, that while he was serving as priest before God in the order of his division,
>
> 9   according to the custom of the priesthood, his lot fell to burn incense when he went into the temple of the Lord.

10   And the whole multitude of the people was praying outside at the hour of incense.

11   Then an angel of the Lord appeared to him, standing on the right side of the altar of incense.

12   And when Zacharias saw *him*, he was troubled, and fear fell upon him.

13   But the angel said to him, "Do not be afraid, Zacharias, for your prayer is heard; and your wife Elizabeth will bear you a son, and you shall call his name John.

14   "And you will have joy and gladness, and many will rejoice at his birth.

15   "For he will be great in the sight of the Lord, and shall drink neither wine nor strong drink. He will also be filled with the Holy Spirit, even from his mother's womb.

16   "And he will turn many of the children of Israel to the Lord their God.

17   "He will also go before Him in the *spirit and power of Elijah* [emphasis mine], *'to turn the hearts of the fathers to the children,'* and the disobedient to the wisdom of the just, to make ready a people prepared for the Lord."

Using the Bible principle of "...by the mouth of two or three witnesses every word shall be established" when we put these two passages together, we see that Jesus said, that "if you are willing to receive it, John is Elijah." Now we have an angel from God who says in Verse 17, "He will also go before Him in the spirit and power of Elijah...." Who will? Zacharias and Elizabeth's son, whose name was John, called the Baptist. So there are two confirming witnesses that John is Elijah — not the physical Elijah that went up in the chariot, but the Elijah who was going to come as a prophet of God with the same anointing, the same power, the same spirit, as the Elijah who walked the earth.

Now, if John is Elijah, then Jesus couldn't be Elijah! And if Jesus couldn't be Elijah, then Elijah and Jesus are not one and the same. Whose report will you believe?

Jesus said that John the Baptist was Elijah, and Mr. Farrakhan says Jesus and Elijah are one and the same. Who should know better, Jesus or Mr. Farrakhan? Obviously, when God said, "I'll send you Elijah," He didn't mean Elijah — the one who went up in the chariot. That is confirmed by what we just read, by what Jesus said about John the Baptist, and by what the angel said about John the Baptist. That's the way you let Scripture prove Scripture. If you take it literally, like the statement in Malachi, the only conclusion you can come to is that Elijah, physically, is coming back. But is that what God meant? He couldn't have, because God sent Jesus from Him with His word, and Jesus said John was Elijah. Clearly, then, this statement in Malachi, where God says, "I'll send you Elijah the prophet," did not mean the Elijah who went up in the chariot, but rather someone like that prophet, in the power and the spirit of that prophet, just like Elijah.

A further reference is found in Matthew 17:1-3:

1   **Now after six days Jesus took Peter, James, and John his brother, led them up on a high mountain by themselves;**

2   **and He was transfigured before them. His face shone like the sun, and His clothes became as white as the light.**

3   **And behold, Moses and Elijah appeared to them, talking with Him.**

This occurred in the spirit, because Moses and Elijah were in the spirit world. When Moses died, his spirit and soul went down to Hades, the place of the departed spirits of the dead, to the paradise section of the underworld. Elijah, on the other hand, never died, but was carried into heaven in a whirlwind. Those who had died waited in Hades, the paradise section of the underworld, for the great day of redemption so that they could be transferred to the heavenly paradise in the third heaven where God lives. God allowed Moses to come up because he was still spiritually — though not physically — alive. (You never die in the sense of ceasing to consciously exist.) God allowed them to appear in glory — Moses from the underworld and Elijah from heaven — representing a prophetic profile of both those "dead in Christ" and those "alive in Christ" in the end times, which means that they did not appear in the flesh. They were in a glorified state.

Matthew 17:4 goes on to say:

Then Peter answered and said to Jesus, "Lord, it is good for us to be here; if You wish, let us make here three tabernacles: one for You, one for Moses, and one for Elijah."

Look down at Verses 10-13:

10   And His disciples asked Him, saying, "Why then do the scribes say that Elijah must come first?"

11   Jesus answered and said to them, "Indeed, Elijah is coming first and will restore all things.

12   "But I say to you that *Elijah has come already,* [emphasis mine] and they did not know him but did to him whatever they wished. Likewise the Son of Man is also about to suffer at their hands."

13   Then the disciples understood that He spoke to them of John the Baptist.

My question to you is, Who speaks for Jehovah God? Mr. Farrakhan or Jesus the Christ? Whose report will you believe?

Let's continue with Mr. Farrakhan's comments:

...We were scanning the horizon, looking for Elijah Muhammad to return. I was scanning with you, but I didn't know that at the end of my three years down, when I rose up, Elijah would rise up in me. *I am that Elijah* [*emphasis* mine] that was to come and now is. That Elijah that says God is not to come but He's present. What is your function, Elijah? To turn the children and their hearts back to their father. Who is your father? Elijah Muhammad is the father of this knowledge, and you were turned away from him. But Elijah comes to do what? Elijah must first come and restore all things. You can only restore what was taken away. What was taken away from you in your fall? It is this little Elijah that is restoring it back to you, that you may rise again.... I'm not talking about myself, because it's not good. But I'm really not talking about myself; I'm talking about something that God has done for you, for me, for us. White people want to know why so many black people are moved by Farrakhan. What is it about Farrakhan that he touches the essence of black people? That even if they don't agree with everything that he says, nobody meets him and remains the same? What is it about him? People say he's an orator. Yes, I'm that. But orators don't transform human life. I'm more than an orator with good oration. I came to you today with no notes. Nothing is written; it is all coming from within....

I want you to look at your brother [meaning Farrakhan himself], this Easter, who while he is speaking to you, is in the first phase of his crucifixion. Were you there when they crucified my Lord? We're always there. We usually take part in it.... You're looking for Jesus. I'm telling you as your brother, I'm the son of my father...because when He speaks He opens their eyes by God's permission. When He speaks, he unstops their ears by God's permission. When He speaks if you listen to what I say and say what you hear me say, God will put a tongue in your mouth and you that were dumb yesterday, but you speak with wisdom today, if you speak after what I say. Whether you like it or not, I'm your connecting link to the Honorable Elijah Muhammad. To deny me is to deny him! To accept me is to accept him! You will never be successful, even in what he taught you, if you don't connect me in there, then the power to (…?) the word won't be with you. This is not vanity. I'm among you. Man, open up your eyes and look and see what God is doing in the midst of you….

…My job is to hook you up with the Christ. "Now, Farrakhan, how can you hook somebody up to Christ if you ain't hooked up?" Check me out! If I'm not hooked up, then nobody in America or in the world is hooked up. I'm more hooked up to Christ than the Pope is…. I'm hanging on a cross right now. I'm on Calvary right now. "Aw, come on, Farrakhan, let's not be melodramatic." Any other black leader catching this kind of hell? Not one! No! I'm beginning to hang here now and it's around the first hour. They want to strip me of my robe…. The more I suffer, the more our people are raised in consciousness. Just by their beating on me and my being able to take it, black people beginning to say, "What are they beating on that man for? What are they…?" I mean, and people are getting angry now. Well, what's raising you? It is the cross. It is my suffering that is undeserved. I did nothing to deserve this. But it is out of my love for him and for you that I am suffering. And I'm ready to go all the way, because I know that by my stripes every one of you will be healed. You don't have to look anywhere for your Jesus, I represent Him!…This journey to that hour when he says, it is finished; it don't mean he died; it means I have done what you brought me into the world to do. It's finished! I've ran my course, and now it's laid up for me the crown and I'm going to get my crown. And what is my crown? You will see me again! Man, I'm so happy, I'm so happy, that my blessed mother, who is not alive to see her son today, but that blessed black woman may (…?) for Mary

again, laid a foundation in her son. I was born to die
for you. I love the thought of dying for you.

This might seem lengthy, but I want you to read what this man
says. Mr. Farrakhan is an eloquent speaker, and people are listening to
him. You might want to pick up the videotape series *Race, Religion &
Racism,* because we include the actual video of this speech within that
series, so you can see for yourself what a forceful, convincing speaker he
is.

We can go along with "forceful" or "charismatic," but we
have to separate truth from error. This gets us close to some of the
areas I want to deal with, but you have to get an idea of the person's
modus operandi, or how a person operates. Mr. Farrakhan is saying
some things about us, as Christians, and using things from the Bible
and about Jesus. You have to look past the delivery and the "cha-
risma" and examine the message, not the messenger. Is the message
valid? You can't afford to be sold on a product just because of an
attractive package. If you have to eat cereal, you can't just go on the
appearance of the box! You may starve to death if that cereal isn't
edible, or if there's sawdust inside. You must be sure.

Mr. Farrakhan has strongly implied, or so it seems, that he is
Jesus. He states that he is being crucified right now, for you. He
doesn't use the exact phrase, "I am Jesus," but you be the judge. He
says he is dying for us, and that he can "hook us up." I submit to you,
especially anyone who watches the video, that the tone, style, and
implication of his comments can mean nothing except that he is claiming to be Jesus. The gist of this section appears to be that the Jesus
we worship only "prefigured" Mr. Farrakhan, who, it is implied, is
the "real" Messiah or the "prophetic Jesus." Is this not what he means
when he talks about Jesus being only a "historical Jesus" and that
there still is a Messiah who "is to come?"

Does Mr. Farrakhan not imply — and again, you be the judge
— that the "crown" Jesus received was that you would "see me
again?" And does not the rest of the passage suggest that indeed
Mr. Farrakhan is Jesus incarnate? ("You don't have to look anywhere for your Jesus, I represent Him!") He says, "This is not van-

ity. I'm among you. Man, open up your eyes and look and see what God is doing in the midst of you...." Again, this does not appear to point to Jesus Christ as the One who will return, but to one who is "among us" now, does it not?

The Bible has a completely different message. Jesus said He is the Messiah, not Mr. Farrakhan. Whose report will you believe?

I must emphasize that the biblical principle is **"by the mouth of two or three witnesses every word shall be established."** Mr. Farrakhan has made some rather bold statements, but has given us no scriptural proof — no way to check things out. He said "check *me* out," but he didn't tell us to "check the Scriptures out." Jesus, on the other hand, was very clear. He said, **"search the Scriptures."** He didn't just say, "read the Scriptures," but **"search the Scriptures," "...for in them** [the Scriptures] **you think you have eternal life; and these are they** [the Scriptures] **which testify of Me"** (John 5:39).

Mr. Farrakhan goes on to say an astounding thing:

> ...Seventy-five percent of what you read in the Bible referring to Jesus is referring to a future man. And 25 percent of what you read is referring to the man of 2,000 years ago who is considered a type. But the real question is, "Who is Jesus? Where will you find Him?" This the scholars are going to have to sit down and meet on. If the scholars agree that the Jesus of 2,000 years ago prefigured or gave us a picture of the real Jesus, then the historical Jesus is not the real Jesus, but the real Jesus is the one that the historical Jesus prefigured or gives us a type of.[4]

> The historical Jesus was not the Messiah! The prophetic Jesus is the Messiah. The historical Jesus prefigured the

---

[4] It should go without comment that just because "scholars" agree on something hardly makes it right. "Scholars" agreed for hundreds of years that the world was flat, and that the sun rotated around the earth.

> Messiah and that's why the Jews have never accepted
> the historical Jesus; they continue to look for the Mes-
> siah. They are not wrong....

I did not detect any scriptural references in Mr. Farrakhan's assertions. He said that 25 percent of the Bible that mentions Jesus is talking about a historical Jesus and 75 percent of what the Bible says about Jesus is referring to a future man. That is not in the Bible. That is not correct, and that is inaccurate information. It is also dangerous. If what he said was true, I should be able to find it in the Bible. I should be able to find Scripture that says that 25 percent of what is written is talking about the Jesus that came 2,000 years ago, the "historical Jesus," as he says, and 75 percent of what is written refers to a future Jesus — a "prophetic Jesus," as he calls Him. But that is incorrect, and is not biblically supportable.

Mr. Farrakhan said, "25 percent of what the Bible says about Jesus is talking about the historical Jesus, the man of 2,000 years ago, and 75 percent of what the Bible says about Jesus is talking about a future man...." So we should not find any Scripture about Jesus being the Messiah, because Mr. Farrakhan said that the "historical Jesus" (the one we know as the real Jesus, the man of 2,000 years ago) was *not* the Messiah. The "historical Jesus" means Mary's son, the One they nailed to the cross, the One who was resurrected. That's the "historical Jesus." The "historical Jesus" is the One who turned water into wine. The "historical Jesus" is the One who walked on the water. The "historical Jesus" is the One who raised Lazarus from the dead after Lazarus had been dead for four days and his body had already begun to decompose. That "historical Jesus," that Jesus — Mr. Farrakhan said is *not* the Messiah.

We want to examine this historical and prophetic Jesus. If Mr. Farrakhan's words are of God, we shouldn't find anything in the Bible that would contradict what Mr. Farrakhan said. But if we find something to the contrary, it should tell us that Mr. Farrakhan's information is flawed!

So let's look at Matthew 2:1-6:

1   Now after Jesus was born in Bethlehem of
     Judea in the days of Herod the king, behold,
     wise men from the East came to Jerusalem,

2   saying, "Where is He who has been born King
     of the Jews? For we have seen His star in the
     East and have come to worship Him."

3   When Herod the king heard *this*, he was
     troubled, and all Jerusalem with him.

4   And when he had gathered all the chief priests
     and scribes of the people together, he inquired
     of them where the Christ was to be born.

The word *Christ* comes from the Greek term *Christos*, which
means "Messiah" or "the anointed of God." So Herod was in essence
saying, "where is the Messiah to be born?" When he said "the Christ,"
he was talking about the "anointed of God," the "Messiah." Both
words mean the same thing. Let's continue:

4   And when he had gathered all the chief priests
     and scribes of the people together, he inquired
     of them where the Christ was to be born.

He did not inquire where the "historical Jesus" was to be
born. He wanted to know where the "Messiah" was going to be born.
Verses 5 and 6 clarify this even further:

5   So they said to him, "In Bethlehem of Judea,
     for thus it is written by the prophet:

6   *'But you, Bethlehem, in the land of Judah, are
     not the least among the rulers of Judah; for out
     of you shall come a Ruler who will shepherd
     My people Israel.'* "

183

Remember, our mission is to find out what the Bible says, what the writers of the Bible wrote — who did *they* think that this Jesus was, the one Mr. Farrakhan calls the "historical Jesus." It seems reasonable that those who actually wrote about Him should know.

In Matthew 16:13-16, we find these words:

13   **When Jesus came into the region of Caesarea Philippi, He asked His disciples, saying, "Who do men say that I, the Son of Man, am?"**

14   **So they said, "Some *say* John the Baptist, some Elijah, and others, Jeremiah or one of the prophets."**

15   **He said to them, "But who do you say that I am?"**

16   **Simon Peter answered and said, "You are the Christ, the Son of the living God."**

Peter said, in essence, "you're the Messiah," because we've seen that is what the word *Christ* means, "anointed of God."

In fact, if you look closely, notice that Peter directly contradicted Mr. Farrakhan's claim that Jesus was Elijah by saying, **"...some** [say you are] **Elijah."** In essence he is saying, "You're not Elijah. **You are the Christ....**" It is interesting that, given the opportunity to identify Jesus as Elijah, Peter specifically mentioned that He wasn't Elijah! Then look at what Jesus added to Peter's comments in Verses 17 to 20:

17   **Jesus answered and said to him, "Blessed are you, Simon Bar-Jonah, for flesh and blood has not revealed *this* to you, but My Father who is in heaven.**

18   **"And I also say to you that you are Peter, and on this rock I will build My church, and the gates of Hades shall not prevail against it.**

19   "And I will give you the keys of the kingdom
         of heaven, and whatever you bind on earth will
         be bound in heaven, and whatever you loose
         on earth will be loosed in heaven."

20   Then He commanded His disciples that they
         should tell no one that He was Jesus the Christ.

Jesus commended Peter for figuring out, by the Holy Spirit, that He was the Christ, the Son of God, and now that "the cat was out of the bag," so to speak, Jesus, in Verse 20, **commanded His disciples that they should tell no one that He was** *Jesus the Christ* [emphasis mine]. Once again, the "historical Jesus" was in fact "the Christ." Now, who do you think should know who Jesus is? Jesus or Mr. Farrakhan?

I could close my case and be biblically correct, but we're not going to stop there. We're going many steps beyond. In Matthew 26:63-64, we find another statement by Jesus as to His identity, during His questioning by the high priest:

63   But Jesus kept silent. And the high priest
         answered and said to Him, "I put You under
         oath by the living God: Tell us if You are the
         Christ, the Son of God!"

64   Jesus said to him, *"It is as* you said...."

Now how do you interpret that answer? He said, "You got it! I'm Jesus the Christ the Son of God." Isn't that right? That makes three witnesses, but we will move on to still more. Look at Luke 4:14-21:

14   Then Jesus returned in the power of the Spirit
         to Galilee, and news of Him went out through
         all the surrounding region.

15   And He taught in their synagogues, being
         glorified by all.

185

16   So He came to Nazareth....

Pause here for a moment and consider, Who do you think it means when it says "He" came to Nazareth? Wouldn't that be the person spoken of in Verse 14? So let's make this clear when we look at it this time:

16   So He [Jesus] came to Nazareth, where He had been brought up. And as His custom was, He went into the synagogue on the Sabbath Day, and stood up to read.

17   And He was handed the book of the prophet Isaiah. And when He had opened the book, He found the place where it was written:

18   *"The Spirit of the Lord is upon Me, because He has anointed Me to preach the gospel to the poor; He has sent Me to heal the brokenhearted, to proclaim liberty to the captives and recovery of sight to the blind, to set at liberty those who are oppressed;*

19   *to proclaim the acceptable year of the Lord."*

20   Then He closed the book, and gave *it* back to the attendant and sat down. And the eyes of all who were in the synagogue were fixed on Him.

21   And He began to say to them, "Today...."

Realize that Jesus was in the synagogue on the Sabbath, and when He was there it was "today" for Him. That day that He said the Scripture quoted above was "today" when He said it.

21   And He began to say to them, "Today this Scripture is fulfilled in your hearing."

What does this mean? Go back to Verse 18: **"The Spirit of the Lord is upon Me, because He has anointed Me...."** We just saw that the word *Christ* means "anointed of God," and that *Messiah* means "the anointed one." With that in mind, look at Verse 21 again: **And He began to say to them, "Today this Scripture is fulfilled...."** We want to be specific — what Scripture was fulfilled? That God had anointed Jesus — Jesus had just read from Isaiah, who had prophesied about the Messiah. Do you see the deep truth here?

If something is fulfilled, there is nothing coming after it. It's over. If the prophecy is fulfilled, it is completed. Note again, this is Jesus Himself speaking — not Fred Price, and not Mr. Farrakhan, but Jesus the Christ. He said, **"Today."** That "today" chronologically refers to a day some 2,000 years ago! Jesus who read that Scripture is the same Jesus Mr. Farrakhan says is the "historical Jesus," but Whom Mr. Farrakhan says is not the Messiah, but only "prefigures" the Messiah! But that is not what Jesus said. He said, **"Today this Scripture is fulfilled in your hearing."** "Today," not some future date, but today, meaning that day 2,000 years ago! Whose report will you believe?

Yet there is still more evidence that Jesus was the Messiah (the Christ). In Luke 4:40-41 Jesus encountered people who were sick and possessed of demons:

> **40** **When the sun was setting, all those who had any that were sick with various diseases brought them to Him; and He laid His hands on every one of them and healed them.**
>
> **41** **And demons also came out of many, crying out and saying, "You are the Christ, the Son of God!" And He, rebuking *them*, did not allow them to speak, for they knew that He was the Christ.**

This is especially significant, because demons are disembodied spirits, who operate in the spirit world. It isn't that I want you to take demons at their word, but in this case, they were blurting out something that indicated they knew who Jesus was. They didn't say He was the "historical" Jesus "prefiguring" the prophetic Jesus who was coming later. Oh no! **And demons also came out of many, crying out and saying, "You are the Christ...."** [in other words, "You are the Messiah, You are the anointed of God"] **And He,** [Jesus] **rebuking** *them*, **did not allow them to speak,** [why?] **for they knew that He was the Christ.**

Yet again, we have in Acts 2:36, the following:

> **"Therefore let all the house of Israel know assuredly that God has made this Jesus, whom you crucified, both Lord and Christ."**

"Lord and Christ." "You are the Christ." "For they knew He was the Christ." "If you are the Christ, the Son of God...It is as you say."

Despite these statements by Jesus as to His identity, there are still those who say He did not say He was the Messiah or the Son of God. Such comments are hard to understand, given the statement Jesus made to His disciples in John 17:3, when He prayed for them: **"And this is eternal life, that they may know You** [the Father], **the only true God, and *Jesus Christ* [emphasis mine] whom You have sent."** Notice that Jesus refers to Himself as **"Jesus Christ, whom You** [God] **have sent."** A reasonable paraphrasing of this would be, "...that they may know that You, Father, are the only true God and that they may know that I am Jesus the Messiah and that you sent me to them." This is awesome! Jesus confirmed that He was the Messiah. You can't miss this!

This is overwhelming evidence. We have seven witnesses: 1) Herod wanted to know where the "Christ" was born; 2) Peter straightaway called Jesus "the Christ," and Jesus confirmed Peter's comment; 3) the High Priest called Jesus the Christ, and again, Jesus confirmed it; 4) Jesus Himself told the people in the synagogue that He was the Anointed One (i.e., "Messiah"); 5) Peter said again that Jesus was "Lord and Christ;" 6) even the demons confirmed He was the Christ; and 7) Jesus plainly said His name and title was "Jesus Christ," or Jesus "the Anointed One."

In basketball this is called a slam dunk. But Mr. Farrakhan says the "historical Jesus" is not the "prophetic Jesus," who is the Messiah. Whose report will you believe?

If Mr. Farrakhan claims that Jesus was not the Messiah, what is the position of Islam on Jesus Christ as the Son of God? After all, Mr. Farrakhan might not be relating Islam's position accurately. But in fact, it's quite simple: The Koran says Jesus is not the Son of God. To establish this, remember I am using two versions of the Koran. The first is entitled *The Koran,* translated with notes by N.J. Dawood; the second, *The Meaning of the Glorious Quran*, by Abdullah Yusuf Ali.[5] Again, the Koran does not have chapters, but divisions called suras [literally, rows]. So we are reading from Sura 4:171:

> "O People of the book, commit no excesses in your religion: nor say of God, aught but the truth. Christ Jesus the Son of Mary was (no more than) an apostle of God...."[6]

This is Allah, Almighty God to the Muslims, speaking his word to Muhammad, saying, "...Christ Jesus the Son of Mary was no more than an apostle of God...." If Jesus is "no more than an apostle," then He's certainly not a savior and definitely not a redeemer, right? The Koran continues in the same Sura 4:171:

> ....And His Word, which He bestowed on Mary, and a Spirit proceeding from Him: so believe in God and His apostles. Say not "Trinity": desist: It will be better for you: For God is One God: Glory be to Him: Far Exalted is He above having a son....[7]

---

[5] Abdullah Yusuf Ali, *The Meaning of the Glorious Quran*, 2 vols. (Cairo: Dar Al-Kitab Al-Masri, 1938).
[6] Ali, 1:233-234.
[7] Ali, 1:234.

In other words, it's beneath Almighty God's dignity to have a son. That's awesome, and it is vitally important to any Christian to understand this! Sura 171 finishes as follows:

> ...To Him belong all things in the heavens and on earth and enough is God as a disposer of affairs.

But let's be fair. We have already seen that we have various translations of the Bible that can render different interpretations. We've certainly seen in Volume 2 of *Race, Religion & Racism* with the Dake's Bible that an erroneous translation can lead to all kinds of bondage. So we need to validate that we are dealing with Islam fairly here. So I am going to provide a second citation — another translation of the Koran, which I have already used, by N. J. Dawood. Again, Sura 4:171:

> ...People of the Book, do not transgress the bounds of your religion. Speak nothing but the truth about God. The Messiah, Jesus the son of Mary, was no more than God's apostle and His Word which He cast to Mary; a spirit from Him. So believe in God and His apostles and do not say "Three." Forebear, and it shall be better for you. God is but one God; God forbid that He should have a son.[8]

So Mr. Farrakhan and both versions of the Koran agree that Jesus is not the Messiah. But I find it interesting that the first translation of the Koran calls Him "Christ Jesus," but goes on to say that He was "(no more than) an apostle of God." The second translation of the holy book of the Muslims calls Him "...the Messiah, Jesus...." but says He "was no more than God's apostle...." Why use such terms as *Christ* and *Messiah* to identify Jesus and then deny that the terms apply to Him? Remember, we saw that the Greek term *Christ* translates into "anointed of God" and the Hebrew word *Messiah* translates into

---

[8] Dawood, 78.

"the anointed one." In effect, both words mean Messiah. These descriptions in the Koran come off as contradictory and confusing. Can you imagine the Holy Bible calling Muhammad "the anointed one"?

Following Mr. Farrakhan's argument, since the "prophetic Jesus" has not yet come, we don't know what his mother's name is going to be. But we do know the name of the mother of the "historical Jesus" — Mary. Clearly, then, this translation is referring to the "historical Jesus," because it mentions that His mother was Mary. So that we make this absolutely unmistakable, read passage 171 again:

> People of the Book, do not transgress the bounds of your religion. Speak nothing but the truth about God. The *Messiah* [emphasis mine], Jesus the son of Mary, was no more than God's apostle and His Word which He cast to Mary: a spirit from Him. So believe in God and His apostles and do not say: "Three." Forbear, and it shall be better for you. God is but one God, God forbid that He should have a son![9]

Allah's word, through the prophet Muhammad, says "...God forbid that He should have a Son...." The Koran, then, explicitly states that God does not have a son. Compare this with Luke 4:41 again: **And demons also came out of many, crying out and saying, "You are the Christ, the Son of God!..."** It would have been enough for this verse to say, "And demons also came out of many, crying out and saying, 'You are the Christ,' " period. Isn't it interesting that the demons said **"You are the Christ, the Son of God!..."** So we have a serious contradiction here! The Koran says (which means Muhammad said, which means Allah, God of the Muslims, said), "...God forbid that He should have a son...."

The Bible records that both Peter and the demons said, **"You are the Christ, the Son of God!..."** Not just "the Christ," but "the

---

[9] Dawood, 78

Christ, the Son of God." At this point, it is clear that the Jehovah God of the Bible and the God of the Koran, Allah, are most definitely not the same.

There is more, and this next spiritual reference is the icing on the cake. Recall that Mr. Farrakhan said that the "historical Jesus" was not the Messiah. In John 4:21-26, Jesus is conversing with the woman at Jacob's well in Samaria. In the course of their discussion, they both make a statement that cements this issue of who the "historical Jesus" really was:

21   Jesus said to her, "Woman, believe Me, the hour is coming when you will neither on this mountain, nor in Jerusalem, worship the Father.

22   "You worship what you do not know; we know what we worship, for salvation is of the Jews.

23   "But the hour is coming, and now is, when the true worshipers will worship the Father in spirit and truth; for the Father is seeking such to worship Him.

24   "God *is* Spirit, and those who worship Him must worship in spirit and truth."

25   The woman said to Him, "I know that Messiah is coming (who is called Christ). [Note that she put both names together!] "When He comes, He will tell us all things."

26   Jesus said to her, "I who speak to you am *He*."

"Am He" who? Christ and Messiah! Jesus confirmed to the woman that "**I who speak to you am *He*** [the Christ and Messiah]." If anyone should know who He is, it is Jesus.

According to Mr. Farrakhan, the Messiah hasn't come yet. But Jesus said, *"...I am He..."* in response to the woman's statement that

"Messiah is coming." Put another way, Jesus said, "I am that one whom you expect to come." Whose report will you believe?

But there is more evidence. In John 6:66-69, we find this revelation:

66   **From that *time* many of His disciples went back and walked with Him no more.**

67   **Then Jesus said to the twelve, "Do you also want to go away?"**

68   **But Simon Peter answered Him, "Lord, to whom shall we go? You have the words of eternal life.**

69   **"Also we have come to believe and know that You are the Christ, the Son of the living God."**

So the demons acknowledged that Jesus was **"the Christ, the Son of God,"** and Peter confirms to Jesus that he knows **"You are the Christ, the Son of the living God."** Yet the Koran said "God forbid that He should have a son."

If you are planning to commit your life to Islam, this is a serious situation. These are serious contradictions, and they demand an answer. No one can think that Allah and Jehovah are the same person based on these references.

Look at Verses 66 to 69 again:

66   **From that *time* many of His disciples went back and walked with Him no more.**

67   **Then Jesus said to the twelve, "Do you also want to go away?"**

68   **But Simon Peter answered Him, "Lord, to whom shall we go? You have the words of eternal life.**

69   "Also we have come to believe and know that
        You are the Christ, the Son of the living God."

These men walked with Jesus and observed Him. Isn't it amazing that they came to know that He was the Christ, the Son of the living God, and yet here comes Muhammad, 600 years later, saying "God forbid that He should have a son." These statements are diametrically opposed — you can't straddle the fence with this! Whose report will you believe?

But I'll give you yet another witness. Again, the Word says, **"by the mouth of two or three witnesses,"** but for something this important the Holy Spirit left no doubt. John's Gospel records an encounter between Jesus and Mary and Martha. In John 11:24-27, we see this exchange:

24   Martha said to Him, "I know that he will rise
        again in the resurrection at the last day."

25   Jesus said to her, "I am the resurrection and
        the life. He who believes in Me, though he may
        die, he shall live.

26   "And whoever lives and believes in Me shall
        never die...."

Understand that Jesus was speaking about never dying spiritually. If you believe in Him and are born again spiritually, you'll never die spiritually. This does not refer to never dying physically, but rather never dying spiritually.

26   "And whoever lives and believes in Me shall
        never die. Do you believe this?"

27   She said to Him, "Yes, Lord, I believe that You
        are the Christ, the Son of God...."

Notice how often the terms *Christ* and *Son of God* appear together in these verses? Yet the Koran says, "...God forbid that He should have a son…." So we have the Bible, where **She** [Martha] **said to Him, "Yes, Lord, I believe that You are the Christ…."** and at that point, she could have ended her sentence just like Peter could have. All that was necessary for her to say was "…I believe that You are the Christ." End of statement. So why does the Holy Spirit record the fact that these witnesses always seem to add "the Son of God?" And not "a" Son of God, but "the" Son of God. It is obvious that Mr. Farrakhan cannot be born again, with all this in the Bible. It is clear he does not know the Word, and has some bad information.

Now look at John 17:1-5:

1   **Jesus spoke these words, lifted up His eyes to heaven, and said: "Father, the hour has come. Glorify Your Son, that Your Son also may glorify You,**

2   **"as You have given Him authority over all flesh, that He should give eternal life to as many as You have given Him.**

3   **"And this is eternal life, that they may know You, the only true God,** [apparently there are some other gods, but they must not be true!] **and Jesus Christ whom You have sent.**

4   **"I have glorified You on the earth. I have finished the work which You have given Me to do.**

5   **"And now, O Father, glorify Me together with Yourself, with the glory which I had with You before the world was."**

This is awesome! Jesus clearly said "Father." And a person who calls someone father is either a daughter or a son. Since Jesus is a man, then He must be the Son of God! Again, we have multiple witnesses, capped off by Jesus' own testimony of who He is! Peter said **"You are the Christ, the Son of the living God,"** Martha said **"You are the**

Christ, the Son of God," and Jesus called God "Father" and spoke of the **"glory which I had with You before the world was."** This really isn't a close call: Whose report will you believe?

It is important for us as Christians and it's also important for Muslims, especially black Muslims, to get correct information. Notice again how conspicuous by its absence is the fact that Mr. Farrakhan gave no scriptural or biblical references to authenticate his position. He is such an eloquent speaker, such a charismatic personality, that people will believe what he says simply because of the rhetoric and presentation. This is not about the man, but rather the content of his message.

Let's review part of the statement Mr. Farrakhan made on the tape:

> ...That 75 percent of what you read in the Bible referring to Jesus, is referring to a future man. And 25 percent of what you read is referring to the man of 2,000 years ago, who is considered a type. A type is like a sign of the real. So when you're looking at a type, you see in minuscule what the real is going to look like. So when you look at and study the type, then you won't be able to miss the real when the real comes....

Notice this "75 percent, 25 percent" reference. There is nothing in the Bible that supports this. He could not have gotten this from the Bible, because you won't find it there. Again, if there is a "historical Jesus" and a "prophetic Jesus," that means there were two Jesuses. My Bible only speaks of one. But let's continue with Mr. Farrakhan's comments:

> But the real question is, who is Jesus? Where will you find Him? This, the scholars are going to have to sit down and meet on. If the scholars agree that the Jesus of 2,000 years ago, prefigured or gave us a picture of the real Jesus, then the historical Jesus is not the real Jesus, but the real Jesus is the one that the historical Jesus prefigured or gives us a type of. I want you to

> follow me, this may be a little difficult for those who are
> not biblical scholars, but it's going to come right clear to
> you. You say, "Well brother Farrakhan, as much hell as
> we're catching, I mean, what are you troubling us with
> Jesus for? You know, I mean, can't we talk about how to
> get out of the hell that we're in? I mean, why you gotta
> waste our time, trying to see about a historical or pro-
> phetic Jesus, I ain't got no bread on my table and I have
> very little sense in my head, can you tell me why you
> fooling around with this Jesus question?" Well, I mean
> you might be thinking like that.

One of the things Mr. Farrakhan said was, "…I want you to follow me. This may be a little difficult for those who are not biblical scholars, but it's going to come right clear to you…." What I gather from that is that Mr. Farrakhan *is* a biblical scholar. Did you get that? "…I want you to follow me. This may be a little difficult for those who are not biblical scholars, but it's going to come right clear to you." Without coming right out and saying it, he is claiming that he is a biblical scholar, who is able to make things "right clear" to the people.

Well, if you are a biblical scholar then you should give me biblical information! Give me chapter and verse so I can check you out. Just because you say you are a spokesman for God does not make you that: Jesus said in Matthew 12:33, **"…a tree is known by *its* fruit."** Jesus also said in John 5:39, **"…search the Scriptures, for in them you think you have eternal life; and these** [the Scriptures] **are they which testify of Me."** Mr. Farrakhan went on to say:

> And there is nothing wrong with your thinking like that,
> because that's very real; I mean, we waste a lot of time
> with scripture and whatnot….

I must reiterate my earlier point that Mr. Farrakhan is not a Christian. If he were a Christian he would never say "…we waste a lot of time with Scripture…." You can't waste time with Scripture, because Scripture is all we have. If it's a waste of time, we are in serious trouble.

Moreover, we have it straight from Jesus (we read it above) to **"...search the Scriptures, for...[these Scriptures] are they which testify of Me."**[11] Again, we are back to whose report will you believe: Mr. Farrakhan or Jesus Christ?

Mr. Farrakhan continued:

> And there is nothing wrong with your thinking like that, because that's very real; I mean, we waste a lot of time with scripture and whatnot and the people saying.... People upset; people hungry, people naked, people out of doors; people beaten and killed every day, man, "don't waste my time on something that has no relevance to me." But, I would not waste your time, so it does have relevance because the Jesus that is, is the Jesus that saves. The Jesus that was, is pointing to the Jesus that saves, that will get us all out of the condition that we are in, will get the world out of the condition the world is in....

So we are back to the "historical Jesus" and "prophetic Jesus." All you Christians need to get this, and all you Black Muslims need to get this, and all Muslims, period, need to get this. If what Mr. Farrakhan says is true, none of us is saved. Not one Christian is saved — we are all lost and standing on the brink of hell. I'm not saved, and you're not saved — if what Mr. Farrakhan says is true. Let's read that again, because it touches on the very foundations of Christianity! He said: "...Because the Jesus that is,

---

[11] Paul, in 2 Timothy 2:15, also commands us, through the Holy Spirit to **"Be diligent** [also translated as "study"] **to present yourself approved to God, a worker who does not need to be ashamed, *rightly* dividing the word of truth** [emphasis added]." The purpose of the study – of "being diligent" – is to avoid these kinds of problems, so that you "rightly divide" the word of truth. Well, clearly, then you can "wrongly divide" the word of truth if you do not do what Jesus said and **"search the Scriptures."** So again, we have by the mouth of two witnesses, one of them Jesus, that studying Scripture is not a "waste of time."

is the Jesus that saves. The Jesus that was [the "historical Jesus"] is pointing to the Jesus that saves [i.e., the "prophetic Jesus"]...." Mr. Farrakhan is saying that the "Jesus that saves" is yet to come; and the "Jesus that was," who is the "historical Jesus," was not the one who saves!

What does the Bible have to say on this issue? In John 3:16, **"For God so loved the world that He gave His only begotten Son."** It doesn't say God "is going to give" in the future, but "gave" in the past tense. It is a done deal. Again, not "going to give," but **"He gave His only begotten Son...."** It is clear from this that the action in question already took place. It is not a future event about to happen, but has already occurred. But let's read on to John 3:16-18:

> 16   **"For God so loved the world that He gave His only begotten Son,** [for what purpose?] **that whoever believes in Him should not perish but have everlasting life.**
>
> 17   **"For God did not send** [again, note that it isn't "God is going to send"] **His Son into the world to condemn the world, but that the world through Him might be saved.**
>
> 18   **"He who believes in Him is not condemned; but he who does not believe is condemned already, because he has not believed in the name of the only begotten Son of God."**

Also see this: If this Jesus, the "historical Jesus," is the only begotten Son of God as the verse states, then it means that God doesn't have a second son, because he already gave His **only begotten Son.**

Mr. Farrakhan claimed that the "historical Jesus" does not save, that it is the "prophetic Jesus" — the future Jesus — who saves. The Bible says that Jesus saves, period. The "historical Jesus, the prophetic Jesus" — there was and is only one Jesus. So whose report will you believe?

In fact, from a biblical perspective, Mr. Farrakhan makes a gross error, a deadly error! If people do not believe what God said here, they will be busy looking for someone in the future, and they'll miss the Savior that's in front of their eyes.

Recall that we have examined Mr. Farrakhan's view that the "historical Jesus" is not the Messiah, and that we have that "historical Jesus" and a "prophetic Jesus." According to my mathematical understanding, historical and prophetic adds up to two. So there also must be two Messiahs, based on what Mr. Farrakhan said. If such a thing can be proved in the Bible, I don't have a problem with that idea. But is it actually in the Bible? There is more that the Bible has to say on this issue of the Messiah than we've already established.

Many ministers have pointed this out but it bears repeating. Either Jesus is who He said He is or He's the greatest deceiver, most outlandish egotist, or outrageous liar that ever lived. He said of Himself things that no other human has ever said. For instance, in John 14:1-6, Jesus says:

1   **"Let not your heart be troubled; you believe in God, believe also in Me.**

2   **"In My Father's house are many mansions; if *it were* not so, I would have told you. I go to prepare a place for you.**

3   **"And if I go and prepare a place for you, I will come again and receive you to Myself; that where I am, *there* you may be also.**

4   **"And where I go you know, and the way you know."**

5   **Thomas said to Him, "Lord, we do not know where You are going, and how can we know the way?"**

6   **Jesus said to him, "I am the way, the truth, and the life. No one comes to the Father except through Me."**

Jesus didn't say, "I am one of the many ways." No, He said, **"...I am the way."** So, again, either He's who He said He is or He's the biggest egotist who ever lived. If He isn't who He said He is, He is in need of psychological help, because no one else has ever, to my knowledge, made this kind of statement: **"I am the way, the truth and the life."** He said, **"No one comes to the Father except through Me."** The man is either a complete kook, a liar, or the biggest egotist in the world...or, He's who He says He is!

Mr. Farrakhan said that "the historical Jesus was not the Messiah...." What does the Bible say? Don't take my word for anything, any more than you take Mr. Farrakhan's word for anything. Check it out. I'm human. I could make a mistake. That is why you need to check everything out in the Bible. In John 1:35-41, it says:

35   **Again, the next day, John stood with two of his disciples.**

36   **And looking at Jesus as He walked, he said, "Behold the Lamb of God!"**

37   **The two disciples heard him speak, and they followed Jesus.**

38   **Then Jesus turned, and seeing them following, said to them, "What do you seek?" They said to Him, "Rabbi (which is to say, when translated, Teacher), where are You staying?"**

39   **He said to them, "Come and see." They came and saw where He was staying, and remained with Him that day (now it was about the tenth hour).**

40   One of the two who heard John *speak*, and fol-
           lowed Him, was Andrew, Simon Peter's brother.

41   He first found his own brother Simon, and
           said to him, "We have found the Messiah
           (which is translated, the Christ)."

Mr. Farrakhan claims that Jesus wasn't the Messiah, but the Bible
says He was. Andrew said Jesus was the Messiah, and Andrew was a
Jew. Notice that he didn't say, "*I* have found the Messiah." He said, "*We*
have found the Messiah...." This means that Andrew and someone else,
at least, "found the Messiah."

Salvation, saving, Messiahship — Christianity hinges on this!
If none of these claims are true, all that you have is another religion.
Jesus did not say, "*I* have come that you might have religion." He
said, **"...I have come that they may have life, and that they may have
it more abundantly"** (John 10:10). Man may have made this into a religion, but Christianity is a relationship with a man named Jesus.

Jesus says He is the Messiah. The Bible says Jesus is the
Messiah. Andrew said Jesus is the Messiah. Peter said Jesus is the
Messiah. Even the demons said Jesus is the Messiah. Mr. Farrakhan
says Jesus is not the Messiah. Whose report will you believe? But
we are only getting started. In the next chapter, I will close the case,
and there will be no doubt in your mind that Jesus — the "historical
Jesus" — is the same Jesus who is the Messiah, Anointed One, Lord,
Redeemer, and Savior.

7

Closing the Case

We have a fundamental disagreement. On the one hand, we have the Bible, the Word of God, which gives us certain information. And on the other hand, we have Mr. Farrakhan, who gives us contradictory information. We need to know not only who is right here, but also if Mr. Farrakhan's claims about what the Bible says are true. We have already seen that Mr. Farrakhan compared himself to — or, more accurately, implied that he *is* — Jesus Christ. How can he possibly say such an outrageous thing? Let's look at how he gets to that conclusion. Again, this is taken from the video *Farrakhan: Charismatic Beacon or Cult Leader?* You can see the speech, which we have incorporated into the *Race, Religion & Racism* video series. This is a partial transcript from that video, with Mr. Farrakhan speaking:

> ...that 75 percent of what you read in the Bible referring to Jesus, is referring to a future man. And 25 percent of what you read is referring to the man of 2,000 years ago, who is considered a type. But the real question is, "Who is Jesus? Where will you find him?" This the scholars are going to have to sit down and meet on. If the scholars agree that the Jesus of 2,000 years ago prefigured or gave us a picture of the real Jesus, then the historical Jesus is not the real Jesus, but the real Jesus is

203

the one that the historical Jesus prefigured or gives us a type of.

> The historical Jesus was *not the Messiah!* [italics mine] The prophetic Jesus is the Messiah. The historical Jesus prefigured the Messiah and that's why the Jews have never accepted the historical Jesus; they continue to look for the Messiah. They are not wrong....[1]

That's an awesome statement! But people need to know the Bible's side of this. You're reading Mr. Farrakhan himself saying this. You're not reading me. I have quoted him verbatim. And I have in my possession the videotapes to prove it! So let's read this again: "...the historical Jesus was not the Messiah...." Did you see that? "The prophetic Jesus is the Messiah...!" So according to my limited mathematical understanding, historical = one, prophetic = one. That means there are two Jesuses.

He said, "...the historical Jesus was not the Messiah...." Do you realize that condemns every person who has lived for the last 2,000 years who has staked his or her life on the fact that Jesus was the Christ? Mr. Farrakhan has just buried all of us. We have no Messiah, if he is correct. We have been believing, confessing, singing, and praying in the name of a Jesus who is not the real Messiah. Now, my brothers and sisters in the Lord, that is awesome stuff! If Jesus the Messiah is not who He says He is, then we are yet in our sins. We are without hope in the world.

Mr. Farrakhan says: "...The historical Jesus prefigured the Messiah. And that's why the Jews have never accepted the historical Jesus; they continue to look for the Messiah. They are not wrong...." Now Mr. Farrakhan definitely didn't get his facts from the Bible. Let's go to Scripture and approach this along a different path.

We will start our journey in the book of Deuteronomy 18:15-18, which is God speaking through His prophet, Moses:

---

[1] *Farrakhan: Charismatic Beacon or Cult Leader*, Appendix B, pages 352-356.

15   "The LORD your God will raise up for you a Prophet like me from your midst, from your brethren. Him you shall hear,

16   "according to all you desired of the LORD your God in Horeb in the day of the assembly, saying, 'Let me not hear again the voice of the LORD my God, nor let me see this great fire anymore, lest I die.'

17   "And the LORD said to me: 'What they have spoken is good.

18   'I will raise up for them a Prophet like you from among their brethren, and will put My words in His mouth, and He shall speak to them all that I command Him.' "

Now, understand this. God is saying to Moses that He's going to raise up a prophet *like* him. My question is, who was Moses to the children of Israel? In other words, what was his role? Do you remember that the children of Israel were in bondage and slavery for 430 years, under the Egyptians? They cried out to Jehovah for relief. Jehovah God heard their cry and sent Moses to be their deliverer. Through ten mighty plagues, God manifested His power to Pharaoh, king of Egypt. Pharaoh let the people go. They left. They came to the Red Sea and this huge body of water was stopping their progress. The Egyptians changed their minds and began to pursue them to destroy them. Moses stretched his rod out at the direction of Jehovah over the water, and the waters parted. The wind blew all that night and dried the ground. The water congealed on both sides so that it would not come back upon them. They went across on dry land. Moses was their deliverer. In essence, Moses was their savior. Moses was their messiah.

Remember, **"The LORD your God will raise up for you a Prophet like me...."** In order to be like Moses, you would have to be a deliverer. You would have to be a redeemer. In essence, you would have to be a savior. He had to be someone who would take them out of death, as it were, and put them into life. Not just a prophet, because Isaiah or Jeremiah could have fulfilled that office. But there was no one else like Moses, because Moses was the deliver of the children of Israel out of Egyptian bondage. Keep that in mind.

Jehovah God confirms this by saying, **"I will raise up for them a Prophet like *you*** [Emphasis mine]...." The deliverer. So does Jesus fit this description? Look at John 1:43-45:

> 43   **The following day Jesus wanted to go to Galilee, and He found Philip and said to him, "Follow Me."**
>
> 44   **Now Philip was from Bethsaida, the city of Andrew and Peter.**
>
> 45   **Philip found Nathanael and said to him, "We have found Him of whom Moses in the law, and also the prophets, wrote — Jesus of Nazareth, the son of Joseph."**

Mr. Farrakhan said that the "historical Jesus" was not the Messiah, but that He "prefigured" the Messiah that was "yet to come." The people who lived in the day that Jesus lived believed He was the Messiah. Mr. Farrakhan was not there. They were. They said right here, **"We have found Him of whom Moses in the law, and also the prophets, wrote...."**

Don't you think it is significant that the only person's name mentioned when they said **"we have found Him"** was Moses's name? How many prophets were there? Daniel, Isaiah, Jeremiah, Zachariah, Hosea, Haggai, Jonah, and so on — yet the only name that is mentioned is that of Moses. That is because Moses himself had said that God Almighty was going to raise up a Prophet "like me." Again, these are people who lived in the day that Jesus lived. Mr. Farrakhan did not live in that day. They did, and they should know who they thought they were following.

Let's examine Verse 45: **Philip found Nathanael and said to him, "We have found Him of whom Moses in the law, and also the prophets, wrote...."** The law is the first five books in the Bible, technically known as the Pentateuch: Genesis, Exodus, Leviticus, Numbers, and Deuteronomy. We just read from Deuteronomy, which is often called "The Law," where God said **"I will raise up for them [Israel] a Prophet like you...."** Moses said to them himself, **"The Lord your God will raise up for you a Prophet like me...."**

Put these verses together. In John 1:45, we read:

> **Philip found Nathanael and said to him, "We have found Him of whom Moses in the law, and also the prophets, wrote — Jesus of Nazareth, the son of Joseph."**

They're saying that Jesus of Nazareth, the son of Joseph, is the prophet whom Moses said God would raise up, and that person was the Messiah. But Mr. Farrakhan says that the "historical Jesus" was not the Messiah? Now whose report will you believe?

Mr. Farrakhan said "...the historical Jesus prefigured the Messiah...." So the "historical Jesus," if He prefigured the Messiah, was not in fact the Messiah himself. (That means there would have to be two Jesuses.) Look at it again: "...the historical Jesus prefigured the Messiah and that's why the Jews have never accepted the historical Jesus; they continue to look for the Messiah. They are not wrong!"

In fact, the Jews *were* wrong. They were wrong not to have received the "historical Jesus," because the "historical Jesus" *is* the Messiah. Why did they not receive Him? There has to be a reason. To understand this, we need to dissect Mr. Farrakhan's statement a little. He said "...that's why the Jews have never accepted the historical Jesus...." When you say "the Jews," does that mean all the Jews? Does it mean every Jew? If you said "some Jews," that would be one thing. But to say, "…the Jews never accepted Jesus…" you are saying none of the Jews accepted Him, and, supposedly, they did not accept Him because He wasn't the Messiah. That's totally inaccurate.

I have a question for you: Who was Peter? Wasn't he a Jew? Who was John? Wasn't he a Jew? Who were Andrew, and James, and Paul? Weren't they Jews? Yes they were, every one of them. And every one of them accepted Jesus as the Messiah. We ought to be more accurate and say that the religious establishment Jews did not accept Jesus as the Messiah, but the Bible says that the common people heard Him gladly. Religious leaders have always been a pain in the backside and a stumbling block for the masses of people. As for the Jews, it was only the Pharisees and Sadducees, the Jewish leaders, who would not accept Jesus.

Why do you suppose the religious leaders of the day didn't accept Jesus as the Messiah, when all the rest of the Jews did? Here is why, in Isaiah 53:1-12:

> 1 **Who has believed our report? And to whom has the arm of the LORD been revealed?**

> 2 **For He shall grow up before Him as a tender plant, and as a root out of dry ground. He has no form or comeliness; and when we see Him, *there* is no beauty that we should desire Him.**

> 3 **He is despised and rejected by men, a Man of sorrows and acquainted with grief. And we hid, as it were, *our* faces from Him; He was despised, and we did not esteem Him.**

> 4 **Surely He has borne our griefs** [literally, "sicknesses"] **and carried our sorrows** [literally, "pains"]; **yet we esteemed Him stricken, smitten by God, and afflicted.**

5   But He *was* wounded for our transgressions, *He was* bruised for our iniquities; the chastisement for our peace *was* upon Him, and by His stripes we are healed.

6   All we like sheep have gone astray; we have turned, every one, to his own way; and the Lord has laid on Him the iniquity of us all.

7   He was oppressed and He was afflicted, yet He opened not His mouth; He was led as a lamb [remember this word *lamb*] to the slaughter, and as a sheep before its shearers is silent, so He opened not His mouth.

8   He was taken from prison and from judgment, and who will declare His generation? For He was cut off from the land of the living; for the transgressions of My people He was stricken.

9   And they made His grave with the wicked — but with the rich at His death, because He had done no violence, nor was *any* deceit in His mouth.

10   Yet it pleased the Lord to bruise Him; He has put *Him* to grief. When You make His soul an offering for sin, He shall see *His* seed, He shall prolong *His* days, and the pleasure of the Lord shall prosper in His hand.

11   He shall see the labor of His soul, *and* be satisfied. By His knowledge My righteous Servant shall justify many, for He shall bear their iniquities.

12   Therefore I will divide Him a portion with the great, and He shall divide the spoil with the

strong, because He poured out His soul unto death, and He was numbered with the transgressors, and He bore the sin of many, and made intercession for the transgressors.

The reason the Jewish religious leaders did not, and still today do not, accept the historical Jesus as the Messiah is because in their minds when Moses said the Lord will raise up for you a deliverer like me, a prophet like me, those religious leaders could only see the Red Sea parting. All they could see was the pillar of cloud by day, and the pillar of fire by night. All they saw was the supernatural instantaneous deliverance that God wrought through Moses from Egyptian bondage.

They did not understand that sin had to be dealt with. They only saw themselves from a political point of view, set free from the bondage of the Roman Empire, and they missed God's true purpose. They're still looking for a conquering hero; they're still looking for someone to come and take the yoke off them and restore them to be the apple of God's eye, to make them the leading nation of the world. They did not understand the spiritual significance because they were spiritually dead, just like Mr. Farrakhan.

I don't mean that unkindly — but I'm talking about the fact that he is not spiritually born again. He is therefore what the Bible calls "spiritually dead." He cannot understand the message of the Book because he has no spiritual antennae, and neither did the Jewish leaders of Jesus' day. That is why they didn't accept Him. Returning to Isaiah 53:7: **He was oppressed and He was afflicted, yet He opened not His mouth; He was led as a *lamb* [emphasis mine] to the slaughter....** Why didn't it say "goat?" Why didn't it say "heifer?" Why did it say "lamb?" I'll tell you why it said lamb. It's all revealed in John 1:29, where John the Baptist saw Jesus coming and said, **"...Behold! The Lamb of God who takes away the sin of the world!"**

The Jewish leaders, the Pharisees and the Sadducees, didn't understand that any more than Mr. Farrakhan understands it. They don't understand the sin situation. Instead, they're looking for some political deliverer. But you have to have the cross before the crown, and you have to have salvation before you have the Kingdom. So in dealing with Mr. Farrakhan's statement that the "Jews did not receive Jesus," we need to look at what the Bible says.

Were there some Jews who commented on Jesus? If so, what did they say? In John 3:1-2, we find:

1   There was a man of the Pharisees named Nicodemus, a ruler of the Jews.

2   This man came to Jesus by night and said to Him, "Rabbi, we know that You are a teacher come from God; for no one can do these signs that You do unless God is with him."

Mr. Farrakhan said that the Jews did not receive Jesus, but note that the Bible says, **This man came to Jesus by night and said to Him, 'Rabbi, *we know*...[italics mine]."** Nicodemus did not say, "We're guessing," or "we're making a 60/40 wager," that you are from God. Notice again, Nicodemus says *we know*.... [italics mine]." Note also that he didn't say, "I know." Nicodemus wasn't speaking just on his own behalf. He said, "we know." Who was the "we?" It had to refer to the other religious leaders he associated with. By saying, "we know," and not saying "I know," he was speaking on his own behalf *plus someone else's*, correct? He says, "we know" — know what? — **"that You are a teacher come from God; for no one can do these signs that You do unless God is with him."** Then in Verse 3:

Jesus answered and said to him, "Most assuredly, I say to you, unless one is born again, he cannot see the kingdom God."

Let me clarify this. Jesus said, "Unless one is born again...." Look at Verse 4, and then I'll explain it:

Nicodemus said to Him, "How can a man be born when he is old?..."

Obviously, Nicodemus thought Jesus was talking about physically going back and starting over in his mother's womb as a baby, because he said **"...how can a man be born when he is old?"**

He understood Jesus to mean physical birth. If this was not his understanding, he would not have made the statement, **"How can a man be born when he is old? Can he enter a second time into his mother's womb and be born?"** How did he get there the first time? Physically, through his mother's womb, correct? Clearly, his perception of Jesus' comment was in physical terms.

Now look at Verse 5:

Jesus answered, "Most assuredly, I say to you, unless one is born of water and of the Spirit, he cannot enter the kingdom of God."

Notice that in Verse 3, Jesus had said, **"He cannot *see* the kingdom** [italics mine]" Again, **"...unless one is born again he cannot see the kingdom."** In Verse 5, though, He says **"...unless one is born of water and the Spirit, he cannot *enter* into the kingdom** [italics mine]...."

The English language that our Bibles are written in unfortunately does not always convey the full impact of the original language. When Jesus said in Verse 3, **"unless one is born again,"** literally in the Greek this means "born from above." Nicodemus was right when he said, **"Can he enter a second time into his mother's womb?"** — because that was how he got here the first time. Man is born from his mother's womb, which is a physical birth on a horizontal plane.

But Jesus was talking about spiritual things. Nicodemus had already had a "horizontal birth." Now he needed a "vertical birth." He needed to be born from above, not from his natural physical mother and father. In Verse 5, Jesus uses similar terminology, referring to being **"...born of water and of the Spirit...."** The word *water* is being used symbolically or emblematically, in reference to the Word of God. In Luke, Chapter 8, Jesus taught a parable about the sower who went out to sow. Some seed fell by the wayside and the birds ate it up. Some fell on stony ground, some fell among thorns, some fell on good ground and brought forth a crop.

The disciples asked Jesus to interpret the parable for them. Jesus made an awesome statement that fits exactly what we are talking about. He said in Luke 8:11: **"The seed is the word of God."** In order to be born, you have to have a sperm and an egg come together. You need something from a male and something from a female, right? It also takes two things to make a spiritual life: the Word, which is the seed, and the Holy Spirit, who impregnates that Word, if you will. You need both the Holy Spirit and the Word of God to bring forth spiritual life.

Without that spiritual life, you cannot understand the Bible. You might *read it* in your native language, but you will not understand its message. Notice that the first time the word *Spirit* is used it is capitalized, exactly as it ought to be, referring to the Holy Spirit. The second time it is used, *spirit* is in the lower case, referring to man's spirit. Jesus said in John 3:6, **"That which is born of the flesh is flesh…."** and that which is born of the Holy Spirit is man's spirit. Therefore, the new birth is the rebirth of the human spirit and does not affect your physical body. Why? Because all flesh can do is reproduce more flesh; that's why Jesus said you have to be born from above.

You need to have your spirit changed so you can understand that which comes from the Holy Spirit of God, which is the Bible. And unless that happens, you will be like the religious leaders, both in Jesus' day and today. They are not born again, and therefore they cannot understand. Mr. Farrakhan is not a Christian; he is a devout Muslim, and therefore he has not been born again. Consequently, he cannot understand the message of the Bible. He can read it at face value, but he cannot understand its message.

Is there a confirming Scripture? The Bible says by the mouth of two or three witnesses every word shall be established, so I need to give you at least two Scriptures to confirm what I have said. Remember what Jesus said: **"…unless one is born again, he cannot see…."** The words *cannot see* in English connote visual perception, right? When you say to someone, "see," the first thing they think of is what they can perceive visually. But we also know in our language that the words *I see* may have nothing to do with our eyes. When someone says, "Oh, I see!" it means "Oh, I understand! I get it!" So when the Bible says **"unless one is**

born again, he cannot see…" the literal Greek meaning is "he cannot come to know the kingdom of God." That's why in John 3:7, Jesus said, "You must be born again." It's a necessity. He didn't say it was optional! He said you *must* be born again.

People have trouble with this simple principle. Yet people have sense enough to know that if you want to take a flight on an airplane, you have to be on board the plane when it lifts off the ground or you are not going to your destination. No one has a problem with that idea. If you want to go to New York City on TWA Flight 99 at nine o'clock a.m., leaving from Los Angeles, you must be on board that plane when it lifts off the ground. You can't be home in bed and still go to New York on that flight. You'll never get there. Well, if you want to get into the Kingdom of God, you must be born again. God won't *make* you get born again, any more than TWA is going to make you get on that flight at nine a.m. But if you choose that flight to New York, you have to be on that plane when it lifts off the ground. If you want to understand the Bible, you must be born again. Otherwise, you'll never understand the Kingdom of God.

In 1 Corinthians, Chapter 2, we have a demonstration of this concept of spiritual-versus-natural perception or understanding. In 1 Corinthians 2:11 we see, **For what man knows the things of a man except the spirit of the man which is in him? Even so no one knows the things of God except the Spirit of God.** That is why you must be born again, by the Spirit of God, so that you can be connected to the Spirit of God and can know what the word of God means. Otherwise, you can't know it. If only the Spirit of God knows the things of God, then Mr. Farrakhan doesn't know.

But let's continue in 1 Corinthians 2:12-14, and you'll see this quite clearly:

> **12   Now we have received, not the spirit of the world, but the Spirit who is from God, that we might know the things that have been freely given to us by God.**

13   These things we also speak, not in words which man's wisdom teaches but which the Holy Sprit teaches, comparing spiritual things with spiritual.

14   But the *natural* [emphasis mine] man does not receive the things of the Spirit of God, for they ["the things"] are foolishness to him; nor can he know *them*, because they are *spiritually discerned* [emphasis mine].

This clearly tells us that if you're not born again, then you can't understand the Word. You don't have the Spirit who is from God, so you can't discern the things that are spiritually discerned. That is why the Jews are still looking for a Messiah who already came — because they weren't spiritually minded, and they thought Jesus was not the Messiah.

This is the same mistake Mr. Farrakhan is making: because he's not a Christian, he's not "born again," and yet he's trying to interpret the Bible.

Based on what Mr. Farrakhan said, the Messiah is yet to come. Of course, that is what the Jewish religious leaders of today are still looking for — the Messiah, a man like Moses, to deliver them. They don't understand that the sin question had to be dealt with first. They don't understand the fact that **all have sinned and fall short of the glory of God** (Romans 3:23). They don't understand the fact that **the wages of sin** *is* **death, but the gift of God** *is* **eternal life in Christ Jesus our Lord** (Romans 6:23). They do not understand even today that a man "must be born again." They still don't accept that a person must be born from above in order to know the Kingdom of God.

Back to our main point, though: If the historical Jesus was not the Messiah that Christians believe He is, the Bible ought to say that. It says just the opposite.

In Acts 2:36, Peter spoke on the day of Pentecost, saying:

"Therefore let all the house of Israel know…[Just a point of reference here. Who is "the House of Israel?" Aren't those Jews? Mr. Farrakhan said that the Jews never accepted the historical Jesus as the Messiah.] **assuredly that God has made this Jesus, whom you crucified,** [It is unmistakable that the reference is to the "historical Jesus," because He's the One they crucified.]…**both Lord and Christ."**

There is still more evidence in Acts, Chapter 4. This is the account of Peter going into the temple at the gate called Beautiful. A lame man was laid at that gate every day, asking alms of people who went into the temple. As Peter and John were going into the temple, the man asked alms of them. Peter ministered to him, and the man was instantaneously and miraculously healed — this 40-year-old man had been lame from his mother's womb. Not only did the miracle get everyone's attention, it rocked the boat of the religious leaders, who were upset that the apostles healed the man. Peter was called before the religious leaders to present his defense (Acts 4:10):

"let it be known to you all, [meaning the religious leaders challenging him] **and to all the people of Israel…."**

I recall that Mr. Farrakhan said the Jews did not accept the historical Jesus as the Messiah and that "…they continue to look for the Messiah. They are not wrong." Here is Peter, speaking to Jews, about the Messiah, in Acts 4:10:

…that by the name of Jesus Christ of Nazareth, whom you crucified, whom God raised from the dead, by Him this man stands here before you whole.

Again, Mr. Farrakhan said the "historical Jesus" was not the Messiah, yet Peter qualifies exactly, and without question, who the "historical Jesus" really was because he specifies **Jesus Christ of**

Nazareth, whom you crucified…. We know that the One they crucified was the "historical Jesus." No question about that. Even Mr. Farrakhan agrees with that — the Man crucified was the historical Jesus. But notice how Peter qualifies and identifies Jesus even further:

> **"…that by the name of Jesus Christ of Nazareth** [not "Jesus of Nazareth," but "Jesus *Christ* of Nazareth"]**…"**

Keep in mind that the word *Christ* is the same as *Messiah* is the same as *Anointed of God* or *Anointed One*. Peter, unequivocally, was saying "Jesus the Christ, Jesus the Messiah, Jesus the Anointed One of Nazareth, was the One whom you crucified…." Peter walked with Jesus for three and a half years. I would think he would know better than Fred Price or Mr. Farrakhan who Jesus was, wouldn't you agree?

In Acts 4:23-28, the account continues:

> 23   **And being let go, they went to their own**
>   ***companions* and reported all that the chief**
>   **priests and elders had said to them.**

> 24   **So when they heard that, they raised their voice**
>   **to God with one accord and said: "Lord, You**
>   ***are* God, who made heaven and earth and the**
>   **sea, and all that is in them,**

> 25   **who by the mouth of Your servant David have**
>   **said: *'Why did the nations rage, and the people***
>   ***plot vain things?***

> 26   ***'The kings of the earth took their stand, and the***
>   ***rulers were gathered together against the Lord***
>   ***and against His Christ.'***

This last phrase, "His Christ," that would mean "His Messiah;" that would mean "His Anointed One." In Verses 27 to 28, this is further amplified:

27   **"For truly against Your holy Servant Jesus, whom *You anointed* [emphasis mine], both Herod and Pontius Pilate, with the Gentiles and the people of Israel, were gathered together**

28   **"to do whatever Your hand and Your purpose determined before to be done."**

Peter and the apostles said that the "historical Jesus" was Jesus Christ of Nazareth. If what Mr. Farrakhan says is true — that there is another "prophetic Jesus" coming — where is He going to be born? Acts 4:10 said, "Jesus Christ of Nazareth," so we know this isn't "Jesus of Chicago," or "Jesus of the South Bronx," or "Jesus of Tijuana." Peter clearly identified Jesus Christ as coming from Nazareth. To emphasize this again: Mr. Farrakhan says that the "historical Jesus" is not the Messiah, but so far every piece of evidence, and every Scripture we have from the Bible, shows that what he said is untrue!

In Acts 5:41-42, we have another revealing statement:

41   **So they departed from the presence of the council, rejoicing that they were counted worthy to suffer shame for His name.**

42   **And daily in the temple, and in every house, they did not cease teaching and preaching Jesus *as* the Christ.**

There it is again: **they did not cease** (they did not stop) **teaching and preaching Jesus.** Not just Jesus, but *Jesus as the Christ* [emphasis mine]. They thought He was the Christ.

Still again, in Acts 9:20-22:

20   **Immediately he [Saul/Paul] preached the Christ in the synagogues, that He is the Son of God.**

21   **Then all who heard were amazed, and said, "Is this not he who destroyed those who**

> called on this name in Jerusalem, and has come here for that purpose, so that he might bring them bound to the chief priests?"

> **22** But Saul [who we later come to know as the Apostle Paul] **increased all the more in strength, and confounded the Jews who dwelt in Damascus, proving that this** *Jesus* **is the Christ.**

Not "a" Christ. Not "one of many" Christs. But *proving that this Jesus is the Christ* [emphasis mine].

We could read that as follows, "...proving that this Jesus is the Messiah, is the Anointed One." I know I'm giving you an abundance of Scripture on this point, but it is vitally important. Mr. Farrakhan violated the biblical principle of **"...by the mouth of two or three witnesses every word shall be established"** (2 Corinthians 13:1). I've given you at least ten direct statements, including Jesus' own testimony, that indicate that He was the "Christ" or "the Messiah." But we aren't finished.

In Acts 17:1-3 we find:

> **1** Now when they had passed through Amphipolis and Apollonia, they came to Thessalonica, where there was a synagogue of the Jews.

> **2** Then Paul, as his custom was, went in to them, and for three Sabbaths reasoned with them from the Scriptures,

> **3** explaining and demonstrating that Christ [Messiah] had to suffer and rise again from the dead, and *saying*, "This Jesus whom I preach to you is the Christ."

Paul says Jesus is "the Christ," (or) "the Messiah." Mr. Farrakhan says He's not. Whose report will you believe?

If we examine the writings of Paul, and his experience on the Damascus Road in the ninth Chapter of Acts, you will know that when he refers to Jesus as the Christ, he is referring to Jesus of Nazareth, the same One they nailed to the cross. That is the "historical Jesus." And again, Mr. Farrakhan said that the "historical Jesus" is not the Messiah. Paul said He was. Peter said He was.

But we aren't finished presenting our case from Acts yet. Acts 18:5 records the following:

> **When Silas and Timothy had come from Macedonia, Paul was compelled by the Spirit, and testified to the Jews *that* Jesus *is* the Christ.**

Paul testified that Jesus is the "Anointed of God," that He is "the Messiah." We find this throughout the Bible. Look at Acts 18:28: **for he** [Paul] **vigorously refuted the Jews publicly, showing from the Scriptures that Jesus is the Christ.** This verse not only makes clear that Paul did this publicly, but that he **vigorously refuted the Jews publicly,** *showing from the Scriptures…*[emphasis mine]. I've given you more than a dozen biblical references that the "historical Jesus" was in fact the Messiah, the Christ, the Anointed One. But I will give you still more evidence.

In Romans 6:4, it says:

> **Therefore we were buried with Him through baptism into death, that just as Christ was raised from the dead by the glory of the Father, even so we also should walk in newness of life.**

If Christ was **raised from the dead**, then Christ must have been alive and somehow died in order to be raised from the dead. Of course, He did die at the instigation of the Jewish religious leaders, and was crucified at the hands of the Roman government. He died, was buried, and rose from the dead. The Jewish religious leaders did not understand this. That's why they are still looking for the Messiah. They were looking for the conquering hero — the Jesus of the Book of Revelation, Who comes riding in on a white stallion with a great sword in His hand, the armies of heaven following behind Him. The religious leaders did not understand that someone had to do something about Adam's sin.

Jesus had to. Christ had to. Messiah had to. Messiah had to die to take upon Himself the sin of the world. That is what John the Baptist meant when he saw Jesus and said, **"Behold! The Lamb of God who takes away the sin of the world!"** (John 1:29). He did not say "sins of the world." Jesus did not die to take away your "sins" but your "sin." We are responsible for doing something about our "sins" (plural) but God was responsible through Christ to deal with the sin problem, because it is "sin" that causes "sins." That is why in 1 John 1:9, we are told that if we confess our "sins," He is faithful and just to forgive us of our "sins" and cleanse us from all unrighteousness. Jesus, on the other hand, when He died, took care of the "sin" question. S-i-n is the predisposition to commit s-i-n-s. Without sin — a "sin nature" — there would be no sins. Jesus died to take care of the sin, and to place man in a position where he could come to God and be free from the penalty of sin.

The Jewish religious leaders of the day didn't understand that Christ had to die first to take care of the sin. He *is* coming back — the same Jesus. It won't be a "prophetic Jesus." It will be the same Jesus that left here. In 1 Corinthians 1:17, Paul writes:

> **For Christ did not send me to baptize, but to preach the gospel, not with wisdom of words, lest the cross of Christ should be made of no effect.**

So there was a cross in reference to Messiah — the "cross of Christ" (i.e., the "cross of the Messiah").

Let me show you a verse that will explain why the Jews, Mr. Farrakhan, and others have a problem with the "historical Jesus." In 1 Corinthians 1:23, Paul writes, **but we preach Christ** [Messiah] **crucified, to the Jews a stumbling block and to the Greeks foolishness.** The word *Greeks* here means "Gentiles," and encompasses anyone who is not a Jew. The Gentiles/Greeks think Christ crucified is fool-ishness, while to the Jews it's a stumbling block. Why do they stumble? They stumble because they don't understand the cross before the crown — they don't understand that the sin question had to be dealt with first.

Notice the words *Christ* (Messiah) and *crucified*. Now we know without a doubt that Paul is talking about the "historical Jesus." If the "prophetic Jesus" hasn't come yet, He couldn't be crucified yet. Here is another challenging Scripture, 1 Corinthians 2:2: **For I [Paul] determined not to know anything among you except Jesus Christ and Him crucified.** "Jesus the Anointed One, and Him crucified." "Jesus the Messiah, and Him crucified." Mr. Farrakhan said that the "historical Jesus" was not the Messiah. Whose report will you believe?

In 1 Corinthians 8:11, Paul continues to dwell on Christ, the Messiah, dying for the sin of man: **And because of your knowledge shall the weak brother perish, for whom Christ died?** We have many verses here linking Jesus — the "historical Jesus" — to the fact that He is the Messiah/the Anointed One. Now Paul squarely puts the Christ, the Messiah, together with crucifixion. And that, historically, validates who we are talking about, even among people who aren't Christians, who nevertheless have heard about Jesus Christ on the cross.

Now look at Galatians 3:1: **O foolish Galatians! Who has bewitched you that you should not obey the truth, before whose eyes Jesus Christ was clearly portrayed among you as crucified?** There it is yet again: Jesus, the Messiah, the Anointed One crucified.

Paul was a Jew. Let's see what he thought about Jesus. In Ephesians 1:15-20, Paul writes:

15   **Therefore I also, after I heard of your faith in the Lord Jesus and your love for all the saints,**

16   **do not cease to give thanks for you, making mention of you in my prayers:**

17   **that the God of our Lord *Jesus Christ*** [emphasis mine — and notice how the Holy Spirit put the words *Jesus Christ* in there, and note also that the word *Christ* is the Greek word for the Hebrew word *Messiah* or *Anointed One*], **the Father of glory, may give to you the spirit of wisdom and revelation in the knowledge of Him,**

18   **the eyes of your understanding being enlightened; that you may know what is the hope of His calling, what are the riches of the glory of His inheritance in the saints,**

19   **and what *is* the exceeding greatness of His power toward us who believe, according to the working of His mighty power**

20   **which He worked in Christ** [Messiah] **when He raised Him from the dead and seated *Him* at His right hand in the heavenly *places*,**

Paul said that Jesus Christ, who is the Messiah, is the one God raised from the dead. So look at Verse 20 again: **which He** [God] **worked in Christ** [Messiah or Anointed One] **when He** [God] **raised Him** [Christ, Messiah] **from the dead and seated *Him*** [Christ, Messiah, or Anointed One] **at His** [God's] **right hand in the heavenly places.**[2]

---

[2] Peter confirmed this in his lengthy speech in Jerusalem (Acts 2:14-36), where he preached to the Jews there: **(14)"...Men of Judea and all who dwell in Jerusalem . . . ." (22) ". . . Jesus of Nazareth, a Man attested by God to you by miracles, wonders, and signs which God did through Him in your midst, as you yourselves also know – (23) "Him, being delivered by the determined purpose and foreknowledge of God, you have taken . . . have crucified, and put to death; (24)**

Mr. Farrakhan says that the "historical Jesus" was not the Messiah, but God Almighty, Creator of the heavens and the earth, says He was. That's awesome!

In 2 Timothy 3:16-17, it says:

16   **All Scripture *is* given by inspiration of God, and *is* profitable for doctrine, for reproof, for correction, for instruction in righteousness,**

17   **that the man of God may be complete, thoroughly equipped for every good work.**

How much is left out of "all?" None. That means that from Genesis to Revelation, all of that is Scripture. **All Scripture is given by inspiration of God....** So if God inspired it to be given, I doubt seriously that He would inspire an inaccurate record to be given.

In Philippians 2:5, Paul writes under the inspiration of the Holy Spirit, **Let this mind be in you which was also in Christ Jesus.**

"whom God raised up, having loosed the pains of death, because it was not possible that He should be held by it." Peter then quoted David: **(30) " . . . being a prophet, and knowing that God had sworn an oath to him that of the fruit of his body, according to the flesh, He** [God] **would raise up *the Christ*** [emphasis mine — the Messiah, the Anointed One] **to sit on his** [David's] **throne, (31) "he** [David], **foreseeing this, spoke concerning the resurrection of the Christ** [the Messiah, the Anointed One] **. . . ."** In case there were any Jews in the audience who were hard of hearing, or plain old dull, Peter spelled it out so no one could miss it: **(36) "Therefore let all the house of Israel know assuredly that God has made this Jesus, whom you crucified, *both Lord and Christ"*** [emphasis mine, but I think we can assume that at this point Peter had probably raised his voice!]. Peter leaves no doubt that it is "this Jesus," not a "prophetic Jesus" or a "future Jesus," whom they had crucified, whom God raised up and made **"both Lord and Christ."**

Notice again how "Christ" (Messiah) and the name Jesus are always used together. God inspired Paul to call Jesus the Christ, the Messiah, the Anointed One. Paul continues in Verses 6 to 8:

> **6   who, being in the form of God, did not consider it robbery to be equal with God,**

> **7   but made Himself of no reputation, taking the form of a bondservant, *and* coming in the likeness of men.**

> **8   And being found in appearance as a man, He humbled Himself and became obedient to *the point of* death, even the death of the cross.**

I wanted to put this together so that you can see that this Jesus — this "historical Jesus" as Mr. Farrakhan would call Him — this Christ, this Messiah, this Anointed One is the same person they nailed to the cross. Mr. Farrakhan says there is a "future Jesus," who is yet to come. God says otherwise. God says that the "historical Jesus," the Jesus of Nazareth, the One they nailed to the cross some 2,000 years ago *is* the Messiah, the Christ, the Anointed One. Whose report will you believe?

Mr. Farrakhan has been given inaccurate information by someone. I can't believe — I refuse to believe (and it's my choice) — that he is deliberately trying to deceive people. Because if he is, then he is a deceiver. But if he's a truly honest man, then he'll make a correction. Having been given the facts now — evidential weight that would carry in any court in the land — if he doesn't make a correction, then he's a dishonest man. And not just him, but you, me, anyone who is given the truth and refuses to change course, that person is dishonest. I've given you enough evidence that only a flatly dishonest person could refuse to see that Jesus of Nazareth is the Messiah, the Christ. But I'm going to run up the score and pile it on.

In Philippians 3:17-18, there is still more evidence:

17   Brethren, join in following my example, and note those who so walk, as you have us for a pattern.

18   For many walk, of whom I have told you often, and now tell you even weeping, *that they are* enemies of the cross of Christ:

There it is again: the "cross of Christ." So Christ was the Messiah. He was the Anointed One and we know that Jesus of Nazareth was the One they nailed to the cross. So the Bible confirms the fact that Jesus is the Messiah. Mr. Farrakhan says there is a future Messiah coming. That's not what we read.

Another important Scripture is found in 1 Peter 3:18. Please note carefully:

For Christ also suffered once for sins, the just for the unjust, that He might bring us to God, being put to death in the flesh but made alive by the Spirit.

Now, in that same chapter, go to Verse 21:

There is also an antitype which now saves us — baptism (not the removal of the filth of the flesh, but the answer of a good conscience toward God), through the resurrection of Jesus Christ [or Jesus the Messiah].

God inspired this word to be written, and God is calling Jesus "Messiah." How dare I call Him something else? And how dare anyone call Him something else when God Almighty calls Him "Messiah." Let's amplify something in 1 Peter 3:18, though: **For Christ also suffered once for *sins*.** I have made a point about the difference between *sin* and *sins*. If you aren't careful, this will look like a contradiction.

Remember earlier when I referred to John the Baptist saying, **"Behold! The Lamb of God who takes away the sin of the world!"**

and I mentioned that Jesus did not take away the "sins" of the world? He took away the S-I-N. When Adam, in the garden, sinned or rebelled against God, he allowed sin to come into the world. So every child that Adam fathered, from a spiritual point of view, inherited Adam's sin nature — not his specific "sins" but his sin nature. It is that nature that fosters the sins (plural). Jesus died to undo what Adam did in the garden; in other words, to right the wrong Adam did. What happens when a person accepts, receives, and confesses Jesus Christ as his or her personal Savior and Lord, from a spiritual perspective? That person goes back to the same spiritual condition that Adam was in before he sinned.

Now, if, after you become a Christian and you commit an act of transgression, you are responsible for doing something about your particular *sins*. But Jesus has already done something about the *sin* question — about your sin nature. If I sin after I have become a Christian, I have 1 John 1:9: **If we** [meaning Christians, not sinners] **confess our sins, He is faithful and just to forgive us** [Christians, not sinners] *our* **sins and to cleanse us from all unrighteousness.**

This verse, 1 John 1:9, has been misapplied throughout Christian history as a salvation verse. It is not for sinners. If that verse is for sinners, then a Christian has no way out of the sins that he or she has committed since becoming saved. Sinners are never, anywhere in the Bible, required, compelled, or even requested to confess their sins in order to get saved. That is a fallacy. The Bible says in Romans 10:9, **that if you confess with your mouth the Lord Jesus and believe in your heart that God has raised Him from the dead, you will be saved.** That's what gets you saved — not confessing your S-I-N-S, because if you had to confess your S-I-N-S, you would have to confess every one you ever committed. You can't possibly remember what you were doing 25 years ago at 10:30 in the morning. And if you sinned and didn't confess it, you couldn't get saved. We have to do something about our S-I-N-S by confessing our sins when we commit them. That is what keeps us clean before God. But Jesus took care of the S-I-N problem.

Returning to 1 Peter 3:18, I want to show you something: **For Christ** [that's the Messiah, the Anointed of God] **also suffered….** Notice what it does not say. It does not say Christ died for S-I-N-S, but it says "suffered" for S-I-N-S. John said **"Behold! The Lamb of God who takes away the S-I-N of the world!"** Now what does that mean that **Christ also suffered**? He did die for S-I-N, but He suffered for the S-I-N-S, the sins that had accumulated since Adam throughout history. That's why He was harassed, falsely accused, persecuted, and lied about. That is why demons tried to get on His case and why the religious leaders came against Him. It was the result of the S-I-N-S in the world — He *suffered* for the *sins*, but He *died* for the *sin*. Now you have to be spiritually minded to get that.

There is an awesome statement in 1 John 5:1 that we must consider in light of Mr. Farrakhan declaring that the "historical Jesus" is not the Messiah: **Whoever believes that Jesus is the Christ** [or the Messiah] **is born of God….** Consequently, the opposite would have to be true, that whoever *doesn't* believe that Jesus is the Christ, is *not born of God.* Therefore, Mr. Farrakhan is not born of God. I didn't say it, so don't get upset with me. The Bible said it. He who believes that Jesus is the Messiah is born of God, but the opposite is also true, whether implied or stated, that he who doesn't believe that Jesus is the Messiah is not born of God.

Further evidence for the fact that the "historical Jesus" *is* the Messiah, *is* the "prophetic Jesus," is found in Matthew 1:17:

> **So all the generations from Abraham to David *are* fourteen generations, from David until the captivity in Babylon *are* fourteen generations, and from the captivity in Babylon until the Christ *are* fourteen generations.**

Wait a minute! **"Until the Christ"**? Doesn't that also mean "until the Messiah" and until the "Anointed One?" So right there that means that you can count the generations from Abraham *to…!*

To what? The word "from" indicates there is a starting point, and if something has a starting point, it has an end. What is the end? Look again at Verse 17:

> **So all the generations** *from* **Abraham** *to* **David** *are* **fourteen generations,** *from* **David** *until* [or "to"] **the captivity in Babylon** *are* **fourteen generations, and** *from* **the captivity in Babylon** *until* [or, again, "to"] **the Christ** *are* **fourteen generations.** [all emphases and explanations mine]

Notice that nothing follows "until the Christ." There are no "froms" or "tos" after the phrase, **"...until the Christ are fourteen generations."** There is no "prophetic Jesus" coming in the future. The only Jesus coming in the future is the same Jesus who left here 2,000 years ago! The angel said it as the "historical Jesus" (Jesus of Nazareth, the Messiah, the One they crucified, and the One who rose from the grave) ascended to Heaven in Acts 1:11: **"...Men of Galilee, why do you stand gazing up into heaven? This *same* Jesus, who was taken up from you into heaven, will so come in like manner as you saw Him go into heaven."** You can't get much plainer than that. This same Man. This same Jesus. This same "historical" Jesus. He *is* the Messiah.

But I'm not finished. Read Matthew 1:17 again:

> **So all the generations from Abraham to David** *are* **fourteen generations, from David until captivity in Babylon** *are* **fourteen generations, and from the captivity in Babylon until the Christ** *are* **fourteen generations.**

This not only makes it absolutely clear that it started with Abraham and ended with Christ, but also that we can accurately count the years (the "generations") before the Messiah came! It's not guesswork or interpretation, because Matthew, through the Holy Spirit, gives us our "earthly timeline yardstick" by pinpointing two events that we know the specific dates of — Abraham's life and the captivity.

Now, if the Holy Spirit didn't do that — if He used some symbolic term like *the time of great tribulation*, then it would be hard to say with certainty exactly *when* the Messiah came. But the Holy Spirit gave us a clear road map, from Abraham to the captivity in Babylon are fourteen generations, and so we know almost to the year how long those fourteen generations were. It is not a symbolic number, it is a real reference to a period of time, which we can count. And **from the captivity in Babylon until the Christ *are* fourteen generations** makes it absolutely clear that whoever the Messiah was, He had to walk the earth fourteen generations from the captivity. That leaves out a "prophetic Jesus" still to come! It started with Abraham, it ends with Christ, and that's it!

Look at Matthew 1:18: **"Now the birth of Jesus Christ....** [Jesus the Messiah, Jesus the Anointed One]. This spells out clearly who that Messiah is, the Man called Jesus. That is it, that's the end of the story. We know that the Jesus Christ Matthew refers to here is the Jesus who was born of the virgin Mary, the "historical Jesus" whom they nailed to the cross, and the One born fourteen genera-tions after the captivity in Babylon. You have to hire yourself some-one to help you miss this!

Yet Mr. Farrakhan said Jesus is not the Messiah. The Bible says He is. So let's add some more evidence. In Luke 2:25-32, it is written:

> 25   **And behold, there was a man in Jerusalem whose name was Simeon, and this man was just and devout, waiting for the Consolation of Israel, and the Holy Spirit was upon him.**

> 26   **And it had been revealed to him by the Holy Spirit that he would not see death before he had seen the Lord's Christ** [Messiah].

That was written 2,000 years ago. So if it was revealed to Simeon by the Holy Spirit that he, Simeon, would not see death before he had seen the Lord's Christ — the Lord's Messiah, the Lord's Anointed One — then that means that for Mr. Farrakhan to be correct, Simeon must still be alive today, making him the oldest human ever to walk the earth. Look at Verses 26 and 27 again:

> **26**   **And it had been revealed to him by the Holy Spirit that he would not see death before he had seen the Lord's Christ.**

> **27**   **So he came by the Spirit into the temple. And when the parents brought in the Child Jesus....**

So if the parents brought the Child Jesus, then the parents were Mary and Joseph, and these are the parents of the One they nailed to the cross.

> **27**   **So he came by the Spirit into the temple. And when the parents brought in the Child Jesus, to do for Him according to the custom of the law,**

> **28**   **he [Simeon] took Him [the Child, Jesus] up in his arms and blessed God and said:**

> **29**   **"Lord, now You are letting Your servant depart in peace, according to Your word;**

> **30**   **For my eyes have seen Your salvation**

> **31**   **which You have prepared before the face of all peoples,**

> **32**   **a light to *bring* revelation to the Gentiles, and the glory of Your people Israel."**

These verses speak of Jesus — the One they nailed to the cross. Mr. Farrakhan says that Jesus is not the Messiah. Whose report will you believe?

Now I have another Scripture, and it is crystal clear. It is awesome! I must warn you that you should be sitting down before you read this Scripture. Remember what Mr. Farrakhan said: "the historical Jesus was not the Messiah?" We find something different in 1 John 4:1-3:

1   **Beloved, do not believe every spirit, but test the spirits, whether they are of God; because many false prophets have gone out into the world.**

2   **By this you know the Spirit of God: Every spirit that confesses that Jesus Christ has come in the flesh is of God,**

3   **and every spirit that does not confess that Jesus Christ has come in the flesh is not of God. And this is the *spirit* of the Antichrist, which you have heard was coming, and is now already in the world.**

That is heavy.

Remember 2 Timothy 3:16: **All Scripture *is* given by inspiration of God....** This is God speaking. **Beloved, do not believe every spirit, but test the spirits....** So I have a right — actually, a duty — to test the spirits! Not to try to find fault, but to be sure that I am listening to the right spirit.

Again to 1 John 4:1-2:

1   **Beloved, do not believe every spirit, but test the spirits, whether they are of God; because many** [look at this — not *some*, but *many*!] **false prophets have gone out into the world.**

2   **By this you know the Spirit of God....**

This is how you can know. God has not left us in the dark, or resigned us to our own puny knowledge. You can check this stuff out. If you get deceived, it is because you let yourself be deceived. There is a way to check this out. God doesn't want you deceived or tricked — that's why He put this Scripture in the Bible.

Here is how you can know:

> 2   **By this you know the Spirit of God: Every spirit that confesses that Jesus Christ....**

Not Christ, but Jesus Christ. So we know that this refers to the "historical Jesus," the One who came fourteen generations after the captivity in Babylon, the One seen by Simeon. That Jesus! This is clearly referring to the Jesus Christ who has already been here.

> 2   **By this you know the Spirit of God: Every spirit that confesses that Jesus Christ** [Jesus the Messiah, Jesus the Anointed One] **has come....**

Did you see that? **...has come....** Not will come. Not future tense, but past tense: **has come.** You need to test the spirits to see if the spirit confesses that Jesus Christ "has come" already!

> 3   **and every spirit that does not confess that Jesus Christ has come in the flesh is not of God. And this is the *spirit* of the Antichrist, which you have heard was coming, and is now already in the world.**

I didn't write this. We did not read this from the Book of First Frederick, or the Gospel of Frederick K.C. Price. It is from the inspired Word of God. Any honest seeker of truth will see through these numerous references that there is, and always has been, only one Jesus Christ. Only one Jesus the Messiah. Only one Jesus, Savior, Lord, Anointed of God.

To conclude this discussion, let me give you one final Scripture. I've referred to it before but I want to emphasize it a little more here. In Acts 1:4-11 we see the resurrected Jesus speaking to the disciples:

4 And being assembled together with them, He commanded them not to depart from Jerusalem, but to wait for the Promise of the Father, "which," *He said*, "you have heard from Me;

5 "for John truly baptized with water, but you shall be baptized with the Holy Spirit not many days from now."

6 Therefore, when they had come together, they asked Him, saying, "Lord, will You at this time restore the kingdom to Israel?"

7 And He said to them, "It is not for you to know times or seasons which the Father has put in His own authority.

8 "But you shall receive power when the Holy Spirit has come upon you; and you shall be witnesses to Me in Jerusalem, and in all Judea and Samaria, and to the end of the earth."

9 Now when He had spoken these things, while they watched, He was taken up, and a cloud received Him out of their sight.

10 And while they looked steadfastly toward heaven as He went up, behold, two men stood by them in white apparel,

11 who also said, "Men of Galilee, why do you stand gazing up into heaven? This *same* Jesus [This same Jesus. Not a prophetic One, not another One, *this One!*], who was taken up from you into heaven, will so come in like manner as you saw Him go into heaven."

Closing the Case

Case closed. There is no other Jesus coming. Jesus the Messiah, Jesus Christ, Jesus the Anointed One — the "historical Jesus" born fourteen generations after the captivity in Babylon, the "historical Jesus" testified to as the Messiah by John the Baptist, Peter, John, Paul, Andrew, Simeon, and all the others, and the same "historical Jesus" identified by the angel as the One who **"will so come in like manner"** — this is the same Jesus returning for us!

8

The Color of Jesus

Without question, Mr. Farrakhan specifically and the Black Muslim movement in America generally have played upon the notion that Christianity is "the white man's religion." They are able to do so because for so long we have only seen images of the Jews, Moses, David, Samson, and especially Jesus, as a lily-white, light-haired, white person. Black people have been hammered over the head with portrayals in movies and books and by artists that God is white, Jesus is white, Gabriel is white, all the angels are white, but the devil is black! Partly in reaction to this, in recent years we've seen some pictures of a black Jesus. I believe that is simply reactionary.

Now I don't need a black Jesus, I don't need a red Jesus, I don't need a yellow Jesus, I don't need a brown Jesus, and I don't need a white Jesus — I need a *real* Jesus. I do have a problem if you take the truth and twist it, then use it against me for social control or monetary gain. The truth is that Jesus was not white. I don't mean that unkindly, but it has not hurt the self-esteem of white people all these years to know that God, the angels, and Jesus were white. And if you say it's not important to you whether He was white, then let's just make Him black now. If it doesn't make any difference, it won't matter, right?

The important thing is that we find out exactly what the Bible says. Jesus was not white. White people have been lied to. They have been led to think He was white and that has allowed Whites to perpetrate the fraud of inferiority on others who are not white. According to Michelangelo, everyone was white. If you go to Rome, to the Vatican, and visit the Sistine Chapel, everyone is portrayed as white. God, the angels, the disciples — everyone is European white. Again, in response to that, some have gone so far as to portray Jesus as a black man. I reject that idea as much as the notion that He was European white. Both of them are wrong, and it is going from one extreme to the other to try and make Jesus into an African black man. Now, again, I don't care what color Jesus was. I want the real Jesus to be seen, not a fabricated Jesus to be used against me as a person of color.

What are the facts as the Bible presents them? One thing is certain: Jesus was pure human. What do I mean by that? I believe Jesus was a composite man. I believe Jesus was everything that everyone else is, all rolled up into one body. Why? Because He came to redeem the whole human race, so why wouldn't He have been a composite man, made up of the whole human race? Without question, Jesus had some black in Him, which I will show from the Bible. I have to zero in on that part in order to help Blacks and Whites alike.

But I haven't had much experience with red, brown, or yellow people, because I wasn't raised with them. I didn't go to a red, yellow, or brown school. Everything I have dealt with in this country has basically been with Whites and Blacks. So I will leave it to the yellow, red, and brown folks to deal with these issues where their ethnicity is concerned. I'm not trying to leave anyone out, but I just can't speak with definitive, experiential knowledge about them. But I can speak about Blacks and Whites.

Ham was in Jesus. Why would I say that? Because the Bible says that. In his book, *All God's Children*, Steven L. McKenzie, associate professor of Hebrew Bible Old Testament studies at Rhodes College in Memphis, Tennessee, makes the following observation:

Most of the genealogy for Jesus in Matthew comes straight out of the Old Testament, so that the names in it would have been familiar to its readers. Again, there would have been no finer pedigree among Jesus' Jewish contemporaries. But one feature of this genealogy may have stood out to Matthew's original audience, namely the fact that it contains references to several women. A survey of other genealogies in the Bible shows that they are usually traced strictly through the male ancestors. Matthew mentions five women: Tamar (1:3), Rahab (1:5), Ruth (1:5), Bathsheba, called "the wife of Uriah" (1:6), and Mary (1:16)....A final observation about the women in Jesus' genealogy according to Matthew is especially germane to our study of racism. Three of the five women mentioned here — Tamar, Rahab and Ruth — were non-Israelites."[1]

It should be noted then that Jesus could not have been a pure Jew if three of the women in the genealogy were not of Israel.

Tamar and Rahab were Canaanites, Ruth a Moabite. Again, there is a subtle point, particularly relevant for Matthew's original audience. The royal, Davidic line which Jesus represented was never "pure" Israelite or Jewish — all three of these women were in fact ancestors of David. Jesus represents and redeems all people.[2]

There is another interesting point regarding the genealogy of Jesus that is valuable for us to pursue. In 2 Samuel, Chapter 11, we have a familiar story, one that has been the subject of several movies: David and Bathsheba. Historically, it is clear that David was a Hebrew, and we would place him in the "white" category. Bathsheba probably was a dark-skinned woman that we could classify as black. Certainly the KKK would classify her as black! Why do I say that she was dark-skinned or black?

[1] Steven L. McKenzie, *All God's Children: A Biblical Critique of Racism* (Louisville, Ky.: Westminster John Knox Press, 1997), 41-42.
[2] McKenzie, 41-42.

Notice that almost every time the Bible refers to Bathsheba, it says **"...Bathsheba...the wife of Uriah the Hittite"** (2 Samuel 11:3). This phrase "the Hittite" locates her geographically and indicates her skin color, because the Hittites were black (and, as you will see, I have Scripture supporting that). But to return for a moment to my point, isn't it interesting that the Bible doesn't just say "Bathsheba," but "Bathsheba...the wife of Uriah the Hittite?" Why mention her "Hittite-ness"? Why tell me Uriah and Bathsheba were Hittites unless there is a point here? Maybe that point is that Bathsheba was black!

In the story of David and Bathsheba, David took this (probably) black woman and had her black husband killed so that he could have her sexually. As a result of the sexual union between David and Bathsheba, there were four children born to this union. All of this is relevant to Jesus, but let's follow it step by step, because some members of the white church will automatically reject this. Let's set the stage in 1 Chronicles 3:1-5:

1　　Now these were the sons of David who were born to him in Hebron: The firstborn *was* Amnon, by Ahinoam the Jezreelitess; the second, Daniel, by Abigail the Carmelitess;

2　　the third, Absalom the son of Maacah, the daughter of Talmai, king of Geshur; the fourth, Adonijah the son of Haggith;

3　　the fifth, Shephatiah, by Abital; the sixth, Ithream, by his wife Eglah.

4　　*These* six were born to him in Hebron. There he reigned seven years and six months, and in Jerusalem he reigned thirty-three years.

5　　And these were born to him in Jerusalem: Shimea, Shobab, Nathan, and Solomon — four by Bathshua the daughter of Ammiel.

The word *Bathshua* is also pronounced and spelled "Bathsheba." If you search this out, you'll find it to be so.[3]

Remember the names *Nathan* and *Solomon*, two of the four sons that were born to David in Jerusalem by Bathshua, or Bathsheba. These names are recorded in both the genealogies of Matthew and Luke. For example, in Matthew 1:6, it says, **"and Jesse begot David the king. David the king begot Solomon...."** You could have stopped right there and we would have known that David begat Solomon. But look at the first part of Verse 6: **"and Jesse begot David...."** Did you notice that it didn't tell us who Jesse begot David *by*? It simply says **"Jesse begot David...."** So why didn't it just say David begot Solomon, and we would have known David begot Solomon and Solomon was the child of David and David was Solomon's father, right? We would have known that. But isn't it interesting how the Holy Spirit put this tidbit there in Verse 6:

> **and Jesse begot David the king. David the king begot Solomon by her *who had been the wife* of Uriah.**

There it is again. I wonder why He's telling us that?

I believe the Holy Spirit has a reason for this. Let's look at Luke 3:31, because this is where we have the other genealogy of Jesus the Messiah: ***the son* of Melea, *the son* of Menan, *the son* of Mattathah, *the son* of Nathan, *the son* of David.** Remember, we read in Chronicles that David had four children by Bathshua/Bathsheba in Jerusalem and one of those was named Nathan. Now consider this: Jesus was not the result of the sexual conduct of Mary and Joseph. However, Joseph was the legal father of Jesus, and Mary was His natural mother. Get these two terms — *natural/legal*. Jesus was the natural son of Mary but He was the legal son of Joseph and both of them, Mary and Joseph, had Bathsheba in their blood. So if

---

[3] See 2 Samuel 11:3; 1 Chronicles 3:5.

Mary had Bathsheba in her bloodline, and Jesus was the natural son of Mary, Jesus had Bathsheba in Him.

At this point someone might object that there is no need for any recognition of a black presence in Christ, especially since most people agree that He transcends the cultural debate. Our culture has in varying degrees viewed blackness as a curse. So to show that Jesus had black in His blood is to destroy that perception and its psychological legacy once and for all, because in Christ we find sinless Man and sinless Savior. This knowledge can free Blacks from an inferiority complex, while at the same time freeing Whites from a superiority myth. In Christ, as I said before, we all find our heritage.

To further substantiate the fact that Jesus had Bathsheba's bloodline and was partly black, let's look at King Solomon, who was probably black because he was the son of David by Bathsheba, "the wife of Uriah the Hittite." In 2 Samuel 12:24, we find this statement:

Then David comforted Bathsheba his wife, and went in to her and lay with her. So she bore a son, and he called his name Solomon. Now the LORD loved him...

That statement, **Now the LORD loved him** [Solomon], stands out. It seems irrelevant. Why is it in there? It makes it appear that this is the only person God ever loved up to that time. Look at it again: **Then David comforted Bathsheba his wife, and went in to her and lay with her. So she bore a son, and he called his name Solomon.** Period. That's it — that's all the Bible needed to say if the point of the story was only that Bathsheba bore a son to David named Solomon. Why add, **"Now the LORD loved him"**? I believe that God put this in to let white people know that if He could love a black boy, so can you! Otherwise, there is no reason to include that phrase. Remember that God is no respecter of persons, so we can say that God should have put this phrase in every time there was a man and woman in the Bible who had a son. God should have loved them, too, so why just this one case?

241

Bathsheba was the wife of Uriah the Hittite. The Hittites were descendants of Heth, who was the son of Canaan. Genesis 10:15 tells us that **Canaan begot Sidon his firstborn, and Heth**. Now, remember that it is claimed that Ham was cursed black, but it really wasn't Ham who was cursed, even though he was the one who saw the nakedness of his father. Noah could not put a curse on Ham, because God had just blessed Ham when he came out of the Ark, so Noah cursed his grandson, Ham's son, Canaan. And the Hittities were descendants of Heth, who was the son of Canaan.

Genesis 10:15, again, says **Canaan begot Sidon his firstborn, and Heth**. If Canaan was black, Sidon and Heth would have to be black too. So the Hittites, the descendants of Heth, were descendants of Canaan. That would make the Hittites black, it would make Uriah the Hittite black, and it would make Bathsheba, Uriah's wife, almost certainly black. And that would make Solomon, the son of a black woman, black!

Why tell us he was a Hittite? The purpose is so that people can trace the lineage of Jesus back. That's why genealogies are important. When most of you pick up the Bible and you start reading the genealogies, they are just plain boring: "So-and-so begot so-and-so…." But God didn't put superfluous rhetoric in His Word. It's there so we can find out who was who, instead of having to accept the lies of one group of people or another. We have a record right in God's Word. We just have to take the time to sort through it and extract the information we need.

If the religious leaders and artists had paid attention to the genealogies, we would never have had a lily-white Jesus hanging in the windows of Bible bookstores, or pale-skinned English actors with blue eyes playing Jesus in movies. In all the famous Hollywood films, virtually everyone was white: David, Bathsheba, Moses — all white. Pharaoh, white. Israelites, white. Everyone was white. But that isn't what the Book indicates.

Two of the four sons of David, Nathan and Solomon, are recorded in the genealogy of Matthew and Luke. Let's examine them in detail, because it's as important for white people that we destroy the myth of white superiority as it is for black people to destroy the myth of black inferiority. Neither is healthy, neither is right, and neither is scriptural.

Even today, many Blacks are still bound by these myths. Many black people want to do that which pleases the white man, because they still feel inferior. Every other group in America maintains some of its cultural identity. There are St. Patrick's Day parades, Columbus Day events, German festivals, even Cinco de Mayo. But black people have been hesitant to claim African culture or to celebrate blackness.

Some Blacks, even today are still ashamed of their skin color and would like to turn themselves white! For years, black society has itself been segregated into lighter-skinned and darker-skinned Blacks. In New Orleans, there used to be black — *African-American* — nightclubs that had a "paper bag test": if your skin was darker than a brown paper bag, they wouldn't let you in — *to a black club!* Historically, black universities have had a social class structure based on the skin shade. These are clearly people ashamed of black skin. So we need to defuse the myth of white being right all the time. White has its place, but it shouldn't have all the places!

We will begin this analysis of Jesus' color in Matthew's genealogical record. Remember that Jesus the Christ was born into the world in, to say the least, an unusual circumstance called the virgin birth. Mary, His mother, was not impregnated by Joseph, her husband-to-be. When she was told about the honor she was to be entrusted with, the angel Gabriel said to her, **"...*The* Holy Spirit will come upon you, and the power of the Highest will overshadow you..."** (Luke 1:35). Jesus was connected to David through His mother Mary. We have two genealogies. Matthew records the genealogy of Joseph. And remember the two boys? Nathan and Solomon? These were David's sons by Bathsheba, the wife of Uriah the Hittite, and the Hittites were black. So in Matthew 1:1, it says:

The book of the genealogy of Jesus Christ....

If this is the genealogy of Jesus Christ, it means that we are going to trace his heritage, right? This is important, because God wants us to have connective information, so that when we take a stand of faith on His Word and we believe something, we'll be able to connect it so that it makes a beautiful mosaic, a beautiful puzzle with no missing pieces. I love jigsaw puzzles and the worst thing in the world is to think that you have all the pieces, work yourself into a frazzle to complete the picture, then get to the end and find out you have a piece missing. "Oh no! The picture's spoiled." With just one or two missing pieces, the picture is incomplete.

Back to Matthew 1:1-16:

1   **The book of the genealogy of Jesus Christ, the Son of David, the Son of Abraham:**

Verse 2 starts the genealogy with the family line of Joseph, the legal father of Jesus:

2   **Abraham begot Isaac, Isaac begot Jacob, and Jacob begot Judah and his brothers.**

3   **Judah begot Perez and Zerah by Tamar, Perez begot Hezron, and Hezron begot Ram.**

4   **Ram begot Amminadab, Amminadab begot Nahshon, and Nahshon begot Salmon.**

5   **Salmon begot Boaz by Rahab, Boaz begot Obed by Ruth, Obed begot Jesse,**

6   **and Jesse begot David the king. David the king begot Solomon by her *who had been the wife* of Uriah.**

7   **Solomon begot Rehoboam, Rehoboam begot Abijah, and Abijah begot Asa.**

8   **Asa begot Jehoshaphat, Jehoshaphat begot Joram, and Joram begot Uzziah.**

9   Uzziah begot Jotham, Jotham begot Ahaz and Ahaz begot Hezekiah.

10   Hezekiah begot Manasseh, Manasseh begot Amon, and Amon begot Josiah.

11   Josiah begot Jeconiah and his brothers about the time they were carried away to Babylon.

12   And after they were brought to Babylon, Jeconiah begot Shealtiel, and Shealtiel begot Zerubbabel.

13   Zerubbabel begot Abiud, Abiud begot Eliakim, and Eliakim begot Azor.

14   Azor begot Zadok, Zadok begot Achim, and Achim begot Eliud.

15   Eliud begot Eleazar, Eleazar begot Matthan, and Matthan begot Jacob.

16   And Jacob begot Joseph the husband of Mary, of whom was born Jesus who is called Christ.

Notice carefully the name *Joseph* where it says, **Joseph the husband of Mary,** then go back two spaces to "Jacob." Jacob begat Joseph. That means whoever Jacob was, this was Joseph's father. This is the genealogy on Joseph's side (again, Joseph as the legal, but not natural, father of Jesus) as presented by Matthew.

Now let's look at Luke, Chapter 3, and notice something interesting. Matthew records the genealogy of Jesus from Abraham forward, but Luke starts with Jesus and goes all the way back to Adam. Question: Who was Joseph? Joseph was the legal father of Jesus and therefore the husband of Mary. And who was Joseph's father Jacob? Lets look at this in Luke 3:23:

> **Now Jesus Himself began *His ministry at* about thirty years of age, being (as was supposed) *the* son of Joseph, *the son* of Heli,**

Here it would appear that "Heli" was Joseph's father. But we just read in Matthew that Jacob was Joseph's father. Now how do we reconcile this? Joseph was the legal father of Jesus. Almost all Hebrew genealogies are traced through the male line. The only time women are mentioned in these Bible references is when it has a direct bearing upon Christ in the future. Now notice what it says here in Verse 23:

> **Now Jesus Himself began *His ministry at* about thirty years of age, being (as was supposed) *the* son of Joseph, *the son* of Heli....**

Actually, when it says, **being (as was supposed) *the* son of Joseph, *the son* of Heli**, that really refers to Mary's family, but since the Jews did genealogies from the male line, they left out Mary's name and instead referred to *her* father.

Remember when we read from Abraham, we got to Jesse and then we got to David. And remember that David had a number of sons by other wives, but he had four sons by Bathshua, or Bathsheba. Now when we get in Matthew's line, descending from Abraham down to Jesus, it only mentions one of David's sons, and that was who? Solomon. It didn't mention anything about the other sons, just Solomon. Let's follow this in Luke 3:23-32:

> 23   **Now Jesus Himself began *His ministry at* about thirty years of age being, (as was supposed) *the* son of Joseph, *the son* of Heli,**

> 24   ***the son* of Matthat, *the son* of Levi, *the son* of Melchi, *the son* of Janna, *the son* of Joseph,**

> 25   ***the son* of Mattathiah, *the son* of Amos, *the son* of Nahum, *the son* of Esli, *the son* of Naggai,**

26   *the son* of Maath, *the son* of Mattathiah, *the son* of Semei, *the son* of Joseph, *the son* of Judah,

27   *the son* of Joannas, *the son* of Rhesa, *the son* of Zerubbabel, *the son* of Shealtiel, *the son* of Neri,

28   *the son* of Melchi, *the son* of Addi, *the son* of Cosam, *the son* of Elmodam, *the son* of Er,

29   *the son* of Jose, *the son* of Eliezer, *the son* of Jorim, *the son* of Matthat, *the son* of Levi,

30   *the son* of Simeon, *the son* of Judah, *the son* of Joseph, *the son* of Jonan, *the son* of Eliakim,

31   *the son* of Melea, *the son* of Menan, *the son* of Mattathah, *the son* of Nathan, *the son* of David,

32   *the son* of Jesse....

This account doesn't mention Solomon, but it mentions the other son, Nathan. Both boys, Nathan and Solomon, were the sons of Bathshua/Bathsheba the wife of Uriah the Hittite. I submit to you that Jesus had black blood in Him, because He inherited His blood through the line all the way back to David and Bathsheba.

I said it before, Jesus was the natural son of Mary, the legal son of Joseph, and both of them had Bathsheba in their veins. So Bathsheba, and her blood, must have been in Jesus too. So we have a dilemma. We know that Bathsheba was married to Uriah the Hittite, that the Hittites were black, and that therefore she was probably black. And it is interesting that the Bible always puts in "Uriah the Hittite." That is because God wants you to check it out. Bathsheba was the wife of Uriah the Hittite, and the Hittites were descendants of Heth, who was the son of Canaan.

We heard for years the lie that the curse of Ham was the curse of black skin. Who started that lie? It wasn't black people who started the lie that Ham was cursed black. He couldn't possibly have been cursed white! No, the assumption was that Ham was cursed black.

Noah, his wife, their three sons, and the sons' wives were in the ark. When the flood was over, God opened the ark and they came out. God blessed Noah and his three sons, Shem, Ham and Japheth. Then Noah planted a vineyard, became intoxicated, passed out, and was found naked in his tent by his son Ham. Ham went out and told his other brothers. The brothers then took a sheet and walked backwards so they wouldn't see the nakedness of their father. When Noah awoke from his wine, supposedly he cursed Ham. However, he couldn't possibly have cursed Ham, because God had blessed Ham. So he cursed Ham's son Canaan. (I dealt with this extensively in Volume 2.) The white clergy has told us that the curse of Ham was blackness. Since Canaan was cursed and not Ham, that would mean one of two things: that Canaan himself was cursed black and that was the end of that and none of his children came forth black, or that all of his posterity would retain the same curse into perpetuity!

Let's get back to the genealogies. We will follow the line of Ham in Genesis 10:15. The Bible says about Ham's son Canaan, who was supposedly cursed black, **"Canaan begot Sidon his first-born, and Heth...."** If Canaan was cursed black, Heth couldn't have come out white. Not European white. I would think it is reasonable to assume, and I think genetically we can support this, that he would have to inherit whatever his father had. So if Heth was black and out of Heth came the Hittites, then the Hittites were black. And if Bathsheba was the wife of Uriah the Hittite, it's plausible and likely that Bathsheba was black, and that's what caught the attention of that Hebrew king up on top of the house, watching that black naked woman bathing, when he should have been out on the battlefield fighting with his men.

In 2 Samuel 12:24, we see:

**Then David comforted Bathsheba his wife, and went
in to her and lay with her. So she bore a son, and he
called his name Solomon. Now the LORD loved him...**

I alluded to this before, but it's so rare that I want to revisit it:
"Now the LORD loved him...." I wonder why God put that in there?
That statement was totally irrelevant to the issue at hand. It was
about who begot so-and-so. It's almost like saying that God didn't
love anyone else before, and of course, that isn't true. Why all of a
sudden did He love this boy? This boy was probably black. So if
God loved black, then maybe white people ought to love black, unless
they are more spiritual than God.

The fact that Solomon was likely black, because he came
from Bathsheba, the wife of a (black) Hittite, let's look at the Song
of Solomon in detail. We will find that there has been some deliberate mistranslation of the Bible to take the "blackness" out of certain
passages related to the genealogy of Jesus.

The Song of Solomon contains a series of juxtaposed state-
ments by Solomon and by the Shulamite woman, Solomon's lover.
The speaker is indicated by a title preceding the verses. Song of
Solomon 1:1-6:

1	**The song of songs, which *is* Solomon's.**

[The Shulamite]

2	**Let him kiss me with the kisses of his mouth
	— for your love *is* better than wine.**

3	**Because of the fragrance of your good
	ointments, Your name *is* ointment poured
	forth; therefore the virgins love you.**

4	**Draw me away!**

[The Daughters of Jerusalem]

We will run after you.

[The Shulamite]

The king has brought me into his chambers.

[The Daughters of Jerusalem]

We will be glad and rejoice in you. We will remember your love more than wine.

[The Shulamite]

Rightly do they love you.

5   **I *am* dark, but lovely** [The traditional King James Version says "...black, but comely...."], **O daughters of Jerusalem, like the tents of Kedar, like the curtains of Solomon.**

6   **Do not look upon me, because I *am* dark** [KJV says "black"], **because the sun has tanned me. My mother's sons were angry with me; they made me the keeper of the vineyards, *but* my own vineyard, I have not kept.**

This gives the impression that the skin was "tanned" temporarily dark by the sun. But let's look at the Song of Solomon 5:11: **His head *is like* the finest gold; his locks *are* wavy, *and* black as a raven.** You have never heard anyone say "dark as a raven." That phraseology is always black as a raven, because a raven is jet black and shiny. Now the same Hebrew word that is translated "black" in the fifth chapter is translated "dark" in the first chapter. I wonder why?

Another point I'd like to stress is that in the Song of Solomon, Solomon is not speaking in every verse. Before I embarked on this study I had always thought that everything in this book was talking about Solomon, in particular, Chapter 1, Verse 5, where it stated, "I am dark…" (KJV, "I am black"). But it's not. This is almost like a play — a dialogue. There are three primary actors in this section. The daughters of Jerusalem, the Shulamite woman, and Solomon. Let's look at Verse 5 again. It says, **"I *am* dark, but lovely…."** (And again, the KJV says, "I am black, but comely…."):

5   **I *am* dark, but lovely, O daughters of Jerusalem, like the tents of Kedar, like the curtains of Solomon.**

6   **Do not look upon me, because I *am* dark [KJV, "black"], because the sun has tanned me. My mother's sons were angry with me; they made me the keeper of the vineyards, *but* my own vineyard I have not kept.**

This is the Shulamite woman speaking. She was "dark" ("black," according to the KJV). They can't bring themselves to say "black" so they used "dark" to play it down. As I asked before, Why? Because it would negatively affect the preconceived ethnic and theological denominational points of view. I point out from Chapter 5, Verse 11, that it says, **"His head *is like* the finest gold…."** [This is the Shulamite woman speaking of her lover]. So "his head," meaning Solomon's head, **"is like the finest gold; his locks are wavy, and black as a raven."**

It is interesting that they changed the term from *black* to *dark* between these verses. In Song of Solomon 5:11 the word is *black*, but in 1:5 the term is *dark* — yet they are the same Hebrew word! In fact, the Hebrew word literally means "swarthy black." Why not call them both either "black" or "dark?" If both words were *black*, it would be clear that the woman was black, and as a black woman, it would seem natural that she would be attracted to a black man. This especially seems to fit in that Solomon was the son of David through

Bathsheba (or Bathshua), who was the wife of Uriah the Hittite, who himself was black.

In Chapter 5, Verse 10, there is another interesting point: It says, **"My beloved *is* white and ruddy, Chief among ten thousand."** Again, this is the Shulamite woman talking about her lover. So now it would seem that what I had said about Solomon being black, or certainly having black in him, would be disproved by the statement, **"My beloved is white...."** Well, believe it or not, the word *white* in that verse is not referring to the color of the skin. You can figure this out because the word *ruddy* is a color. You can't be both white and ruddy. You can't be both yellow and red, you are one or the other.

Let's look at what *Strong's Concordance* tells us about this word, because it's quite interesting. Also notice that the white comes first, before the ruddy. Now who translated this? Black people or white people? *Strong's Concordance*, number 6703, in the Hebrew section of the concordance, examines the word *tsach* (also spelled *tsakh*).[4] It originates, as all Hebrew words do, from a handful of root words, and this root word, number 6705 in *Strong's*, literally means "dazzling," — sunny and bright, figuratively speaking. Let me give you an illustration. Have you ever heard someone say, "My, that's a bright young man!" And they weren't talking about him being white as in skin color. No, Verse 10 is expressing figuratively that the person is bright, effervescent, and intelligent. Solomon dazzled this woman!

Several other translations of the Bible treat this word *white* differently than the *King James Version* or the *New King James Version*. Case in point, in the *New International Bible*, these same two words that we see in our *King James* as *white* and *ruddy* are translated "radiant and ruddy." Radiant is not a skin color, but a personality trait. The *New American Standard Bible* translates those same two words as "dazzling and ruddy," while the *Amplified Bible*

---

[4] James Strong, *The Exhaustive Concordance of the Bible* (Peabody, Massachusetts: Hendrickson Publishers, n. d., circa 1990), #6703, 99.

translates them "fair and ruddy." Likewise, the *Holy Spirit Encounter Bible* translates "My lover is dark and dazzling." Now the others didn't want to say it like that, but that word *white* in the *King James Version* of the Bible is not talking about white skin or skin color, but a personality type.

Getting back to the genealogy of Jesus. During the time that I taught this book as a series in my church, I received an interesting note that raised a question that those of you reading this book might also have. I think it is an important issue:

Pastor Price,

I have a question about Jesus having black blood in Him. I understand that Joseph is the legal father of Jesus and didn't impregnate Mary. I also understand that Jesus didn't receive Joseph's sinful nature, but what about Mary? Wouldn't Mary's sinful nature be placed in Jesus since she was used to bring Jesus into the world? Did God use Mary's egg to bring Jesus in? If God didn't use Mary's egg and just placed Jesus inside Mary's womb, then how can Jesus be related to David, Solomon, etc. Help please."

(Name withheld)

This is a legitimate question and I think worth answering, so that everyone can understand. This thing is so deeply entrenched in the Church, particularly in the white segment of the Church, that we need to bring out the facts.

The writer said, "I understand that Joseph is the legal father of Jesus and didn't impregnate Mary." Correct. "I also understand that Jesus didn't receive Joseph's sinful nature, but what about Mary?" This is a good question, and many have had the same idea — the notion that sin is transmitted in the blood. But it's not. Keep in mind sin is a spiritual problem, not a physical one. Sin has to do with the real you, the person who lives on the inside of the physical body.

That is exactly why God had to circumvent the normal procedure of the human male and female coming together. It's not until a male and female come together that the new spirit person is released from heaven to take up residence in a human body.

When a male and female, man and woman, come together, the male sperm fertilizes the female egg. Conception takes place. A new life is conceived. The spirit of that male/female combination comes from God. After all, where do you think spirits originate? They are not in the blood, or transmitted genetically. Spirits come from God and there is no place for a spirit to inhabit until a male and female come together. When Adam sinned, though, all of his children inherited his sin nature, which simply means that spiritually they were cut off from God. Once they reach the age of accountability — which is no specific age but a different age for each person — God holds them accountable for their sin. How does that relate to our genealogy of Jesus?

God had to bypass Joseph, because if Jesus was the product of Joseph and Mary, then that Spirit that came from God would also be cut off, legally speaking, and Jesus would be in need of a savior Himself. Therefore, God supernaturally impregnated Mary by the power of the Holy Spirit, and there was no sin nature transferred to the embryo to the new fetus, to the child, to the baby.

Let me clarify the "sin nature" issue. Where do babies come from? I mean, where does the spirit of a baby come from? God, correct? Yet there is a verse in the Bible (Romans 3:23) that says **for all have sinned and fall short of the glory of God.** How many are left out of "all?" If all have sinned, wouldn't that mean that an innocent baby is a sinner? Think about it this way: That cannot be true, because that would mean that heaven is populated with sinful spirits, awaiting a physical body to enter the three-dimensional world.

When the Bible says **all have sinned,** that statement must be qualified. All have sinned from the standpoint that Adam sinned in the Garden of Eden, because he was the representative of man and acted on behalf of the whole human race. So all have sinned in the sense that all have inherited Adam's sin nature. But all have not sinned in the sense of acting or committing sin because, again, a baby with a spirit that comes from God would then come as a sinner. That can't be true because there is no sin in God. How do we reconcile this apparent contradiction? (And this does get back to our question about Mary, Joseph, and Jesus).

I mentioned the age of accountability. It isn't a chronological age, even though some have attempted to say that at age 12 or 13 you reach the age of accountability. Jewish boys have their bar mitzvah at age 13. The biblical revelation, though, is in Romans 7:7-12, where Paul writes:

7   **What shall we say then? *Is* the law sin? Certainly not! On the contrary, I would not have known sin except through the law. For I would not have known covetousness unless the law had said, *"You shall not covet."***

8   **But sin, taking opportunity by the commandment, produced in me all *manner of evil* desire. For apart from the law sin *was* dead.**

9   **I was alive once without the law, but when the commandment came, sin revived and I died.**

10   **And the commandment, which *was* to *bring* life, I found to *bring* death.**

11   **For sin, taking occasion by the commandment, deceived me, and by it killed *me*.**

12   **Therefore the law *is* holy, and the commandment holy and just and good.**

Verse 9 is the key verse. Paul said **I was alive once**. Well, when was he alive?

> **I was alive once without the law, but when the commandment came, sin revived and I died.**

But now wait a minute! How could he have died and he's the one writing the letter? How can a dead man write a letter? This can't possibly be referring to physically dying. It must refer to dying spiritually.

Every baby comes into the world sinless. That is why you don't have to worry if your infant died, or if you had a stillborn child. That baby went right back to heaven! It didn't do anything wrong, so it had to go right back to God. The child never sinned. Spirits come from God, and there is no sin in God, so God isn't in the business of creating spirits with sin in them. When a baby comes here, it is sinless…until the law comes.

Now let's go back to Verse 7:

> **What shall we say then?** *Is* **the law sin? Certainly not! On the contrary, I would not have known sin except through the law. For I would not have known covetousness unless the law had said,** *"You shall not covet."*

That's why God gave Israel the law. You cannot hold any person accountable for something they didn't know they were not supposed to do. It isn't fair, and God is a fair and just God. He could not hold the human race accountable for sin until He gave people a law that said, "Don't do this!" Once He did that, and people broke the law, it would be fair and just to hold them accountable. In fact, that was the purpose of the law: to make it so that sin was seen as sin, and to make it clear to people that they had violated the law.

Now in Verse 8, we see, **But sin, taking opportunity by the commandment, produced in me all** *manner of evil* **desire. For apart**

from the law sin *was* dead [emphasis mine]. Without a law, there can be no sin. You cannot judge someone for a law that is not on the books, nor can you arrest someone for a charge that doesn't exist.

In Verse 9, Paul writes, **I was alive once without the law.** He is referring to the time when he was a baby, a child, when he didn't know the law. But he grew up and became accountable.

Jesus was a Spirit, just like the rest of us are spirits. The only way He could enter this three-dimensional world was through a body. He had to be able to die, and spirits don't die. Jesus had to have a body so that He could die to take away the sin of the world, but He had to have a body that didn't contain a sin nature — a spirit that was not cut off from God. Keep all this in mind relative to the question I was asked:

> ...I have a question about Jesus having black blood in Him. And I understand that Joseph is the legal father of Jesus and didn't impregnate Mary. I also understand that Jesus didn't receive Joseph's sinful nature, but what about Mary...?

Mary couldn't pass on the sin nature, because she didn't have another human like herself to join with. You could not impute sin, because there was no human father with a sinful nature to join with Mary's. But what about Mary? There wasn't anything Mary could do, just as there is nothing any woman can do, without sperm, to get pregnant. She couldn't have a baby on her own. Even if artificial insemination were possible, it is still a sperm from somewhere. The question was, "...wouldn't Mary's sinful nature be placed in Jesus?"

No, because the seed that was planted in her was not from Joseph, so there could be no transfer of the sin nature. We can better understand this by posing another question: Where did Adam get his genetic material? He didn't have a mother, and he didn't have a father, so he couldn't inherit anything. Where did he get his genetic makeup? From God? How could God do that? The fact is, Adam was never a baby. He came here fully grown, didn't he? According to the Bible, he was an adult male. Where did he get his genetic material, then? God put it in him when God created Adam.

The Bible further tells us that Adam needed a helpmeet. So God brought all the animals to Adam for him to name, but there was no helpmeet found for Adam. Then God said, **"...*It is* not good that man should be alone..."** (Genesis 2:18). So He put Adam to sleep and took one of Adam's ribs. Now, *rib* in Hebrew means "curve." It doesn't mean seed.

The point is, since Adam didn't have a mother and father to inherit genetic material from, then any genetic material that he had in him was put in by God when God created him. God put Adam to sleep and took a rib and made a woman. Where did he get her genetic material? She didn't have a mother either. We have to be willing to accept the idea that Almighty God could put genetic coding into Adam when He created him, and that God, by virtue of His creative power, could also take a rib out of a man and make a woman. She would have genetic coding in her, so that when Adam and Eve came together and had a child, the child would receive half of its genetic material from the father, Adam, and half from the mother, Eve. So why do we have a problem with the idea of God being able to put a seed inside Mary and create genetic coding that Jesus would have needed in order to be a real human, like us, but without the sinful nature?

So to answer the question, "Wouldn't Mary's sinful nature be placed in Jesus?" the answer is no. The questioner went on to ask, "...did God use Mary's egg to bring Jesus in? If God didn't use Mary's egg and just placed Jesus inside Mary's womb, then how can Jesus be related to David...?" We find the answer in Matthew 1:1: **The book of the genealogy of Jesus Christ, the Son of David, the Son of Abraham.** God said that Jesus was the Son of David and that he was the Son of Abraham. If we didn't find any other validation for that, it wouldn't make any difference. God said it, and it must be so. But to assuage our curiosity, we will delineate it. I'm reading from the *New King James Version* (NKJV) and it says in Matthew 1:1,

The book of the genealogy.... In the traditional *King James Version*, it does not use the term *genealogy*, but uses the word *generation*. The "generation of Jesus Christ...." That word *generation* literally means "tracing," or, in modern parlance, "tracking" by generation. And the definition that's given in the dictionary is "i.e., genealogy." So that is probably where the *New King James* translators came up with the word *genealogy*.

There are some profound findings here in Matthew, Chapter 1, in reference to the birth of Christ. It is interesting that the chapter begins by discussing the genealogy of Jesus Christ and then the birth of Christ. However, if the genealogy of Jesus Christ represents the genes of Jesus Christ, this order makes perfect sense. If the genealogy of Jesus Christ represents his genetic makeup, then it's appropriate to describe His genes before His birth.

Now, what is a genealogy? It is a historical tracking of the generation preceding an individual. Notice the word *genealogy* begins with *gene*. Again, we could say these are the genes of Jesus Christ — His heredity, His genetic makeup. If Jesus was truly a human, He had to have DNA.

Jesus Christ must have had genes in the body in which He walked the earth. The Greek word for *gene* is *gennan,* and it literally means "to produce." It is the basic unit of heredity. *Taber's Cyclopedic Medical Dictionary* explains that the genes that are found in a normal individual with no genetic defects, come from 46 chromosomes that come from the mother and the father.[5] We are going to validate the birth of Jesus, the life of Jesus, and establish the fact that Jesus was a man in every sense that we are. The offspring receives 50 percent of its chromosomes from the mother and 50 percent from the father. Therefore, 23 chromosomes come from the mother and 23 come from the father. These become 23 pairs, resulting in a total of 46 chromosomes.

---

[5] Clarence W. Taber, *Taber's Cyclopedic Medical Dictionary,* 14th ed., Clayton Thomas, ed. (Philadelphia: F. A. Davis, 1981), "gene."

The sex chromosomes are either XX for a female, or XY for a male. Since Jesus Christ was a male, He must have had the Y chromosome. The mother's XX can only donate an X chromosome to the baby. It is the father (XY) who donates the X chromosome to the female offspring or the Y chromosome to the male offspring.

Therefore, Jesus Christ could not have received 100 percent of His genetic makeup from Mary because she did not have the Y chromosome. The Y chromosome must have come from the genes or the genealogy of Jesus Christ — in other words, from Joseph's side. Jesus Christ must have resembled someone in appearance. It makes sense He would look like a combination of Mary and Joseph. God considered Mary and Joseph to be the parents of Jesus here on earth. Why would God make Mary carry Jesus and make Him look nothing like her? Similarly, why would God have Joseph as the father if Jesus looked nothing like him?

Matthew 1:20 says:

But while he thought about these things, behold, an angel of the Lord appeared to him in a dream, saying, "Joseph, son of David, do not be afraid to take to you Mary your wife, for that which is conceived in her is of the Holy Spirit."

This is important, because the world needed to know the earthly parents of Jesus Christ. He could not be thought of as an illegitimate child that was born to a mother out of wedlock. In order for the world to recognize His parents and to accept His birth — and His lineage, thus fulfilling the prophecies — as legitimate, Jesus had to resemble His parents, and Joseph and Mary needed to be married. And He would resemble them if He had their genes.

I believe the genealogy of Jesus Christ is important because it defines the genetic makeup that Christ received from Joseph. The genealogy of Mary represents the genetic makeup He received from Mary. Only God would know the exact genetic code for the body of Jesus Christ while He walked the earth.

Going back to Matthew 1:20, it says, **"...that which is conceived in her is of the Holy Spirit"** (though not of Joseph physically through sexual transmission). The Holy Spirit must have delivered the genetic makeup from the male side to Mary who already had half of the genetic material. Matthew 1:1 refers to Christ as the Son of David and the Son of Abraham. Jesus had the genes of Abraham and the genes of David, including the entire Davidic genealogy. Therefore, it makes sense when Jesus is referred to as the Son of David and the Son of Abraham. He is the Son of Man because He has mankind's genes.

Remember reading that phrase — *Son of Man*? I guarantee that you were puzzled when you read the New Testament and saw Jesus using the phrase *Son of Man*. That's because He has man's genes in Him. He was a human.

Jesus is the "Son of Man" because He has man's genes, but He is also the Son of God because of the Father. The Holy Spirit made it possible for Jesus to enter the earth (Matthew 1:20), while Jesus' ascension made it possible for the Holy Spirit to dwell in the earth (Acts 1:3-10).

That's what the virgin birth is all about. It can be scientifically validated! There is nothing strange about it at all. Jesus referred to Himself as the Son of Man, because He had David in Him, and David and Bathsheba had Nathan and Solomon in them, and Bathsheba was the wife of Uriah the Hittite, and the Hittites were black. Therefore it is reasonable to assume that Jesus had not only white in Him but black as well! In fact, Jesus was a composite man. He had *everyone* in Him. That makes sense, because He's the representative of all men on the earth before God, so why wouldn't He have everyone in Him in order to represent everyone?

We read the genealogy of Luke and it took us from Jesus all the way back to Adam. Adam and Eve began to have children. Noah was the product of his father and mother who were the product of their father and mother who were the product of...you get the point. This goes all the way back to Adam and Eve. Whatever Adam and Eve had in them was transmitted through the genes to their offspring, and to *their* offspring, all the way down to Noah. Noah had three sons, Shem, Ham, and Japheth, and all our Bible scholars and historians declare that the entire human race we see today is the result of those three boys after the flood, because all other humans up to that time were destroyed by the flood. The only people left on earth were Noah and his wife, and Shem, Ham, Japheth and their wives. Therefore, if Jesus' genealogy had the genes of David and Abraham, He had to have the genes of Canaan and He had to have the genes of Ham, and He had to have the genes of Noah and He had to have the genes of Adam! Jesus has everyone in Him! He represents everyone, both spiritually and genetically!

During my research for this book, I came upon much material that inferred that almost everyone in the Bible was black. There is a Bible in which all the pictures are black — Abraham is black and Jesus is black. To me, that is as extreme as inferring that everyone in the Bible was European white. Yet that position, that everyone in the Bible was white, is what our American religious and artistic traditions have left us with. Many Blacks call Christianity the "white man's religion" because of the image the church, with no small degree of help from Hollywood, has propagated over the years — that of a light-skinned, blue-eyed Jeffrey Hunter-looking Jesus Christ. Nothing against Jeffrey Hunter. He's a fine actor, but Jesus did not look like him.

Christianity is not the white man's religion and it's not the black man's religion. Christianity is for everyone willing to accept Jesus, because of the Scriptures. John 3:16 says, **"For God so loved the world that...whoever believes...."** Not "whoever who is white believes" or "whoever who is black believes" but *whoever.* Instead of being Eurocentric or Afrocentric, I suggest that we become Christo-centric — Christ-centered, in other words.

One thing that has been overlooked traditionally is the fact that there are many persons of color mentioned in the Bible who have received no acknowledgment of their color. The early printers, who had the money and the resources to print the first Bibles with pictures, selected their own image to inject into the art. Instead of a Bible of color — *multicolored* — we have a monochromatic Bible — all white! This is unfortunate, and it is too bad that color should matter, but it does in our society. When you think of the fact that black people in this country have for almost 400 years been told that they were little more than beasts of the field, and that among the peoples of the earth they were inferior, the revelation that they were included by God in His Word is indeed good and welcome news.

If you've never been put down or discriminated against like people of color in this country — and not just in the secular area, but in the Church of the Lord Jesus Christ — then you can't empathize with us. Color should not make a difference, but the facts are that to some people it makes a world of difference, and since it does to some people, and since these, too, are people Christ died for, I think it incumbent upon us to reach them at any cost that doesn't compromise the Word of God.

Some people need this information about Blacks in the Bible. You may say, "It doesn't make any difference." But it does make a difference to some people. Some people need this message. They need to know they are not an afterthought to God. I didn't need it for me. Once I found out how to walk by faith, once I found out my covenant rights, once I found out what the Bible said I was and what I had and what I could do, it delivered me from low self-esteem. I took the Word and overcame those inferior feelings. But there are many people who can't even get to the Word because they have been so beaten down all their life with this idea of inferiority. They need this message.

The Church of the Lord Jesus Christ needs this message. Jesus cannot return until we do something about this racism issue. It is not about making black people feel *better* than anyone else — that is not the point or the purpose. The purpose is to let Blacks feel good about themselves because God feels good about them. Jesus said the truth shall make you free, and the truth can free black people from the bombardment of inferiority they have been shelled with for some 400 years.

It is true that not everyone will need this information, but think about this: You need this information to be able to help others. Many people are incapable of helping others because they are so selfish that they have never taken the time to get the information they need to help someone else. Do you ever think about all the people you will come in contact with who will never come to Crenshaw Christian Center, or never visit our Website, or never watch Ever Increasing Faith television? What about them? Those are people Christ died for, too.

So in equipping the body of Christ to speak to all people, we need to be well-grounded in the facts of the Bible. It would be worth finding out if everyone in the Bible was white, as traditionally portrayed, or if there was some color in the Bible. Can we find any black people in the Bible? I think you'll be surprised.

9

Color in the Bible

I'm not interested in putting black people in the Bible just to have black people there. But given all the attacks on the purported intellectual deficiencies of black people, isn't it relevant that the first great world leader — universally viewed as the "wisest man in the world" — was a black man? Again, I'm not interested in showing you every place in the Bible where a black person is mentioned. I'll show you a representative few. Black people *are* in the Bible.

When I started this study, I wanted to know, is there something in the Bible, in God, in Christianity, about black people? The startling thing is that the information is there — it's in the Bible. And it's not hidden. It's just that for centuries those in power in the Church and the Hollywood moviemakers have lied to us. So by focusing on Blacks, my task has been to correct the traditional portrayals of the Bible that sought to ignore black people. I'm not ignoring other ethnic groups, but they were not part of my specific "marching orders." I have to be confident that God will raise up members of those groups to redress their own wrongs, but that isn't the job I was called to do.

Let's return to Genesis 10:6-12:

**6   The sons of Ham *were* Cush, Mizraim, Put, and
       Canaan.**

7 The sons of Cush *were* Seba, Havilah, Sabtah, Raamah, and Sabtechah; and the sons of Raamah *were* Sheba and Dedan.

8 Cush begot Nimrod; he began to be a mighty one on the earth. [This is Ham's posterity. So if Ham was a black man, and they told us he was, then Nimrod, his offspring, would undoubtedly be what he was.]

9 He was a mighty hunter before the Lord; therefore it is said, "Like Nimrod the mighty hunter before the Lord."

10 And the beginning of his kingdom [This was a black man who had a kingdom!] was Babel, Erech, Accad, and Calneh, in the land of Shinar.

11 From that land he went to Assyria and built Nineveh, Rehoboth, Ir, Calah,

12 and Resen between Nineveh and Calah (that *is* the principal city).

This man was a city builder. He was a mighty hunter. This man had a kingdom and this man was the son of Ham. He was a black man. Now I never heard that in any Church before. I thought Nimrod was white!

In Psalm 105:23 we find: **Israel also came into Egypt, and Jacob dwelt in the land of Ham.** Ham had a land — and not like you own a lot or a plot of ground. The whole land was called the "land of Ham," and that would be Egypt! Egypt was the land of Ham. Ham was black. So we could say that Egypt was the "land of black."

Years ago, before the Lord gave me this assignment to do this series and the accompanying books, I didn't pay much attention to genealogies in the Bible. In fact, I thought the genealogies were a waste of time. I mean, "so-and-so begot so-and-so, begot so-and-so." Some of it would drive you up a wall. But God put it in there for a reason. I didn't know that we were all in there.

God put all of us in there — and if we, the Church, had looked at it, there would never have been any white superiority/black inferiority stuff. The genealogies are in there so that people could locate themselves, so that you wouldn't have to take anyone's word about who you are and who you are not. Remember earlier we found that one of the first public acts that Jesus did was to go to the synagogue and locate Himself in the book of Isaiah? The Word has made available a way that we can locate ourselves in the Bible — to know who we are.

What other black people are in the Bible? The Queen of Sheba came from...well, Sheba. She was a Cushite. Who were the Cushites? Look again at Genesis 10:6-7:

6   The sons of Ham *were* [who?] **Cush, Mizraim, Put, and Canaan.**

7   The sons of Cush *were* **Seba, Havilah, Sabtah, Raamah, and Sabtechah; and the sons of Raamah** *were* **Sheba and Dedan.**

In 1 Chronicles 1:9 we get another view that corresponds to what we just read in Genesis through the writings of Moses:

The sons of Cush *were* **Seba, Havilah, Sabta, Raama, and Sabtecha. The sons of Raama** *were* [who?] **Sheba and Dedan.**

There it is again! James Strong, in his well-known concordance, defines the word *Sheba* as "the name of three progenitors of tribes of an Ethiopian district: called Sheba, Sabeans." Ethiopia is in Africa and Ethiopians are black. The Queen of Sheba was black!

All this touches on another area that we've dealt with before, but I really want to rock the boat. This is something that really hamstrings the body of Christ, namely this business of interracial marriage. As I've said before, I'm not promoting interracial marriage one way or another. I personally don't care about it for me, because I'm already married. But this has been a huge stumbling block in the white Church in America in reference to black people. We need to know that God approves of and condones interracial marriage and He approves of Blacks marrying others than Blacks, and other races marrying black. This has been one of the biggest issues in the white segment of the Church. There are some people who don't mind you hanging around as long as there is no danger of you dating a white person or marrying a white person. What does the Bible say about interracial marriage?

In Genesis 16:1-3, it says:

1   **Now Sarai, Abram's wife, had borne him no *children*. And she had an Egyptian maidservant whose name was Hagar.** [Remember, we just read in Psalms that Jacob dwelled in the land of Ham, and that would be Egypt. So, we could say, the land of black. If Sarai, Abram's wife, had an Egyptian maidservant, she probably was black, because Egyptians are black!]

2   **So Sarai said to Abram, 'See now, the L**ORD** has restrained me from bearing *children*. Please, go in to my maid; perhaps, I shall obtain children by her." And Abram heeded the voice of Sarai.**

3   **Then Sarai, Abram's wife, took Hagar her maid, the Egyptian, and gave her to her husband Abram to** [notice this carefully] **be his wife...."**

Look at Verse 3 again: **Then Sarai, Abram's wife, took Hagar her maid, *the Egyptian*** [emphasis mine].... How many times do we fail to pick up on what God is trying to tell us, and why He does what He does? Notice the third verse again. It could have read: "Then Sarai, Abram's wife, took Hagar her maid, and gave her to her husband Abram." Why bother to tell us she was an Egyptian? What difference does it make? It located her geographically and ethnically, and also makes clear the fact that Almighty God doesn't have a problem with inter-ethnic marriage. Sarai gave her to her husband Abram to be his wife, after Abram had lived ten years in the land of Canaan.[1]

Abraham married an Egyptian when he wasn't an Egyptian himself. So that was an interracial marriage, and it didn't look like God had a problem with it. Actually, if it was important, God could have hidden it from us. Just the opposite — God exposed it so you can't miss it. God doesn't care about which "race" people marry into because to God there is only one race, and that's the human race! The Bible says that out of one blood God made all men to dwell on the face of the earth (Acts 17:26). In fact, the only "mixed marriage" God ever discusses is a marriage of partners who are "unequally yoked" (2 Corinthians 6:14). The phrase *unequally yoked* means

---

[1] Some people will ask, "Didn't we just see that multiple wives under Islam was wrong? So isn't this a contradiction? Abram has two wives here." It is obvious from Genesis 2:24 that it was God's intention from the beginning that a man would have but one wife and that a woman would have but one husband. It is also obvious that God permitted, under the Old Testament, multiple wives, but that it was never His perfect will for man. We must keep in mind that the people under the Old Testament – just like the people under Islam! – were not Christians. In other words, they were not born again, according to John 3:3. Under the New Testament, the principle stated in Genesis 2:24 was reinstated, according to 1 Corinthians 7:2. So to compare Islam, which sanctioned multiple wives, to Judaism under the Old Testament would be somewhat accurate, but neither Old Testament Judaism or Islamic practices of multiple wives are sanctioned under the New Covenant, nor was it God's decreed will according to Genesis 2:24.

a Christian married to a non-Christian — that's God's definition of a mixed marriage! As for Hagar, God didn't have a problem with Sarai giving her Egyptian maid to Abram, the father of the faithful.

Now, let me tell you something you may not know. The word *Egypt* means "Mizraim," and Mizraim was one of Ham's sons. Remember we read in Psalm 105:23, that Jacob dwelt in the land of Ham! Mizraim was Ham's son. And the name *Mizraim* translates out of Hebrew to English as "Egypt." Now let's look at this in Genesis 10:6: **The sons of Ham *were* Cush, Mizraim, Put, and Canaan.** Could we not then, read that verse like this: "The sons of Ham were Cush, EGYPT, Put, and Canaan?" The land of Ham is the land of black, but the Church never told us that.

Let me repeat: Mizraim was the second son of Ham and the name *Mizraim* is the Hebrew word for Egypt. There has been a tremendous campaign in movies and literature to portray Egypt as white. Only recently did we have a movie, *The Prince of Egypt*, where most of the characters were dark-skinned — and that was an animated movie! It is true there were invasions by white-skinned peoples, but when Egypt was founded, after the tower of Babel, when the languages were confused and the people spread out, Ham's sons went into that part of Africa called Egypt, or Mizraim, the land of black.

In Genesis 25:1-6, we have another interesting revelation:

1   **Abraham again took a wife, and her name *was* Keturah.**

2   **And she bore him Zimran, Jokshan, Medan, Midian, Ishbak and Shuah.**

3   **Jokshan begot Sheba and Dedan. And the sons of Dedan were Asshurim, Letushim, and Leummim.**

4   **And the sons of Midian *were* Ephah, Epher, Hanoch, Abidah, and Eldaah. All these *were* the children of Keturah.**

5   And Abraham gave all that he had to Isaac.

6   But Abraham gave gifts to the sons of the concubines which Abraham had; and while he was still living he sent them eastward, away from Isaac his son, to the country of the east.

We don't know that much about Keturah. There is not much said about her in the Bible. Abraham had more children by this woman than he had by Hagar and Sarai. Six nations came out of Keturah. Since we cannot find the genealogy of Keturah in the Bible, we have to trace her lineage through the names of her descendants. In Genesis 25:3, again, **Jokshan begot Sheba and Dedan. And the sons of Dedan were Asshurim, Letushim, and Leummim.**

Jokshan was the second child of Keturah, so Sheba and Dedan were grandchildren of Abraham and Keturah. These two grandchildren possess names that belong to Cushites, or black people.[2] Look again at Genesis 10:6: **The sons of Ham** *were* **Cush, Mizraim, Put, and Canaan.**

Recall that Noah only pronounced his curse on Canaan, not Cush, Mizraim, or Put. The word *Cush* means Ethiopia. What color are the people in Ethiopia? So Cushites were not cursed, yet they were black. This means that if Cush was the father of black races, Cush himself was never "cursed" with "blackness." Keep this in mind — Cush was not cursed![3] Now look at Genesis 10:7:

---

[2] See Chapter 1 of Volume 2 of *Race, Religion & Racism* for a discussion of the fact that *Ham* meant "black" and that Hagar, being an Egyptian, was black. Any descendants of Ham, including those with Canaanite names, would be black-skinned.

[3] This fact alone destroys the notion that black skin was the "curse of Ham," and its corollary notion that slavery was associated with black skin.

The sons of Cush *were* Seba, Havilah, Sabtah, Raamah, and Sabtechah; and the sons of Raamah *were* Sheba and Dedan.

In this verse, Sheba and Dedan are described as being from the Cushite line. Since that is the case, we can safely conclude that the Sheba and Dedan we read of in the descendants of Keturah were also Cushites, meaning black. Now this is indeed strange, because Abraham was of the lineage of Shem, and a natural question would be, "what are these Cushites doing in a Shemite family?" The only conclusion is that Abraham must have married into a Cushite family through his wife Keturah.

It's also of interest to note the fact that God Almighty never scolded Abraham or got on his case for marrying into a Cushite (black) family. Apparently God isn't opposed to interracial marriage. The question is, are you? If you are, why would it matter to you when it doesn't matter to God Almighty who created you? Israelites and Egyptians married each other. Those were interracial marriages — mixed marriages.

There is another illustration that God, our Father, doesn't have and didn't have a problem with interracial marriages. In Leviticus 24:10, it reads:

Now the son of an Israelite woman, whose father *was* an Egyptian, went out among the children of Israel; and this Israelite *woman's* son and a man of Israel fought each other in the camp.

I wanted you to see that again God cleverly puts into the text, **Now the son of an Israelite woman...**when introducing this story about two boys who got in a fight. Why tell us one was an Israelite and one was an Egyptian? What difference does it make? These are the kinds of things that Christians read and miss, or don't read at all. Over and over, God is telling us that He doesn't have a problem with mixed or interracial marriages. Look again: **Now the son of an Israelite woman,**

whose father was an Egyptian…. That is a mixed marriage, right in the camp of Israel.

In Genesis 41:45, we have another important illustration of God honoring an interracial marriage:

> **And Pharaoh called Joseph's name Zaphnath-Paaneah. And he gave him as a wife Asenath, the daughter of Poti-Pherah priest of On. So Joseph went out over *all* the land of Egypt.**

The priest of On was an Egyptian, and the Egyptians were people of color. They were black, not white, despite the fact that many movies have portrayed the Egyptians as white.

In the movie *The Ten Commandments*, Yul Brynner and the rest of the Egyptians were white. It is getting somewhat better. As I said, in the animated movie *The Prince of Egypt*, the Egyptians were dark, and in the movie *The Mummy*, all the Egyptians except the high priest/mummy were dark-skinned and black-skinned people. But traditionally, most Americans have grown up with a view of the Egyptians as white people. That is historically untrue.

Let's deal with Jacob for a moment. Remember Jacob had twelve sons, and one of them was named Joseph. His brothers were jealous of him and sold him into slavery. That sounds familiar! Joseph ended up in Egypt, the land of Ham — or, we could say, the land of black. Joseph was a man of God. He walked in the knowledge he had at that time, and God honored and protected him. He was a servant for an Egyptian household and the woman of the house tried to seduce him, but Joseph would have none of it, and he fled her presence. Scorned, she spread lies about Joseph, telling her husband that Joseph had attacked her. The woman's husband, believing her lies, threw Joseph into prison. God worked while Joseph was in prison to give him favor with the warden. Ultimately, God freed Joseph because of Joseph's interpretation of a dream that Pharaoh had.

At that point, Joseph was given an Egyptian wife from Pharaoh. Joseph was from Jacob, and Jacob from Abraham. They were from the Shemite line. Shem, Ham, Japheth — those were the three sons of Noah. So here is a Shemite marrying an Egyptian, who came out of Mizraim, one of Ham's sons. Joseph had two sons by this woman, Asenath: Manasseh and Ephraim. Let's look at Genesis 41:50-52:

> **50 And to Joseph were born *two* sons before the years of famine came, whom Asenath, the daughter of Poti-Pherah priest of On, bore to him.**
>
> **51 Joseph called the name of the firstborn Manasseh: "For God has made me forget all my toil and all my father's house."**
>
> **52 And the name of the second he called Ephraim: "For God has caused me to be fruitful in the land of my affliction."**

Going back to Verse 50, it says, **And to Joseph were born two sons….** That is the subject of the verse: the fact that Joseph had two sons, period. But notice how God always keeps before us the fact of where these sons came from? This is so we won't be misled about who these people were:

> **And to Joseph were born two sons before the years of famine came, whom Asenath, the daughter of Poti-Pherah priest of On, bore to him.**

Did you notice that? God had already told us that in Verse 45 — that Joseph's wife was named Asenath. We also knew her father was Poti-Pherah, priest of On. Why does God keep telling us this? Because God wants us to zero in on the fact that she was an Egyptian, and God didn't have any problem with a Shemite and an Egyptian marrying and having children.

Not only that but — are you ready for this? — Manasseh and Ephraim became leaders of the Jewish tribes sent as spies into the land of Canaan. I wonder how many Jewish families have told their children that there were some black Jews? I wonder if Jewish families tell their children that there was an all-black tribe?

The fact that this has been here all along is what sticks in my craw. For years the Church has encouraged this image that all the Jews were lily white and spoke with British accents. The Bible has been used to attack marriage between the races, to keep one group superior and another group inferior. How many people have died and gone to hell while looking at Blacks and Whites fight, saying, "You claim to have the answer and look how you are treating each other!" I wonder if in eternity these people will stand and give a testimony that they would have come to Christ, but they saw all the race hatred and the infighting. They saw the discrepancy between the fact that Jesus is the way, yet the Church is divided over something no one had any control over, the color of one's skin.

Let's return to Joseph. Remember, he was a Shemite, and the Egyptians came from Ham, so when Joseph, a Shemite, married an Egyptian, that was an interracial marriage. Joseph had two sons, Manasseh and Ephraim. In Numbers 13:1-2 we find an interesting revelation:

1   **And the Lord spoke to Moses, saying,**

2   **"Send men to spy out the land of Canaan, which I am giving to the children of Israel; from each tribe of their fathers you shall send a man, every one a leader among them."**

Question: How many children did Jacob have? Twelve. They became known as the children of Israel, because Jacob's name was changed to Israel. So there were twelve tribes. Let's look at Verse 2 again: **"Send men to spy out the land of Canaan, which I am giving to the children of Israel** ["Children of Israel," I want you to keep that phrase in mind.]; **from each tribe of their fathers you shall send a man...."** Since there were twelve tribes, that means that there were twelve men. Can you agree with that? Now pay close attention:

> 3   **So Moses sent them from the Wilderness of Paran according to the command of the LORD, all of them men who *were* heads of the children of Israel.**

Now, who did we say the Israelites were? The Jews, right? Let's check these next verses carefully, Numbers 13:4-16:

> 4   **Now these *were* their names: from the tribe of Reuben, Shammua the son of Zaccur;**
>
> 5   **from the tribe of Simeon, Shaphat the son of Hori;**
>
> 6   **from the tribe of Judah, Caleb the son of Jephunneh;**
>
> 7   **from the tribe of Issachar, Igal the son of Joseph;**
>
> 8   **from the tribe of Ephraim....**

Ephraim was a tribe of Israel and Ephraim was the son of an Egyptian and a Shemite, which means an interracial couple. The Egyptians were black, so Ephraim had to have some black in him!

> 8   **from the tribe of Ephraim, Hoshea the son of Nun;**
>
> 9   **from the tribe of Benjamin, Palti the son of Raphu;**
>
> 10   **from the tribe of Zebulun, Gaddiel the son of Sodi;**

11   from the tribe of Joseph, *that is*, from the tribe
of Manasseh....

That's one of Joseph's boys, right? Manasseh was a tribe of
Israel. And if they were ever a tribe, they would have to be a tribe
today!

11   from the tribe of Joseph, *that is*, from the tribe
of Manasseh, Gaddi the son of Susi;

12   from the tribe of Dan, Ammiel the son of
Gemalli;

13   from the tribe of Asher, Sethur the son of
Michael;

14   from the tribe of Naphtali, Nahbi the son of
Vophsi;

15   from the tribe of Gad, Geuel the son of Machi.

16   These *are* the names of the men whom Moses
sent to spy out the land. And Moses called
Hoshea the son of Nun, Joshua.

White people and black people, take note: We were in the
group that spied out the Promised Land. Now they didn't tell us that.
White people didn't tell black people that and black people didn't
know it. **These *are* the names of the men whom Moses sent to spy out
the land.**

Anyone ever hear of Joshua? He fought the battle of Jericho.
Like me, you always thought that Joshua was white. Wrong! Joshua was
black. Look at Verse 16 again: **These *are* the names of the men whom
Moses sent to spy out the land. And Moses called Hoshea the son
of Nun, Joshua.** Where did Hoshea, or Joshua, come from? According
to Verse 8: **from the tribe of Ephraim, Hoshea the son of Nun....**
Well, Nun came from Ephraim. And where did Ephraim come from?

From that black Egyptian woman Asenath and that Shemite man Joseph. And I'm here to tell you, from genetic experience, that if there is black in the genetic makeup, the children are not going to come out European white. They may be light, but not European white. Joshua was one of those sent out to be a spy in the Promised Land.

Our heavenly Father did not leave black people out of the Bible. We are not an afterthought with God. He didn't just wake up one morning and say, "Oh, My, I must do something about those black folk." No! We were in the plan from the beginning. And maybe, just maybe, that's why there are more people of color on the planet than there are people who are not of color.

I've traveled all over the world to minister. I went to India and I saw folk there blacker than me. I mean black skin — not sun-tanned skin, but black skin. Straight black hair. And then I saw some of them with bushy hair and black skin. All over India. All over Africa. All over the islands of the sea. All over the Caribbean, and millions of them here in America. Go to the Fiji Islands and they're not white-skinned. Go to Tonga and they're not white-skinned. All I'm saying is that God must have a purpose in this, because there are more darker-skinned people on the planet than lighter-skinned people. Or, as I like to say, God must like chocolate cake because He made a lot of it.

In 1 Chronicles 7:22-27, it says:

22   **Then Ephraim their father mourned many days, and his brethren came to comfort him.**

23   **And when he went in to his wife, she conceived and bore a son; and he called his name Beriah, because tragedy had come upon his house.**

24   **Now his daughter *was* Sheerah, who built Lower and Upper Beth Horon and Uzzen Sheerah;**

25   **and Rephah *was* his son, *as well* as Resheph, and Telah his son, Tahan his son,**

26   Laadan his son, Ammihud his son, Elishama his son,

27   Nun his son, and Joshua his son.

It's amazing. How many years have we skipped over these genealogies, thinking, "There's nothing interesting in there." Well, it's very interesting! Don't you realize that after Moses left the scene, the man in charge of all twelve tribes was Joshua, the son of Nun, who came out of Ephraim, who was the child of an Egyptian and a Shemite, Joseph's son?

Jacob, or Israel, was the head of his family. The twelve tribes came out of Jacob, and Jacob accepted Ephraim and Manasseh as his own sons. We find this recorded in Genesis 48:1-5:

1   Now it came to pass after these things that Joseph was told, "Indeed your father *is* sick"; and he took with him his *two* sons, Manasseh and Ephraim.

2   And Jacob was told, "Look, your son Joseph is coming to you"; and Israel [or Jacob] strengthened himself and sat up on the bed.

3   Then Jacob said to Joseph: "God Almighty appeared to me at Luz in the land of Canaan and blessed me,

4   "and said to me, 'Behold, I will make you fruitful and multiply you, and I will make of you a multitude of people, and give this land to your descendants after you *as* an everlasting possession.'

5   "And now your two sons, Ephraim and Manasseh, who were born to you in the land of Egypt before I came to you in Egypt, *are*

mine; as Reuben and Simeon, they shall be mine."

Jacob took those two black boys in, just like they were his own blood, because they were, they were from his son. It made no difference. He said, "they're mine," just like Simeon and Reuben, whom he actually fathered. Jacob didn't have a problem taking Manasseh and Ephraim. What's the Church's problem? And Jacob wasn't even born again. Jacob wasn't even filled with the Spirit. And yet he could take those two black boys into his family and say, "they're mine."

Manasseh is not only mentioned in the Old Testament, but Manasseh is mentioned in the New Testament. Every time I think about it I kick myself and say, "How could you have been so ignorant, so blind as not to have seen God's purpose?" And I have read the New Testament over and over, more times than I can count, and I still didn't see it.

Let's read in the New Testament about Manasseh, this son of an interracial marriage. So if it's New Testament, then that means it's for us. We find it in Revelation 7:1-6:

1   After these things I saw four angels standing at the four corners of the earth, holding the four winds of the earth, that the wind should not blow on the earth, on the sea, or on any tree.

2   Then I saw another angel ascending from the east, having the seal of the living God. And he cried with a loud voice to the four angels to whom it was granted to harm the earth and the sea,

3   saying, "Do not harm the earth, the sea, or the trees till we have sealed the servants of our God on their foreheads."

4   And I heard the number of those who were
     sealed. One hundred *and* forty-four thousand
     of all the tribes of the children of Israel *were*
     sealed:

Notice that it does not say that 144,000 of all the "tribes of earth," but the tribes of the "children of Israel." This is a special group for a special situation. The emphasis I want to make and that I want us to see is that these were the children of Israel, whom we have come to know as the Jews.

4   And I heard the number of those who were
     sealed. One hundred *and* forty-four thousand
     of all the tribes of the children of Israel *were*
     sealed:

5   of the tribe of Judah twelve thousand *were*
     sealed; of the tribe of Reuben twelve thousand
     were sealed; of the tribe of Gad twelve
     thousand *were* sealed;

6   of the tribe of Asher twelve thousand *were*
     sealed; of the tribe of Naphtali twelve thousand
     were sealed; of the tribe of Manasseh twelve
     thousand *were* sealed;

Of whom? Of the tribe of Manasseh! Manasseh was a tribe and twelve thousand were sealed out of that tribe and that tribe was called a tribe of the children of Israel. We're in there! Probably many Jews don't even know that Manasseh was one of Joseph's sons who was the result of an Egyptian and a Shemite marriage. So from a scriptural point of view we've got relatives in Israel. I realize there are some people who talk about the black Jews, the Falashas, who come from Ethiopia. I don't know all the history there, but I'm going by what the Bible says, and it says our relatives are among those tribes sealed.

Our heavenly Father wants all of His children to be informed about their origin — about who they are and how He sees them. Consequently, He has placed in His Word all of the necessary information for us to be able to trace our origin through the genealogy. If origin and genealogy were not important, why did God put them in the Bible? If it weren't important to know the lineage that Jesus came from, then why did Matthew and Luke take the time to write down the genealogy about Jesus' ancestors? If it weren't important, why tell us? And if He put it in His Word, He must want us to know it. If it's in there and we don't know it, we have no one to blame but ourselves.

I believe if the Church had done its homework, we never would have had black slavery in America. The Church would never have been divided along racial and ethnic lines. Jesus probably would have already come back. The gospel would have been spread all over the world. But the thing that has hindered its spread has been the ignorance on the part of the body of Christ. It has stifled the Holy Spirit from being able to work through the body of Christ, as He worked through Jesus Christ when He walked the earth. We are the body of Christ and we should be representing Jesus, instead of our own preconceived racial and ethnic agendas.

Look at it this way: When people treat other people as inferior, they are really bringing an accusation against God, because God created us all. If there is anything inferior about anyone — any part of humanity — then it had to come from God. And, as I've said before, if they got it from God, then there must be some inferiority in God. Jesus said that the tree is known by its fruit. Whatever is in the fruit is the result of what is in the tree. God is the tree, and we, men, are the fruit, so if there is inferiority here, it had to come from God. I don't know if you are ready to accuse God of inferiority.

Honest people want the truth, and they will receive this teaching. People who want the status quo won't receive it. They'll chafe a bit. But people who want the truth, the whole truth, and nothing but the truth will rejoice at getting this information. God is not a respecter of persons, and He didn't make any creatures inferior, nor did He make any superior.

Consider a man named Jethro. In Exodus 18:1-6, it says:

1   **And Jethro, the priest of Midian, Moses' father-in-law, heard of all that God had done for Moses and for Israel His people — that the Lord had brought Israel out of Egypt.**

2   **Then Jethro, Moses' father-in-law, took Zipporah, Moses' wife, after he had sent her back,**

3   **with her two sons, of whom the name of one *was* Gershom (for he said, "I have been a stranger in a foreign land")**

4   **and the name of the other *was* Eliezer (for *he said*, "The God of my father *was* my help, and delivered me from the sword of Pharaoh");**

5   **and Jethro, Moses' father-in-law, came with his sons and his wife to Moses in the wilderness, where he was encamped at the mountain of God.**

6   **Now he had said of Moses, "I, your father-in-law Jethro, am coming to you with your wife and her two sons with her."**

We see that this man Jethro, was Moses' father-in-law. I wanted to establish that fact. In Volume 2 we discussed how Moses had married an Ethiopian woman, and Aaron and Miriam, Moses' brother and sister, had criticized him. God struck Miriam with leprosy as a result of coming against God's anointed.

In Numbers, Chapter 10, we find another important fact. We'll begin reading at Verse 29, where we find: **Now Moses said to Hobab the son of Reuel....** This Reuel was actually Jethro, Moses' father-in-law, which is revealed in the latter part of this verse. Let's look at it in detail, Numbers 10:29-32:

29   Now Moses said to Hobab the son of Reuel
the Midianite, Moses' father-in-law, "We are
setting out for the place of which the LORD
said, 'I will give it to you.' Come with us, and
we will treat you well; for the LORD has
promised good things to Israel."

30   And he said to him, "I will not go, but I will
depart to my *own* land and to my relatives."

31   So *Moses* said, "Please do not leave, inasmuch
as you know how we are to camp in the
wilderness, and you can be our eyes.

32   "And it shall be, if you go with us — indeed it
shall be — that whatever good the LORD will
do to us, the same we will do to you."

The Midianites were people of color, and Hobab was Jethro's
son. Midianites were members of a Canaanite tribe. In other words,
the Midianites were people of color. Moses, the Shemite, was telling
this man Hobab, come and go with us, you can be our eyes. In other
words, you will be able to lead us through this area, because you
know this area well. Moses was saying to this black man, come and
be our eyes. That's awesome.

But Hobab said he was going to his own land and his rela-
tives. Now the question might arise, Did Hobab ultimately go with
Moses and the children of Israel? To find out, we need to look at
Judges, Chapter 1. Before we start, though, let me point out that in
Bible times, people might be known by several different names.
Jethro, as we just saw, was also called Reuel. It is the same man.
And Jethro was a Midianite, but the Midianites also went by an-
other name.

In Judges 1:16, it says:

**Now the children of the Kenite, Moses' father-in-law,
went up from the City of Palms with the children of**

**Judah into the Wilderness of Judah, which *lies* in the
South *near* Arad; and they went and dwelt among
the people.**

Apparently Moses' father-in-law and his family did not go back
to their land, but accompanied the children of Israel. I would have to
believe that Hobab went with them. Now, the word *Kenite* literally
means "Midianite," and the Midianites were people of color, because
they were descendants of Canaan.

Did you know that a black man wrote one of the books of
the Bible? Zephaniah was a black man, though most people don't
know that. We've been led to think that Blacks made no contributions to the Bible. What is more tragic is that the Church has
squelched knowledge of the role of black people and their contributions. Zephaniah 1:1:

**The word of the LORD which came to Zephaniah the
son of Cushi, the son of Gedaliah, the son of Amariah,
the son of Hezekiah, in the days of Josiah the son of
Amon, king of Judah.**

Almost all serious students of the Bible, and certainly all
ministers, know about *Strong's Concordance*. Most of them believe
Strong as much as they believe the Bible. If Strong says it, it's so! In
Strong's Concordance, number 3508, the word *Cushi* or *Ethiopian*
is defined as "the name of a son of Ham and of his territory; also of
an Israelite." The word is sometimes spelled *Chush* or *Cush* or
Ethiopia. Do you have any idea what color Ethiopians are?

Zephaniah was from the lineage of Cush, and Cush was one
of Ham's boys. That's exciting to me, after having been told all my
life that black people had never made any positive contribution to
anything. Apparently God thought they did and included Zephaniah
in the Bible.

In the book of Jeremiah 38:7, we see: **Now Ebed-Melech the
Ethiopian....** Even if we didn't read another word, we know that we

are not talking about a Native American. This isn't a red man or a yellow man. In Jeremiah 38:7-13, it says:

> 7   **Now Ebed-Melech the Ethiopian, one of the eunuchs, who was in the king's house, heard that they had put Jeremiah in the dungeon. When the king was sitting at the Gate of Benjamin,**

> 8   **Ebed-Melech went out of the king's house and spoke to the king, saying:** [Now remember the Ethiopians were Cushites, and keep in mind that Cush was Ham's son, and that Ham was black. Here is a black man who had the ear of the king.]

> 9   **"My lord the king, these men have done evil in all that they have done to Jeremiah the prophet, whom they have cast into the dungeon, and he is likely to die from hunger in the place where he is. For *there is* no more bread in the city."**

> 10   **Then the king commanded Ebed-Melech the Ethiopian....**

I pointed this out before, but we need to emphasize it again. By now, I hope you have begun to see these things. Notice how God emphasizes people's ethnicity? He didn't have to tell us that Ebed-Melech was an Ethiopian, and certainly didn't have to tell us more than once. Why not say, "Ebed-Melech...."? Why keep saying, "Ebed-Melech the Ethiopian?" He puts this in the Bible so that black people would realize they are a part of God's equation. They are not an afterthought. And it is in here for white people, too, so that white people would know that Blacks are important — important to God. And therefore we should be important to each other.

> 10   **Then the king commanded Ebed-Melech the Ethiopian, saying, "Take from here thirty men**

with you, and lift Jeremiah the prophet out of
the dungeon before he dies."

11   So Ebed-Melech took the men with him and
      went into the house of the king under the
      treasury, and took from there old clothes and
      old rags, and let them down by ropes into the
      dungeon to Jeremiah.

Where did this black man get enough sense to know what to
let down to the prophet so that the prophet could get out of there?
What do old clothes and old rags have to do with anything?

12   Then Ebed-Melech the Ethiopian said of
      Jeremiah, "Please put these old clothes and
      rags under your armpits, under the ropes."
      And Jeremiah did so.

13   So they pulled Jeremiah up with ropes and
      lifted him out of the dungeon. And Jeremiah
      remained in the court of the prison.

Jeremiah was rescued by a black man, Ebed-Melech the
Ethiopian, who interceded with the king on his behalf.
While we are in Jeremiah, let's go to Chapter 39, Verses 15
to 18:

15   Meanwhile the word of the LORD had come to
      Jeremiah while he was shut up in the court of
      the prison, saying,

16   "Go and speak to Ebed-Melech the Ethio-
      pian...."

There it is again. Why does God keep telling us he's an
Ethiopian? A black man! Why doesn't He just use the name, Ebed-
Melech? That's all he has to say. But He keeps saying, "the Ethiopian."

This is the Lord telling Jeremiah to go speak to this Cushite —
this Ethiopian.

> 16   **"Go and speak to Ebed-Melech, the Ethiopian,
> saying, 'Thus says the LORD of hosts, the God
> of Israel: "Behold, I will bring My words upon
> this city for adversity and not for good, and
> they shall be *performed* in that day before you.**

> 17   **"But I will deliver you in that day," says the
> LORD, "and you shall not be given into the hand
> of the men of whom you *are* afraid.**

> 18   **"For I will surely deliver you, and you shall
> not fall by the sword; but your life shall be as
> a prize to you, because you have put your trust
> in Me," says the LORD.'"**

It looks like the Lord was on this man's side, because this
man was on the Lord's side. So Even though Jerusalem would fall to
the Babylonians, Ebed-Melech survived. That's exactly what
happened historically. Now the reason for this — I want to emphasize
it again — is that the Lord stated that Ebed-Melech trusted Him.
This Cushite trusted in the Lord and was delivered. That shows you
that God is no respecter of persons.

Here's what's awesome about this. This man was given a
prophetic word by God through the Prophet Jeremiah, to let him
know that he would be spared when the city of Jerusalem was taken
by the Babylonians. Think about it: Here is a black man, an Ethiopian, a Cushite, who is going to be saved. Do you know why the city
of Jerusalem was captured, overrun, and taken by the Babylonians?
Because of the Shemites' disobedience to God. Yet this man found
favor with the Lord because he trusted Him when the children of
Israel were trusting in their idols.

It isn't just in the Old Testament that we find black people.
It's amazing how unobservant the Church has been. But you know,

when you're consumed with a superiority mentality or an inferiority mentality, you don't always see things clearly. The truth can be in front of your eyes, yet you miss it. Take the Gospel of Matthew: Matthew, part of the New Testament, gives us clues that, again, are obvious. It is sad that people have missed this evidence for so many years. Matthew 10:1-4:

1   **And when He had called His twelve disciples to** *Him*, **He gave them power** *over* **unclean spirits, to cast them out, and to heal all kinds of sickness and all kinds of disease.**

2   **Now the names of the twelve apostles are these: first, Simon, who is called Peter, and Andrew his brother; James the** *son* **of Zebedee, and John his brother;**

3   **Philip and Bartholomew; Thomas and Matthew the tax collector; James the** *son* **of Alphaeus, and Lebbaeus, whose surname was Thaddaeus,**

4   **Simon the Canaanite....**

We've been reading this for years and never made the connection. Look at this: **Simon the Canaanite....** Here is what is interesting and significant about this. If you don't think that it should be important to you, it was important to God. There are twelve disciples. Each name is given. Only with one man are you given his origin, and he was a Canaanite. Tell me why! See how we've missed it? It's absolutely amazing. Why is it that the only one whose ethnicity is mentioned specifically is the Canaanite, whose origin is derived from Canaan, the son of Ham?

I read this for years and never saw it. I ran right over it because of preconditioning. Three times in the 38th Chapter of Jeremiah we are told that Ebed-Melech is an Ethiopian. It seems reasonable to tell us once. Why does God keep telling us? Because God knew men, and he knew that through brainwashing and acculturation, we, the Church, black and white alike, would miss it.

All of the twelve apostles are named, but we only are told the ethnic origin of one, Simon the Canaanite. That is truly interesting. God put this in just for those of you who thought you didn't need this. God knew racist garbage was going to come, even in eternity past, He knew it would come. He knew that this prejudice issue would divide the Church, so He put it in there as a signpost, so we could all know the truth. Instead, we missed it. Black folks missed it, white folks missed it, everyone missed it.

And there is more. Look at Acts 8:26-39:

26   Now an angel of the Lord spoke to Philip, saying, "Arise and go toward the south along the road which goes down from Jerusalem to Gaza." This is desert.

27   So he arose and went. And behold, a man of Ethiopia, a eunuch of great authority under Candace the queen of the Ethiopians [here's another Cushite], who had charge of all her treasury, and had come to Jerusalem to worship [this Cushite was a proselyte to Judaism],

28   was returning. And sitting in his chariot, he was reading Isaiah the prophet.

29   Then the Spirit said to Philip, "Go near and overtake this chariot."

30   So Philip ran to him, and heard him reading the prophet Isaiah, and said, "Do you understand what you are reading?"

31   And he said, "How can I, unless someone guides me?" And he asked Philip to come up and sit with him.

32   The place in the Scripture which he read was this: *"He was led as a sheep to the slaughter; and as a lamb before its shearer is silent, so He opened not His mouth.*

33   *In His humiliation His justice was taken away, and who will declare His generation? For His life is taken from the earth."*

34   So the eunuch answered Philip and said, "I ask you, of whom does the prophet say this, of himself or of some other man?"

35   Then Philip opened his mouth, and beginning at this Scripture, preached Jesus to him.

How did Philip happen to come into contact with this Cushite? The Holy Spirit told him to go. He didn't say avoid the Cushite because he was black. He didn't say segregate him because he's black. He said, "Go to him." Acts 8:36-39:

36   Now as they went down the road, they came to some water. And the eunuch said, "See, *here is* water. What hinders me from being baptized?"

37   Then Philip said, "If you believe with all your heart, you may." And he answered and said, "I believe that Jesus Christ is the Son of God."

38   So he commanded the chariot to stand still. And both Philip and the eunuch went down into the water, and he [Philip] baptized him [the Cushite].

39   Now when they came up out of the water, the Spirit of the Lord caught Philip away, so that the eunuch saw him no more; and he went on his way rejoicing.

Jesus said in Luke 19:10 that He **"has come to seek and to save that which was lost."** The Ethiopian was lost — I mean, you talk about important! God arranged a special ministry, a personal meeting with pastor Philip, for this Ethiopian, for this Cushite. God could have called him back to the Temple in Jerusalem. Instead, He had Philip meet him on the road by himself. God gave him a special audience with Philip all by himself so that Philip could preach Jesus to him. Don't tell me black people aren't important to God!

Another story appears in Mark 15:16-21:

16   **Then the soldiers led Him away into the hall called Praetorium, and they called together the whole garrison.**

17   **And they clothed Him with purple; and they twisted a crown of thorns, put it on His *head*,**

18   **and began to salute Him, "Hail, King of the Jews!"**

19   **Then they struck Him on the head with a reed and spat on Him; and bowing the knee, they worshiped Him.**

20   **And when they had mocked Him, they took the purple off Him, put His own clothes on Him, and led Him out to crucify Him.**

21   **Then they compelled a certain man, Simon a Cyrenian, the father of Alexander and Rufus, as he was coming out of the country and passing by, to bear His cross.**

Question: Was Simon of Cyrene a black man? We'll soon see. But for now, look at Acts 2:5-10:

5   **And there were dwelling in Jerusalem Jews, devout men, from every nation under heaven.**

6   And when this sound occurred, the multitude came together, and were confused, because everyone heard them speak in his own language.

7   Then they were all amazed and marveled, saying to one another, "Look, are not all these who speak Galileans?

8   "And how *is it that* we hear, each in our own language in which we were born?

9   "Parthians and Medes and Elamites, those dwelling in Mesopotamia, Judea and Cappadocia, Pontus and Asia,

10   "Phrygia and Pamphylia, Egypt and the parts of Libya adjoining Cyrene, visitors from Rome, both Jews and proselytes,"

So Cyrene is adjoining Libya. What color are Libyans today? They aren't white, that's for sure. But look at Acts 13:1 for further confirmation:

Now in the church that was at Antioch there were certain prophets and teachers: Barnabas, Simeon who was called Niger, Lucius of Cyrene, Manaen who had been brought up with Herod the tetrarch, and Saul.

So the question is, Were these men from Cyrene black? It is a possibility, but we can't be absolutely sure. Why does the Holy Spirit keep mentioning Cyrene? William Smith's *Dictionary of the Bible* says Cyrene was:

The principle city of that part of northern Africa, which was anciently called Cyrenaica, lying between Carthage and Egypt, and corresponding with the modern Tripoli.

> Though on the African coast, it was a Greek city and the
> Jews were settled there in large numbers....[4]

Since Cyrene was located in modern-day Libya, and is populated by darker peoples, it is possible that the men we just read about — Simon, who carried the cross of Jesus, and Lucius the prophet — were both black. We can't know for sure, as many Greeks and Jews settled there. But that works both ways: If there was a substantial amount of movement between these Greek/Jewish/Roman colonies, it may mean that black people routinely moved from the African areas to Jewish trading cities as well. Again, we cannot be sure, in the absence of other specific evidence, that many people we read about were not black. It's doubtful that they were, given that it appears that the Holy Spirit has alerted us specifically to people of color, but it is not out of the realm of reason.

However, look again at Acts 13:1:

> **Now in the church that was at Antioch there were certain prophets and teachers: Barnabas, Simeon who was called Niger, Lucius of Cyrene, Manaen who had been brought up with Herod the tetrarch, and Saul.**

Whenever God mentions someone of color, He always mentions the person's pedigree. In other words, all He had to say was, **Barnabas, Simeon, Lucius, Manaen, who had been brought up with Herod the tetrarch, and Saul.** That doesn't say anything about ethnicity. But it is not worded that way. It says, **Barnabas, Simeon who was called Niger, Lucius of Cyrene....** Why didn't He tell us where the other men were from? Cyrene was in North Africa, and it's possible that Lucius was a man of color. Now notice the second man named Simeon was **called Niger**. If we go back to *Strong's*

---

[4] William Smith, *Dictionary of the Bible* (Nashville: T. Nelson, 1986), 132.

Concordance, we find: *"Niger, or Neeg'-er, of lat.or; Black, Niger, a Chr.:-Niger."*[5]

The word *Niger* means black. So this man Simeon was "Simeon who was called black." There was definitely one black man in the Church of Antioch, and he was a prophet and/or a teacher. That meant that he had a position of authority and anointing. Acts 13:2-3:

> **2   As they ministered to the Lord and fasted, the Holy Spirit said, "Now separate to Me Barnabas and Saul for the work to which I have called them."**
>
> **3   Then, having fasted and prayed, and laid hands on them, they sent *them* away.**

Who laid hands on Barnabas and Saul? Who sent them away? Simeon, Lucius, and Manaen laid hands on the Apostle Paul. That meant that Simeon who was called Niger (Simeon a black man), laid hands on Paul to send him out on his ministry assignment! When was the last time you laid hands on Billy Graham? This man was obviously anointed and in a position of power. A black man!

If you look at a map of Africa, right in the heart of the Continent there is a river called the Niger. Where do you think they got that name? France perhaps? Or do you think they got the name *Niger* from Sweden? I don't mean that unkindly, but to focus our attention. Where do you think Nigerians come from? Germany? The Niger River is in the land of black! Egypt, Africa, Niger! Simeon was a Niger. In fact, they called him black — notice it says, **Simeon who was called Niger....** Simeon who was called "the black man."

There is more interesting information in Acts, Chapter 21. Paul had come back to Jerusalem and the Church persuaded him to go with some other brothers into the temple for a period of

---

[5] Strong's, number 3526, 50.

purification. While there, some Jews from Asia saw him. Because Paul had been seen in the city with a Gentile, the Jews from Asia assumed he had brought a Gentile into the temple. So they rushed in and grabbed Paul and were about to kill him. The commander of the Roman garrison came with his soldiers and rescued Paul.

In Acts 21:31-37, it says:

31   Now as they were seeking to kill him [Paul], news came to the commander of the garrison that all Jerusalem was in an uproar.

32   He [the Roman commander] immediately took soldiers and centurions, and ran down to them. And when they saw the commander and the soldiers, they stopped beating Paul.

33   Then the commander came near and took him, and commanded *him* to be bound with two chains; and he asked who he was and what he had done.

34   And some among the multitude cried one thing and some another. So when he could not ascertain the truth because of the tumult, he commanded him [Paul] to be taken into the barracks.

35   When he reached the stairs, he had to be carried by the soldiers because of the violence of the mob.

36   For the multitude of the people followed after, crying out, "Away with him!"

37   Then as Paul was about to be led into the barracks, he said to the commander, "May I speak to you?" He replied, "Can you speak Greek?"

This is an interesting question that the commander asked. Paul must not have looked Greek. He must have looked much different than Greek, and that is why the commander asked, "Can you speak Greek?" That would be like me walking up to the average black man in America and asking him, "Do you speak Russian?" Let's continue in Acts 21:38:

> **"Are you not the Egyptian who some time ago stirred**
> **up a rebellion and led the four thousand assassins out**
> **into the wilderness?"**

How could this centurion have thought that Paul was an Egyptian, unless.... Do you suppose Paul *looked* like an Egyptian? First the commander said, "Do you speak Greek?" so he must have thought Paul did not look Greek. Then he asked him, "Are you not the Egyptian...?" We have always thought Paul was white, but whatever he looked like, he was dark enough to be mistaken for an Egyptian. Remember Egypt was called the land of black, because Ham was black, and Egypt was Ham's land.

Look at Exodus, where we have another interesting account. Moses, you remember, killed a man, thinking that his Israelite brethren would see him as their deliverer. Later, two Israelites were in an argument, and Moses tried to separate them, and one said, "Are you going to kill me as you killed the Egyptian yesterday?" So Moses fled, going into the wilderness, and finally ended up in Midian. Now look at Exodus 2:16-19:

> **16   Now the priest of Midian had seven daughters.**
> **And they came and drew water, and they filled**
> **the troughs to water their father's flock.**
>
> **17   Then the shepherds came and drove them**
> **away; but Moses stood up and helped them,**
> **and watered their flock.**
>
> **18   When they came to Reuel their father, he said,**
> **"How *is it that* you have come so soon today?"**

19   And they said, "An Egyptian delivered us from the hand of the shepherds, and he also drew enough water for us and watered the flock."

Moses was mistaken for an Egyptian? They said, **"An Egyptian delivered us...."** They didn't know where he had come from. The daughters didn't know the story of why he fled. So it must have been his appearance. Now in fairness, it could have been his clothing that gave him away. That is possible. But it also might have been his pigmentation. He was a Hebrew but was taken for an Egyptian!

At every point in the Bible, from Genesis to Revelation, we have seen the color of the Bible. The Word is full of color. Again, my mission has only been to deal with black and white issues, but I'm confident that God has placed every person in the Word, and other researchers can find other colors, other races, and other ethnic groups in the Bible. We have looked at the color of Jesus. We have seen color in the Bible. Now I'd like to turn to color in America, what I call, the "color of achievement."

10

The Color of Achievement

 Over the years, there has been such a tendency to overlook the achievements and even the very presence of black people in society that writer Ralph Ellison published a book called *Invisible Man*.[1] Since the 1950s, it has become somewhat more common to see black people in areas of sports or entertainment, but seldom in science, technology, and business. I think it would be educational, revealing, and inspiring for Blacks and Whites alike to know that people of color have made significant contributions to the development of the United States of America. The only black people most children ever read about in school are Booker T. Washington and George Washington Carver. But there are many others, although you have to look outside the mainstream textbooks to find them.

Again, this is useful, not so that black people feel better than anyone else, but so they feel good about themselves. Also, white people need to know that Blacks have not been a liability to society, but an integral part in advancing the United States, scientifically, technologically, and economically. A common perception is that only

---

[1] Ralph Ellison, *Invisible Man* (New York: Vintage, 1995 [1952]).

black people commit crimes, only black people have high illegitimacy rates, and only black people are on welfare.[2]

If you listen to the news, you'd think there were no white people on welfare. But these stereotypes get perpetuated partly because in the news business, it's easier to go to "the projects" for a quick shot of people on welfare than it is to go out to rural Oklahoma, or deep in the backwoods of Oregon, where there might be Whites on welfare. It is also easier to cover a drug bust in the ghetto than it is to follow the trail of a white man involved in some fraudulent business. Part of it is the nature of the news business, but part of it is deliberate deception. Most news reporters, anchors, and writers are white, and they've come at it with their own prejudices and stereotypes and it just perpetuates the problem. So it is helpful for us black people to find out about ourselves.

If one race in society has no examples of achievement, others naturally tend to get an attitude of superiority. Part of the problem, though, is that the dominant group starts to ignore or downplay achievements of others, making that superiority attitude worse. Black people have made significant contributions to civilization and to our country. For example, Benjamin Banneker, a black man, made the first clock in the American colonies, in 1754.[3] Banneker's father had been a slave. Banneker himself was allowed to enroll in a Quaker school, and he

---

[2] Actually, from 1950 to 1975, when illegitimacy rates in this country soared, they rose far faster among Whites than among Blacks, and overall there have always been more Whites in poverty than Blacks. But because Blacks tended to live in the cities, they were more easily targeted by welfare programs and, thus, were more easily counted. See George Gilder, *Wealth & Poverty* (New York: Basic Books, 1981); Larry Schweikart, *The Entrepreneurial Adventure: A History of Business in the United States* (Ft. Worth: Harcourt, 2000); Warren Brookes, *The Economy in Mind* (New York: Universe 1982), 157-169.

[3] Joan Potter with Constance Clayton, *African-American Firsts* (Elizabethtown, New York: Pinto Press, 1994), 233.

soon impressed everyone as a mathematical genius. He pioneered many crop-production methods, before becoming interested in the stars and skies. In 1792, he wrote an almanac, predicting weather and seasonal changes. When Banneker sent a letter to Secretary of State Thomas Jefferson, arguing that Blacks were the full intellectual equals of Whites, Jefferson continued the exchange. This ultimately led Jefferson to appoint Banneker to help develop plans for a new capital city called Washington, D.C. When the head designer left abruptly, the team members glumly concluded that they had to start from scratch, because Pierre L'Enfant, the man commissioned to head the job, had taken all the plans back to France. Banneker, however, had all the designs imprinted in his memory, and Washington D.C. literally sprang from Benjamin Banneker's mind.

Have you ever heard of the expression, "the real McCoy?" This term is related to a black man, Elijah McCoy, whose parents had escaped slavery and fled to Canada. McCoy returned to the United States to work in Ypsilanti, Michigan, where he was a fireman for the Michigan Central Railroad. This was no menial position, but was akin to a copilot on a modern airliner. Noticing that locomotives stopped frequently to cool their engines because of a weakness in the oil systems, McCoy invented an engine lubricator in 1872. It was so efficient that — imitation is the best form of flattery — a number of similar contraptions showed up. However, McCoy's lubricating system was of such high quality that people began to ask, "Is this the real McCoy?"

In 1920, at the age of 77, Elijah McCoy patented an air-brake lubricator and opened his own company.[4]

Andrew Jackson Beard, from Alabama, worked in the railroad industry at a time that connecting railroad cars was done by

---

[4] *African-Americans: Voices of Triumph* (Alexandria, Virginia: Time-Life Books, 1993), 132; Burton Folsom, "Real McCoy Showed Depth of Black Enterprise," *Detroit News*, February 28, 1996.

hand. Workers had to drop a steel pin through the connectors, and hands and legs were often crushed if the timing was not perfect. Beard patented a device in 1897 called the Jenny Coupler. Every child who has ever played with toy trains knows how this works. It is like two hands, one upside down, fingers gently curved into a hook. As the two "hands" meet, the "fingers" catch, connecting the two cars. Beard also patented many other inventions, including a steam-driven rotary engine and a double plow.[5]

Who invented the first railroad telegraph system? In 1887, Granville T. Woods patented a rail telegraph system designed to avert accidents by allowing messages to be sent between moving trains and railroad stations. Woods, who became known as the "black Edison," had secured more than sixty patents by the time he died in 1902. He also invented the "third rail" still used in subways today.[6]

A black man named Jan Matzeliger received a patent in 1883 for the first lasting machine that would turn out a complete shoe, while the first ironing board was invented and patented in 1892 by an African-American woman named Sarah Boone.[7] She had devised a narrow wooden board with a padded covering supported by legs that could be collapsed. Before Boone's invention, people ironed on tables or boards laid across chairs.

Let's get a little more technical than ironing boards and shoe machines. What about medical science? Ignorant black Africans couldn't know anything about medicine, could they? The extent of black people's medical knowledge would have to be the witch doctor, right? Wrong! Who performed the first open heart surgery? In 1893, an African-American doctor named Daniel Hale Williams made history for that feat. When James Cornish was stabbed in a bar

---

[5] "Andrew Jackson Beard," A Salute to Black Scientists and Inventors, Vol. 2 (Chicago: Empak Enterprises and Richard L. Green, n.d.), 6.

[6] Potter, 241-242.

[7] Potter, 241-242.

brawl and sent to Provident Hospital, Williams used an innovative technique to save his life. Without the aid of X-rays, antibiotics, or blood transfusions, the gifted surgeon made an incision in Cornish's chest and stitched up the wound. The patient recovered completely and the amazing operation made Williams famous.[8]

In the early days of the automobile, traffic was controlled by a policeman sitting in a little tower at intersections, manually operating stop and go signals. This changed when Garrett A. Morgan, a black man, after seeing an accident between an automobile and a horse-drawn carriage on a busy street, invented and patented the first automatic traffic light in November 1923. But already Morgan had come to the public's attention when he used a breathing device, which he invented in 1914, in a dramatic rescue. An explosion in a tunnel below Lake Erie trapped nearly 30 workers and filled the tunnel with smoke. Morgan and his brother, wearing the newly invented device called a "safety hood," went into the shaft and pulled the trapped men to safety. When fire officials around the country heard about the rescue, they put in orders for Morgan's safety hood. Many, however, canceled their orders when they learned of Morgan's color. The U.S. Army saw value in Morgan's invention, and after making a few improvements, had a portable gas mask that saved thousands of lives in World War I.[9]

Dr. Charles R. Drew, a researcher at Columbia University in New York City, set up the nation's first blood plasma bank. While at Columbia, he developed techniques for separating and preserving blood and found that plasma could be stored longer than whole blood. In 1929, Drew set up a plasma bank at Presbyterian Hospital, the first of its kind.[10] Dr. Benjamin S. Carson also made medical history when he was appointed director of pediatric neurosurgery at Johns

---

[8]   Potter, 241-242.
[9]   Potter, 245-246.
[10] Potter, 245-247.

Hopkins University Hospital in Baltimore in 1984 at the age of 33. He was the youngest person in the country to hold that position.

In 1985, he performed a medical procedure known as hemispherectomy, removing half the brain of a four-year-old girl who was suffering 150 seizures a day. The other half of her brain took over all functions, and she went on to grow and develop normally. Carson made news again in 1987 when he led the medical team that, for the first time, successfully separated Siamese twins joined at the head.[11]

Almost everyone knows white jockey Willie Shoemaker. But who was the first jockey to win the Kentucky Derby three times? A black rider. Interestingly, you seldom see black jockeys today. Years ago, however, they put black boys on the horses so that if the horse was wild and threw the rider off, the white boys would not get hurt. Once horse racing became a gambling event with high payoffs, Whites again entered the scene. Some of you might remember this: In certain homes you would see, on the front lawn, a miniature statue of a jockey — always black. If you don't know, you might have thought that was a put-down, but it was a historical testament to the fact that all jockeys were black at one time.

Considered the greatest jockey of the 19th Century, Isaac "Ike' Murphy, who was born near Lexington, Kentucky, in 1861. During his 20-year career, Murphy raced 1,412 times and won an astonishing 628 races. He won his first Kentucky Derby in 1884, winning again in 1890 and 1891.[12]

Another man with an affinity for horses, Bill Pickett, an African American, was born in Texas in 1860. He became one of the most popular rodeo performers of all time, inventing the art of bulldogging. He would ride after a steer, leap from his saddle — grabbing the horns of the steer — and wrestle it to the ground. Pickett and his

---

[11] Potter, 251.
[12] Potter, 259.

horse, Spradly, attracted crowds from around the country to see this new sport. He was inducted into the Cowboy Hall of Fame in 1971, the first black man to receive this honor.[13]

Dr. George F. Grant, a black graduate of Harvard University, invented the golf tee in 1899. Before this invention, golfers balanced the balls on mounds of dirt.[14]

Although no specific person is identified, in J.A. Rogers' book, *Sex and Race*, the author points out that "Archeologists generally agree that it was the Negro who first discovered the secret of iron."[15]

Blacks were a part of the Western frontier, too. James P. "Jim" Beckwourth was a free black "mountain man" who lived (to say the least) a colorful life. A trapper, army guide, saloon owner, and prospector, Beckwourth was welcomed into the Crow Indian tribe, and possibly became a war chief before leaving the tribe for employment as a trader on the Santa Fe Trail.[16] The role of black men and women in opening the American West is just now starting to be appreciated. It was a Negro from St. Domingo, Juan Dusable, who was the founder of the city of Chicago.

We tend to think of black people as being only in sports or entertainment, but Blacks have pioneered major businesses in the United States. Ever hear of a song called "You Keep Me Hangin' On," by the Supremes? Or "ABC" by the Jackson Five? Or "Lonely

---

[13] Potter, 264. Other information on Bill Pickett appears in "Rodeo," in Howard R. Lamar, ed., *The New Encyclopedia of the American West* (New Haven: Yale University Press, 1998), 972.

[14] Potter, 263.

[15] J. A. Rogers, *Sex and Race*, Vol. 1, 9th ed. (St. Petersburg: Helga M. Rogers, 1967), 48, and Vol. 2 (St. Petersburg: Helga M. Rogers, 1970), 177.

[16] Beckwourth, James Pierson in Lamar, 89-90; Elinor Wilson, *Jim Beckwourth: Black Mountain Man and War Chief of the Crows* (Norman: University of Oklahoma Press, 1972).

Teardrops" by Jackie Wilson? These hit songs were all written and developed under a business created by a black Detroit auto worker named Berry Gordy, Jr. Using money loaned to him by his mother — five hundred dollars she was going to use for a new couch — Gordy launched a record company called Motown Records.

He knew that if he only sold to black people he could only tap into 12 percent of the population, so from the outset Gordy was determined to "cross over" into white markets and get airplay on white radio stations. He hired tutors for his acts, gave them lessons in elocution and public relations, and insisted that they always look topnotch. Before long, not only were so-called white stations playing his groups — the Supremes, Smokey Robinson and the Miracles, and the Jackson Five — but Motown Records was dominating the nation's music charts. Gordy also pioneered a "play-time" rule that limited any song to just over two minutes, based on the attention span of youths. This rule remained in effect for nearly fifteen years. By 1972, Motown was the top black-owned business in America.[17]

Most people know of Michael Jordan, the basketball player. But do you know Michael Jordan, the businessman? He has developed his own line of cologne, clothes, ties, and of course, shoes. People who once would pay to see Jordan play basketball are now being employed by him in one of his many business spin-offs. By all accounts he is one of the richest men in all of sports — mainly because he approached basketball as a business.

Many women watch Oprah Winfrey, right? Oprah is likely the wealthiest black woman in America because she is a businesswoman. Her Harpo Productions is a model for achievement and success.

Do you know who Herman Cain is? He is a black man who owned Godfather's Pizza. How he came to own it, though, is a testimony to perseverance and vision. Cain was a mid-level executive at Pillsbury Foods. He had a good job, with middle-class perks, as head

---

[17] Schweikart, 397-398.

of the computer division. (That's mathematics and numbers, in case you don't realize it!) But he was ambitious, and wanted no less than the top position. When he approached his boss and asked, in essence, "How do I get your job?" the man was honest and said that at Pillsbury the company did not promote from the computer side — only from the food division, because that was where the corporation had its emphasis.

If Cain wanted the top job, he had to resign his position and start all over in the food side of things, literally learning the business from the ground up — as a counter person at Burger King! Cain relinquished a company car and an executive position to learn the burger business, and in a few weeks was the regional manager of the Burger King stores. Soon, he had impressed his supervisors so much that they made him the regional manager of the troubled Godfather's Pizza operations, in Pennsylvania. Cain not only turned the franchise around, but was named president in 1986 at only 40 years of age. When Godfather's came on the market, he assembled a team of backers and purchased the company, becoming CEO in 1988, and doubling the value of the company.[18]

In fact, one of the biggest misconceptions propagated in the history books about emancipation is that it freed black people to become workers. The notion is, "Well, now all those black slaves are free to negotiate their own wages." But there is a different way of looking at this: The Emancipation Proclamation, in essence, freed 3.5 million potential business owners and entrepreneurs. Why settle for "workin' for the man" when you can be "the man?" This was a type of bigotry of low expectations — that black people were free, true, but they were all going to stay employees of Whites. Not so!

You have people like Free Frank McWhorter, a slave who purchased his own freedom, then went on to found the town of New

---

[18] Schweikart, 520-521.

Philadelphia, Illinois, managing and owning several businesses.[19] The records of Dun & Bradstreet show that one-fifth of the enterprises in Virginia after the Civil War were owned and operated by black people.[20] Black entrepreneurs have not disappeared. *Ebony* founder John Johnson, Motown's Berry Gordy, media mogul Oprah Winfrey, and pizza king Herman Cain are creating jobs, generating wealth, and improving the material well-being of people all over the country, and, indeed, the world.

Now, everyone isn't cut out to own his or her own business. Some people — white and black — enjoy working for others because there is less pressure and responsibility. But it is a false picture to portray black people as only the servants of others, and never give them their due as scientists, architects, doctors, entrepreneurs, and pioneers.

There is plenty of information out there about the role of Blacks in our nation's history, and I hope that the little I've shared here will inspire you — both Blacks and Whites alike — to pursue the subject on your own. The more truth we know about each other, the easier it will be for us to create a fellowship with each other in Spirit and in truth. The world is dying and it needs the life that Jesus came to bring. But that truth can only be seen through the Church of the Lord Jesus Christ. We *are* the Church: men and women, boys and girls, from every nation, every color, every tribe, and every kindred. Jesus is counting on us. The world needs to see us as Christians, not as black, white, red, yellow, and brown. We are all God has. He is depending on us to proclaim the gospel.

But we've been more concerned about perpetuating our own overblown ideas about self-importance. We have been careful to present

---

[19] Juliet K. Walker, *Free Frank: A Black Pioneer on the Antebellum Frontier* (Lexington: University Press of Kentucky, 1983).

[20] See Robert C. Kenzer, "The Black Business Community in Post Civil War Virginia," *Southern Studies*, new series, 4 (Fall 1993), 229-252.

to the world that white is right and black better get back. This is what we have portrayed in the nation and in the Church. I've said this repeatedly in these three volumes on *Race, Religion & Racism*, but Jesus said it this way: **"You are the light of the world...."** He never said the "light of the Church." He said **"the light of the world,"** so people should be able to look at the Church and see light. Instead of light, we have been presenting division, prejudice, racism, and superiority/inferiority complexes. Jesus said **"You are the salt of the earth...."** He didn't say, "salt of the Church," but **"salt of the earth."** We have been keeping our light hidden under a bushel and it has allowed division to come up and cause great confusion. We have to walk together, to understand that we are one in Christ.

This is the reason, I believe, that God gave me the directive to share the things that I have shared in this book and the previous two volumes in this series. People are people are people. Everyone given the same opportunity and the same tools to work with will produce successfully. God gave mankind different talents and abilities, and no single ethnic group has all of it, although some have tried to act like they have. God would never do that. He'd be unwise to do that, because it would look like he was a respecter of persons. No, He has spread out the talents and abilities and gifts among all the peoples. The Church should be the one organism that displays and demonstrates to the world our unity. But we have been divided.

But I believe there is a new day coming, and in fact that new day is here. I believe that based on this teaching, along with others, we are going to come together and be the Church that the world needs to see and the Church that the Lord Jesus Christ intends for us to be. Jesus' words carry more truth today than ever before. Look at John 13:34-35:

> **34**   **"A new commandment I give to you, that you love one another; as I have loved you, that you also love one another.**

**35   "By this all will know that you are My
disciples, if you have love for one another."**

He's talking to His blood-bought, blood-washed redeemed
people. Obviously, at the time, He spoke to His disciples, but in general
He was speaking to the whole body of Christ. He said this is the way that
the world will know you are disciples. They won't know it because of the
buildings you construct. They won't know it by the great choirs and
wonderful music you have. They won't know it by the universities you
establish. They will know that you're My disciples because you have
love for one another. Well, if you loved me, you'd never consign me to
ride on the back of the bus. If you loved me, you'd never put a sign over
drinking fountains reading "Colored Only." Even in some churches, a
black person to this day is not welcome. I would never lynch those I love.
We in the Church have a long way to go, but the journey begins with the
first step.

Racism, ethnic pride, ethnic prejudice, color prejudice —
these are all learned behaviors. They are not genetically transmitted,
as I've said throughout this series. So we have to decide that we'll
not be racist. We have to set our minds that we will not be racially
and ethnically prejudiced. That is a decision. That is a conscious
choice. I don't care how you were taught. If you were raised wrong,
that is no reason to keep doing it. When you find out the truth, your
responsibility is to act on the truth. That is what God will hold you
accountable for — the truth that is given you. Let's look at Matthew
5:13-14:

**13   "You are the salt of the earth; but if the salt
loses its flavor, how shall it be seasoned? It is
then good for nothing but to be thrown out and
trampled underfoot by men.**

**14   "You are the light of the world. A city that is
set on a hill cannot be hidden."**

That's us. That's our responsibility. We, the Church, can no longer do business as usual. We can no longer see ourselves as we have in the past. Anthony T. Evans, in his book *Are Blacks Spiritually Inferior to Whites?* sums it up brilliantly:

> To refer to oneself as a Black Christian, or a White Christian or a Mexican Christian or a Chinese Christian, is technically incorrect. In these descriptions, the word "Christian" becomes a noun that is modified by an adjective — Black, White, and so on. Our Christianity should never be modified by our culture. It should be just the opposite. We must see ourselves as Christian Blacks, Christian Whites, Christian Mexicans, or Christian Chinese. When we do, our culture will be modified by the nature of our Christian commitment.[21]

That's awesome. I'm not a "black Christian" — I'm a "Christian Black." You're not a "white Christian" — you're a "Christian White." During the time that I taught this subject as a series in my church, I was invited to minister in an Asian country. The city that I was invited to is one of the most beautiful in Asia. It is one of the cleanest cities you will ever see — you can eat off the streets.

Anyway, I was invited to this city, and we were all ready to go. However, the government would not let me come. To show you how strong this issue of racism is, I want to share something with you as an illustration. This is an e-mail that I received from another minister in reference to my coming to his country to minister. It is addressed to my secretary.

> Greetings in Jesus' name. I apologize for my delay in responding to you. I regret to inform you that the authorities have denied Dr. and Mrs. Price a permit to (our

---

[21] Anthony T. Evans, *Are Blacks Spiritually Inferior to Whites?* (Wenonah, New Jersey: Renaissance Publishers, 1992), 144.

country) on the grounds that [he quotes the authorities] "it is our opinion that the individual holds radical and divisive views on the unity of races, and as such, would be unsuitable for the people of our country."

The minister goes on to say,

I assume they [the authorities] are referring to Dr. Price's recent series on race. Although there is no TBN [Trinity Broadcast Network] the authorities must have checked up on the information I supplied them. They are very sensitive to anyone saying anything on such a topic and have been known to be quite unreasonable.

The government has a very tight hold on information coming in or out of the country. The fact that this was to be a religious meeting did not help either. I have not heard anything about Dr. Price's series, but I do trust him as a man of his word. I would not have invited him otherwise. While I have assured the government that no harm would come of the meeting since we will be dealing with faith and have appealed the decision, they are nonetheless unconvinced. I am sorry that they have taken this stand. I believe many people will miss out on the blessings of God's Word as a result of their decision. Please tell Dr. Price that I love him in the Lord and that I am sorry that it did not work out. Please see that he gets a copy of this e-mail. Although I am not able to host Dr. Price at this time, I hope to be able to maintain a line of fellowship with him. Because despite what the government says, the ministry of Dr. Fred Price has very definitely been a blessing to me. I look forward to hearing from you and any comments Dr. Price may have. God bless you sister for all you are doing.

Reverend J. T.

As I mentioned, this e-mail was the result of a correspondence between Reverend J.T. and my secretary. I told her to tell him that I wanted to read the e-mail on nationwide television, but I didn't want to do that if it was going to cause him any flak from the government. This is what he replied:

> Dear Brother Price,
>
> Greetings in Jesus' name. I apologize for my delay in responding to you. Our offices were closed for a staff retreat. Of course, you may share my e-mail with CCC and the television viewers. They have a right to know why their pastor had to cancel an overseas trip. I appreciate your ministry and look forward to keeping in touch with you.
>
> God bless you.

That is why I'm sharing this with you, the reader. I got his permission first. But do you see the subtlety here? And what is interesting is that this is a mixed city with a diverse ethnic makeup. This just goes to show you how strong this racism is.

Now let me share another e-mail I received off the Internet. It is absolutely incredible.

> Dear Black Americans:
>
> After all of these years and all we have been through together, we think it's appropriate for us to show our gratitude for all you have done for us. We have chastised you, criticized you, punished you, and in some cases even apologized to you, but we have never formally nor publicly thanked you for your never-ending allegiance and support of our cause. This is our open letter of thanks to a unique people, a forgiving people, a steadfast people, and a brave people:
>
> Black Americans we will always be in debt to you for your labor. You built this country and were responsible for the great wealth we enjoy today. Upon your backs, laden with stripes we sometimes had to apply for disci-

plinary reasons, you carried our nation. We thank you for that. We thank you for your diligence, and tenacity. Even when we refused to allow you to even walk in our shadows, you followed close behind believing that someday we would come to accept you and treat you like men and women. Your strength in the face of adversity cannot be understated. You are truly a great people, and we thank you so much. We publicly acknowledge black people for raising our children, attending to our sick, and preparing our meals while we were occupied with the trappings of the good life. Even during the times when we found pleasure in your women and enjoyment in seeing one of your men lynched, maimed and burned, some of you continued to watch over us and our belongings. We simply cannot thank you enough. Your bravery on the battlefield, despite being classified as three/fifths of a man, was and still is outstanding and beyond the call of duty. We often watched in awe as you went about your prescribed chores and assignments, sometimes laboring in the hot sun for 12 hours, to assist us in realizing our dreams of wealth and good fortune. You were always there, and we thank you. Now that we control at least 90 percent of all the resources and wealth of this nation, we have black people to thank the most. You were there when it all began, and you are still with us today protecting us from those black people who have the temerity to speak out against our past transgressions. How can we thank you for your dedication? You warned us about Denmark Vesey's plans. You let us know about Gabriel Prosser's plans; you called our attention to Nat Turner. And you even sounded the alarm when old John Brown came calling on Harper's Ferry. Some of you still warn us today. Thank you, thank you, thank you! Now, as we look out upon our enormous wealth, and as we assess our tremendous control of the resources of this country, we can only think of the sacrifices you and your families made to make all of this possible. You are indeed fantastic, and we will be forever in your debt. To think of how you have looked out for us for hundreds of years and to see you still doing the same thing is totally amazing. Thank you for continuing to bring 95 percent of what you earn to our businesses. That is so gracious of you. Thanks for buying our Hilfigers, Karans, Nikkis [sic], and all of the other brands you so adore. Your purchases of these products really makes us feel that we are at least giving something back to you for your patronage. After all, in the past the brands we put on you were quite painful, but those of today can be proudly worn because they give you a sense of self-esteem, right? But it's the least we can do for a people who have treated us so well. Your super rich athletes, entertainers, intellectuals, and business persons (both legal and illegal) exchange most of their money for our cars, jewelry, homes, and clothing. What a windfall they have provided for us!

The less fortunate among you spend all they have at our neighborhood stores enabling us to open even more stores. Sure, they complain about us, but they never do anything to hurt us economically. You are very special people. Thank you. Oh yes, allow us to thank you for not bogging yourselves down with the business of doing business with your own people. We can take care of that for you. Please don't trouble yourselves with it. Yes, you were very successful at it after slavery ended and even as recently as 1960. But you know what happened when you began to build your own communities and do business with one another. Some of the "lower ones" of our kind burned you out time and time again. So why bother?

In today's business environment your own people will not support you anyway. You just keep doing business with us. It's safer that way. Besides, everything you need, we make anyway, even kinte [sic] cloth. You just continue to dance, sing, fight, get high, go to prison, backbite, envy and distrust and hate one another. Have yourselves a good time, and this time we'll take care of you.

It's the least we can do, considering all you've done for us. Heck, you deserve it. Black people, for your labor which created our wealth, for your resisting the messages of trouble-making blacks like Washington, Delaney, Garvey, Bethune, Tubman, and Truth, for fighting and dying on our battlefields, we thank you. For allowing us to move into your neighborhoods, we will forever be grateful to you. For your unceasing desire to be near us and for hardly ever following through on your threats due to our lack of reciprocity and equity. We thank you so much. We also appreciate your acquiescence to our political agendas, for abdicating your own economic self-sufficiency and for working so diligently for the economic well-being of our people. You are real troopers. And, even though the 13th, 14th, and 15th Amendments were written for you and many of your relatives died for the rights described therein, you did not resist when we changed those black rights to civil rights and allowed virtually every other group to take advantage of them as well. Black people, you are something else!

Your dependence upon us to do the right thing is beyond our imagination, irrespective of what we do to you and the many promises we have made and broken. But, this time we will make it right, we promise. Trust us. Tell you what. You don't need your own hotels. You can continue to stay in ours. You have no need for supermarkets when you can shop 24 hours a day. Why should you even think about owning more banks? You have plenty now. And don't waste your energies trying to break into manufacturing. You've worked hard enough in our fields. Relax and have a party. We'll sell you everything you need. And when you die, we'll even bury you at a discount. Now how's that for gratitude? Finally, the best part. You went beyond the pale and turned your children over to us for their education. With what we have taught them, it's likely they will continue in a mode similar to the one you have followed for the past 45 years.

> When Mr. Lynch walked the banks of the James River in 1712 and said he would make us a slave for 300 years, little did we realize the truth in his prediction. Just 13 more years and his promise will come to fruition. But with two generations of your children having gone through our education systems, we can look forward to at least another 50 years of prosperity. Wow! Things could not be better and it's all because of you. For all you have done, we thank you from the bottom of our hearts, black Americans. You're the best friends any group of people could ever have! Sincerely, all other Americans.

Now, as I close this book, I want to end on a positive note. Someone has put into an eloquent story some things that Blacks, Whites, Browns, Yellows, and Reds all need to know about black people. This is excerpted from a little article called "A Day of Absence" (author unknown):

> This is a story of a little boy named Theo, who woke up one morning and asked his mother, "Mom, what if there were no black people in the world?" Well, his mother thought about that for a moment and then said, "Son, follow me around today and let's just see what it would be like if there were no black people in the world." Mom said, "Now, go get dressed and we will get started."
>
> Theo ran to his room to put on his clothes and shoes. His mother took one look at him and said, "Theo, where are your shoes? And those clothes are all wrinkled, son. I must iron them." However, when she reached for the ironing board, it was no longer there. You see, Sarah Boone, a black woman, invented the ironing board, and Jan E. Matzeliger, a black man, invented the shoe lasting machine.
>
> "Oh well," she said. "Please go and do something with your hair." Theo ran in his room to comb his hair, but the comb was not there. You see, Walter Sammons, a black man, invented the comb. Theo decided to just brush

his hair, but the brush was gone. You see, Lydia O. Newman, a black female, invented the brush. Well, this was a sight: no shoes, wrinkled clothes, hair a mess, even mom's hair without the hair inventions of Madam C. J. Walker. Well, you get the picture.

Mom told Theo, "Let's do our chores around the house and then take a trip to the grocery store." Theo's job was to sweep the floor. He swept and swept and swept. When he reached for the dust pan, it was not there. You see, Lloyd P. Ray, a black man, invented the dustpan. So he swept his pile of dirt over in the corner and left it there. He then decided to mop the floor, but the mop was gone. You see, Thomas W. Stewart, a black man, invented the mop. Theo yelled to his mom, "Mom, I'm not having any luck." "Well son," she said, "Let me finish washing these clothes and we will prepare a list for the grocery store." When the wash was finished, she went to place the clothes in the dryer, but it was not there. You see, George T. Samon, a black man, invented the clothes dryer. Mom asked Theo to get a pencil and some paper to prepare the list for the market. So Theo ran for the paper and pencil, but noticed the pencil lead was broken. Well, he was out of luck, because John Love, a black man, invented the pencil sharpener. Mom reached for a pen, but it was not there because William Purvis, a black man, invented the fountain pen. As a matter of fact, Lee Burridge invented the typewriting machine, and W.A. Lovette, the advanced printing press.

Theo and his mother decided to head out to the market. Well, when Theo opened the door he noticed that the grass was as high as he was tall. You see, the lawnmower was invented by John Burr, a black man. They made their way over to the car and found that it just wouldn't go. You see, Richard Spikes, a black man, invented the automatic gear shift and Joseph Gammel invented the super charge system for internal combustion engines. They noticed that the few cars that were moving were running into each other and having wrecks because there were no traffic signals. You see, Garrett A. Morgan, a black man, invented the traffic light. Well, it was getting late, so they walked to the market, got their groceries and returned home. Just when they were about to put away the milk, eggs and butter, they noticed the refrigerator was gone. You see, John Standard, a black man, invented the refrigerator. So they just left the food on the counter. By this time, Theo noticed he was getting mighty cold. Mom went to turn up the heat, and what do you know? Alice Parker, a black female, invented the heating furnace....

It was almost time for Theo's father to arrive home. He usually takes the bus, but there was no bus, because it's precursor was the electric trolley, invented by another black man, Elbert R. Robinson....

He also dropped off the office mail at a nearby mailbox. But it was no longer there because Philip Downing, a black man, invented the letter-drop mailbox, and William Barry, invented the postmarking and canceling machine.

Theo and his mother sat at the kitchen table with their heads in their hands. When the father arrived, he asked, "Why are you sitting in the dark?" Why? Because Lewis Howard Latimer, a black man, invented the light-bulb filament.

Theo quickly learned what it would be like if there were no black people in the world, especially if he were ever sick and needed blood. Charles Drew, a black scientist, found a way to preserve and store blood, which led to his starting the world's first blood bank. And what if a family member had to have heart surgery? This would not have been possible without Dr. Daniel Hale Williams, a black doctor, who performed the first open-heart surgery.

So if you ever wonder, like Theo, where would we be
without black folk? It's pretty plain to see: we would still
be in the dark.

I think now you can see that black people have made a
difference in this country, and that they have made significant
contributions that have improved life for everyone. I have one final
chapter for you, now, which I added as an epilogue based on the
responses to the television show. It will prove that we have come a
long way, and that we still have a way to go.

11

The Color of Love

During and after the completion of the television series *Race, Religion & Racism* on Ever Increasing Faith television, I began to receive a number of letters from viewers. As you might imagine, these covered the entire spectrum, from loving support to outright anger and hostility. Some people were sincerely disturbed that I was reviving racial distrust that had, in their view, died down. Others commended me for broaching a subject that needed to be addressed. One thing was certain: the series touched anyone who took the time to watch it.

Most of the letters revealed a radical life change — an awareness of racism in myriad ways that people had not seen before. Many wrote to tell of similar struggles with racial issues, in and out of the church. Therefore, the Holy Spirit led me to include some of these stories and comments as the finale to this book. I think you can see that those people "who had ears to hear" experienced a life change in a dramatic way, and that the Bible is not about black or white, it is about the color of love.

A powerful, but typical, letter that we read on television came from a married couple whose name and location I will not give, for reasons you will see when you read this:

Dear Dr. Price,[1]

I am writing first and foremost to commend you on your series "Race, Religion and Racism." My husband and I, through the grace of the Lord Jesus Christ, were saved from the accursed clutches of the Ku Klux Klan.... As my husband and I both held very "high ranking" positions within the organization, we know exactly what they teach and feel it is our duty to warn young people as to what this particular organization is all about. All this organization is about is brainwashing the young people of my race and carrying their souls to HELL!

It is only through teaching ["Race, Religion & Racism"] as yours that all false doctrines can be exposed, and the true gospel of the Lord Jesus can be preached....

May God bless you richly for having the courage to teach the gospel correctly. We love you brother!

This couple was actually in the Ku Klux Klan, and now they are calling me "brother!" If that isn't a life changed, I don't know what is. But this couple was not alone in having their lives affected by this series.

Douglas Fierstein, of Nashville, Tennessee, wrote in a similar vein:

Dear Dr. Price,

I am so proud that God has raised up another preacher with the intestinal fortitude to address this volatile issue, Amen.

---

[1] The editor has taken the liberty of eliminating some names, and punctuating and correcting minor errors to standardize the text to our editorial style. We have not changed the content of the quotes.

I am a forty year old white man, ashamed of his race and country. Ashamed of the way our political system, and our religious leaders, as well as our society have treated all peoples of all colors for the last two hundred years.

Until last year, my wife and I resided in an all white upper West Nashville neighborhood. After my baptism, I could no longer tolerate these "Closet Racists." We sold our house and moved to the neapolitan neighborhood of South Nashville. We now live among an equal mix of all races and nationalities. Not people who live in cliques, but people who live together in peace and harmony with one another. Watch out, we are all prejudiced against prejudiced people. I feel that God may be prejudiced in this manner also.

Nowhere in Scripture do I read that God or Jesus frowns against race mixing or interracial marriage.... Dr. Price, I want you to know for what it's worth, I also back you up one hundred percent on this issue. I also want you to know that if a racist bullet were to be fired upon you...I would be proud to stand beside you, for no other reason than to throw my six foot, three hundred-fifty pound, white self between you and that bullet. So that you may "Preach on my Christian Brother."

This is humbling and touching. But lest you think everyone was affected by the series in a positive way, you might want to consider the words of Robert Page of Roan Mountain, Tennessee:

Dear Dr. Price,

You are a racist. The look of smugness and the joy of retaliation are in the faces of your black constituents as you make your animated points against Whites and the views of some of them. Such grandiose and blanket statements you make about "Whites are right" attitudes lump me in with those Whites who think that way, and I don't. You are fomenting a spirit of self aggrandizement and arrogance in your black members equal to that of Whites who do the same thing.

Mr. Page continues:

I was raised in the South in a very prejudicial home. I was poisoned by my environment. I said and did despicable things to blacks. I was converted to Christ at age seventeen. My heart was changed, totally changed. I did not need anyone to "educate" me in order to convict me of my wrong actions and thoughts. The Holy Spirit did it, and it was near instantaneous. Without becoming an "activist," in the normal course of life I met and became close to black individuals and families, some of whom I am still in regular communication. They have spent vacations in my home as recently as last year. One of my children is named after a young black man for whom I felt admiration and affection.

What the hell difference does it make who was what color in the past or present? Isn't it enough that Paul teaches "there is no more Jew nor Greek, bond nor free, male nor female"? "They are all one in Christ." It is a changed life in Christ that your congregation should be cheering about...not that Miriam or Hagar or Muhammad Ali were black. Egos do not need to be inflated by superficial means any more than they should be deflated by racial supremacists.

You impress me as a black Jerry Falwell, only you are a lot funnier.

This is a good example of what we are up against in this demon called racism. I'm sure Mr. Page is indeed born again, and does not think he holds any racist attitudes at all. But I wasn't the one who mentioned Hagar's, or Miriam's, or anyone else's race — *God did*! If you followed the series closely, I pointed out that there had to be a reason that *only* in the case of these black people did the Word mention race, and that all other times names were given without

comment. Anyone watching the series also knows that virtually every time I made a "condemnation," it was never as a blanket statement. I regularly went out of my way to say, "Don't take this personally if it doesn't apply to you."

Let me give you an example of this: when we shop in the grocery store. Let's say there is a little dispensing machine that gives you these manufacturer's coupons and there are coupons for an air freshener. If you plan to buy that air freshener, you take one of those coupons, but if you don't plan to put an air freshener in your cart, you don't — it's not meant for you! This message has been like that. Why in the world would you think comments about bad racial attitudes apply to you if you don't have those attitudes?

Finally, let me reiterate that this series was never about "inflating egos." This was about seeing the truth that has been buried in the Word for generations! This was about getting into the open what the Church — and since most of it has been in control of white people, the white Church — has kept hidden for centuries.

Mr. Page asks: "What the hell difference does it make who was what color in the past or present?" It must make enough of a difference to men that for nearly 2,000 years they never painted a dark-skinned Jesus, or a dark-skinned Solomon, or had a motion picture in which Moses and the Egyptians were dark-skinned. It must make enough of a difference that Hollywood has only chosen English or American (never Jewish or Semitic looking) actors to play Jesus in its major movies about Christ. And it must make enough of a difference that God needed to put in these little "alerts" again and again about color in the Bible.

Mr. Page's letter was not the only one taking me to task for "bringing up" the subject of race and racism. Donna J. Graczyk of St. Albans, West Virginia, wrote:

Dear Pastor Price,

First and foremost I would like to say that I am a white woman who is not prejudiced to any color and/or nationality....

> Up to a few weeks ago, I watched you on TBN [Trinity Broadcasting Network] whenever I could. You preached God's Word, and you preached it hard.... Then all of a sudden a few months ago, every time I saw you...you were not preaching the Gospel and the Word of God any more. You were always talking about prejudice, taking your points far beyond Matthew 5:37 in which the Lord instructs us to let our yes be yes and our no, no for whatever is more than these is from the evil one.

> Pastor Price, you seem to be almost obsessed with this subject. Being prejudiced is certainly not to be taken lightly, but the black people are well aware of how they were and are being treated. I may be reading scripture wrong, but I see scripture as saying not to keep rehashing the past, to forgive and pray for those that do us wrong, and go on. One reason among others is that it will bring even more strife, and in this case may cause the black people to have even more prejudice against the white people than they have now, causing them to sin.

Let me state categorically that I'm not questioning anyone's motives here: I think that these and other critical letters are sincere in their desire to have racial harmony and justice. But as we know, being sincere and being right — as defined by being in line with the Word — can be two different things. **There is a way that seems right to a man, but its end is the way of death** (Proverbs 14:12). For example, the writer refers to Matthew 5:37, which is in the so-called *Beatitudes*. Jesus was giving instructions for general living here, not for studying Scripture or teaching the Word. Quite the contrary, we see Jesus constantly correcting the learned men of the day in the four Gospels. Matthew 5:37 was certainly not a directive to pastors or teachers that they should only say "yes" or "no." Jesus told Peter point-blank: "feed my sheep." Well, sometimes the sheep may not like the taste of the food, but they need it to grow.

Likewise, the writer says Scripture tells us not to keep "rehashing the past." Certainly, Jesus intended us to forgive those who have sinned against us. But He did not mean that we were not to learn from the past — that is the entire purpose for giving us all the examples in the Bible, so that we can see what mistakes others made and avoid them. Paul's "Hall of Fame of the Heroes of Faith" in Hebrews is a giant rehashing of the past, bringing to the peoples' remembrance the faith "superstars" who had gone before them. The United States has "forgiven" Japan for the Pearl Harbor attack, but it's in every history textbook so that we are prepared and don't get caught like that again.

I'll give you just one more example of the types of letters we received by people concerned that the series would inflame racism rather than deal with it in a positive way. Mrs. Winnie Gussie Ramsdell of Villa Hills, Kentucky, wrote:

> Pastor Fred Price:
>
> I feel when I hear you on TV that you are trying to start a war between the two races. This is not God! . . . You should be praising God for what <u>He has done</u>! Not beating down white people. If you'd get that chip off your shoulder and quit bringing back the past, then <u>God</u> can make you the head and not the tail, as you are saying.... Pastor, start teaching the Ten Commandments and the New Birth. This will do your people more good than what you are doing. You are preaching darkness instead of light. I don't feel any love coming from your people when you are digging up smut about us.

I didn't get the assignment to teach this series from the deacons, or from the directors of the church, and least of all, not from my own wish to talk about race. God gave me this assignment, as He gives me all my assignments. If He instructs me to teach on the Ten Commandments, then that is my next series — end of story. But in this case, He gave me this assignment, whether I wanted it or not. Now, I could have been Jonah, and run the other way, so as not to upset people. Or, I could be faithful to His instructions and do what He told me to do. I chose the latter.

A similar letter came from Maxine Wright in Arizona, who said:

Pastor Fred Price,

You scare me. Millions of people are learning this, and many are not receiving it in the manner you intended it. About the time the White people began to gain the confidence of the Black people & beautiful Black people I might add — you are pushing us apart again.... I know how hard headed and stubborn you are, but please listen.

I would never (not now) feel comfortable in your church.... What you have said lately on TV gave me a complex, that I have never had before — now I'm afraid to speak to a Black person for fear of how they feel toward white people so instead of bridging a gap, you work very hard at widening....

Mrs. Wright raises some points worth considering. First, I cannot help how people "receive" what I teach. I have to trust God that He will uphold His end of the bargain, and that His Word will not return to Him void. God said, **"So shall My word be that goes forth from My mouth; it shall not return to Me void, but it shall accomplish what I please, and it shall prosper in the thing for which I sent it"** (Isaiah 55:11). My job is not to chew the food and swallow it for the people. My job is to feed them by preparing the food, making it as appetizing as possible, and setting the table. But I can't eat it for them.

Second, it is interesting that she blames what I said for causing her feelings of "discomfort" toward black people. But what really has changed? The way black people she encountered felt? No, that has stayed the same. What has changed is her awareness of how they might feel. That is what is bothering her — not their feelings, but her comfort level.

You can see through these letters, though, how quickly people will charge you with wanting to cause trouble — "start a war between the races" — if you raise these issues. Jesus didn't say, "Well, Father, I know you want me to heal this crippled man, but it's the Sabbath and I don't want to offend these religious Jews, because they may think I'm trying to start some kind of war here. So I'll just skip this part of My mission." No, He followed His instructions, and that's what I have had to do in this series.

Let me ask you a question. Do you remember when Jesus called the religious leaders vipers? To which religious leaders was He talking? To whom was that term, *generation of vipers*, addressed? All of them? Well, then I have another question. Was Nicodemus — the one who came to Jesus by night — a believer? (We know he couldn't have been born again until after the Resurrection, but he could accept in his heart that Jesus was the Messiah, right?) The Bible tells us that Nicodemus indeed came to be a believer. Was he a viper? So I guess that term Jesus used in describing some — maybe most — of the religious leaders certainly did not apply to all of them. Do you suppose Nicodemus took it personally when Jesus called the others vipers? Not if he wasn't a viper. He just shook it off because it did not apply to him.

If these letters quoted above are examples of some of the critical letters I received, you'll be greatly inspired by some of the letters that came into the ministry about how the series exposed racism in people and changed their hearts.

Mrs. Debra Higginbotham of Mulberry, Florida wrote:

Dear Dr. Price,

I don't go to your Church but I feel such a part of it. I have been watching you for many years and I have learned so much. I am speaking from my heart and would love to have a pastor like you.... You are teaching on Race, Religion and Racism. I feel strongly that this needs to be taught. I am a white woman and feel that we as Christians need to do something about it [racism]. I have been to churches where it is an all white church and if a black couple comes to the church and joins, about half of the people stop coming to the church. That's pitiful.

We are supposed to be like Christ, and this is not something Christ would do. Let's love everyone!!! It starts in the church.... Thank you Dr. Price.

Similar sentiments were expressed in a letter from Patricia L. Smith of Germfask, Michigan:

Dear Brother Price;

After last evening's service on TBN television station, I feel I must write. I did not know of your church problem before last evening. I am ashamed that in today's society such a problem could happen. Thank you and your church for dealing with it in an open and Christian way.

...I am a fifty-five-year-old female mother. I was raised to accept all races and treat them well. About ten months ago I was reading some short stories of Christian peoples' lives. One from an African American hit me hard between the eyes! I wasn't prejudiced, or was I? No way, I felt. I had looked at other touched-by-mixed-race marriages and [did not] judge. God said to me, "Pat — it never has touched you personally. How would you feel if your daughter or son was to marry an African American person?" I was crushed and ashamed. I was guilty. I had prided myself for acceptance and also equality....

Brother Price, I asked God to forgive me and I ask all African American people to forgive me for my self-righteous thoughts.... White people were raised in a society that did not look at skin color as just a color. We were pushed to be superior — this is not a pleasant realization in my life.

This letter is an important response to those people who sincerely think they don't have a "racist bone in their body"...until their son or daughter starts to date a black person! That is why I keep using racial mixed marriages as a barometer. It is what I call a "litmus test" on race. If a person of another race is not good enough to marry, or to have your son or daughter marry, then the chances are pretty good you are a racist, no matter what other views you hold.

Julia A. Bickel, of Millington, Michigan, explains her transformation from a person who initially was angered by the series, then "had ears to hear" the message:

Dear Dr. Price,

In the past four months I have become aware of your program on TV which airs on Friday night here. Although I watch TV only occasionally, I have frequently stopped "channel surfing" when I find you speaking. I have listened attentively and with a careful spirit when you preach. I have sometimes thought you were incendiary, but when you finished the presentation, found you to be faithful to the Scriptures and to the Holy Spirit. Over a long period of time...I have studied diligently and prayed fervently to be able to discern the truth...I have even prepared presentations for the women of my church body to teach how to discern the truth. I am confident that you are a man of God and a faithful preacher.

My "black" brother in Christ, I encourage you to keep "speaking the truth in love" (Ephesians 4:15) to "hold fast to what is good" (I Thessalonians 5:12) to "stand fast therefore in the liberty wherewith Christ hath made us free" (Galatians 5:1). Also remember Philippians 1:29 "For unto you it is given in the behalf of Christ, not only to believe on him, but also to suffer for his sake."

A woman from Oklahoma [Name withheld] echoed Julia Bickel:

> Dear Dr. Frederick Price,
>
> Would like to thank you for the Sunday Morning teachings on prejudice. I am a white, 80 year old widow. As a little girl, I had the same feelings about the injustice that was placed on your people.... Needless to say, I am ashamed and irate about the cruelty your people have suffered from <u>some</u> of my people....

An Arkansas woman celebrated the fact that the *Race, Religion and Racism* series helped bring down a wall that separated the races.

Many times we think we aren't prejudiced, when in fact we have a number of little behaviors that tattle on us. Consider a letter from a Portland, Oregon, woman, who admitted that while she thought she was progressive and tolerant, after watching the series she noticed in herself several traits of which she was not proud, such as grabbing her purse when Blacks passed her on the street. She praised God for the liberation from the oppression of racism that she had even subconsciously experienced.

Here is another example of someone who may not have condoned racism, but who did little to speak out about it until hearing this series. One couple from a Southern California city [Name withheld] wrote:

> Dear Pastor Price,
>
> I'm writing to comment on your present series of Race, Religion and Racism. I believe this is a series long overdue. I am also proud to say that MY pastor is handling it. My wife and I have been members [of CCC] since 1994.... We are both white and do not take offense to the message. However, I've felt embarrassed due to my lack of not standing my ground on my views about

racism around other white people. I'm speaking of the "guilt by association" that you spoke of....

I had an opportunity to change that when I heard my parents make a comment about black people.... I called them on the carpet for that!....

I'm not intimidated to do what's right anymore! All at CCC are my family, even the ones that have given us negative looks across the aisles during this message.

You know, pastor, it's been said that Abraham Lincoln set the black people free. However, I believe that before this series is over, the history books are going to have to be changed, because I know of two white people that you've helped to set free!

One of the reasons I wanted to include that letter was the comment that some people at CCC gave this couple "negative looks across the aisles" during this series. After I read the letter from the Southern Califonia couple to the congregation, I received another letter, from Laurie Drevlow of Anaheim, California:

Dear Dr. Price,

I am writing to you in regards to a letter that you read this past Sunday. I believe a couple...made a brief comment regarding some individuals who have been giving them dirty looks "across the aisles." I just wanted to let you know that they are not the only ones who have experienced negative reactions as a result of being White. I too, have had similar experiences.

I have been a member of CCC for several years now, and prior to last year, I had never experienced any overt negative reactions from CCC members. From the first Sunday I arrived, I was always received with loving open arms. So, as you can imagine, when I returned [from college in Washington, DC, two years later], I was shocked at the response I was receiving from some of the congregants.

...I was shocked not only of the things that were being said, but also by the treatment I was receiving. As you would be ministering, people would quite often yell "AMEN!" in an exceptionally loud voice, and then turn and give me dirty looks. Other times they would simply glare or give me a disapproving "once-over" while shaking my hand. At first, I ignored it, but then it became so frequent, it was difficult to let it go. For the first time in my life, I felt unwelcome in the church I called home.... Prior to that time, people were warm and friendly.... I was a stranger to most, but nevertheless, loved and received as...a sister in the Lord.

I was so hurt...that I sought advice. First, I discussed the situation with some of my close friends...who are African-Americans.... They insisted that it was my imagination and that I should continue to attend church.... However, after several more Sundays of the same treatment, I sought pastoral counseling.... I was comforted in the fact that someone understood the situation, and was convinced I was not over-reacting.... I was considering leaving the church for a season. In some respects, I felt as though I was being abused.... You see, I really believe if our black brothers and sisters knew what most of us white people had to go through in order to attend CCC, they would leave us alone. They would understand that we are playing on the same team.

I wanted to attend CCC when I was a teenager, but it was not allowed. Later, when I became a young adult, I decided that "come hell or high water," I was going [to CCC].... In the process, I was told I was crazy and that I would most assuredly be shot or killed. I distinctly remember people saying things like, "Why do you want to go to church down there?.... Why do you want to go to a black church? What are you, some kind of nigger lover...? Are you trying to get a black man?" No matter what the words...the implications were always the same...that there was something wrong with me....

So, you can imagine how hurt I was when these events transpired.... At any rate.... You generally conclude [your altar calls] by saying..."I'm the pastor of this church, and until I mess over, until I'm mean to you, until I give you dirty looks and won't talk to you...don't leave church...." Your family has never been anything but kind and loving to me.... I said all that to say this...I want to thank you for the kind reprimand you gave the congregation on Sunday. You told people to leave us alone. That if we were down here, then we were okay. You were right when you said that we could be at other churches, but we have CHOSEN to come to Crenshaw.

I want to thank you for protecting your flock, even the white sheep.... There was a one hundred eighty-degree change. It seemed to me as though people were going out of their way to greet me and say hello. The warm and friendly air that infiltrates the Dome was once again present!

I wanted to include these letter so that I make it clear: I did not come against racism, and deal with all these challenges of people resigning from boards and go through all this effort to root out racism only to have it resurface at the FaithDome. But as a pastor, I have to make sure before I act, and sometimes these issues don't come to my attention right away. Also, we need more than one person's word on something — the Bible's "two or three witnesses." But once I had those witnesses, I acted on this and I believe we nipped it in the bud. On the final session of the *Race, Religion & Racism* series, I asked all of our "non-black" (including Whites, Asians and Hispanics) congregation to sit together in the FaithDome. I wanted the members of CCC to acknowledge their faithfulness and courage to stay the course of this series. It was indeed an uplifting service.

I believe one of God's purposes for this series was not only to get people to examine black/white issues in the Word, but to open it up to a re-examination of all the races' place in Scripture. As I have said, my mission was not to trace the genealogy of the Yellow, Red, or Brown people, but I believe God is preparing others to do just that even as you read this.

One of the most powerful letters I received was from a man, who wrote:

> I have watched Dr. Price for a while now, not as much as I would like because my work schedule keeps me away long hours. But his series has touched me deeply. I am a white, and for many years, I despised racists to the point of hating them. After I accepted Jesus, I stopped hating them and merely despised them. Racism...has never been a weakness with me despite growing up white in Mississippi.... I was so full of pride about not being a racist when I started watching Dr. Price. His series showed me that if I'm not being part of the solution, I'm being part of the problem.
>
> Then to cut me down to size, the Holy Spirit showed me some passive prejudice that I harbored in my own heart in the form of stereotypes held about black people. I was stunned to realize this, but now, I could no longer despise those who are given to the sin of racism.... As a white male...in the United States,...I am opposed to racism of any type.... You [Dr. Price] are a living example of what people should be doing and that is to talk about it. Get it out. Understand it. Learn from it and move with the wonderful life that God wanted us to have. I thank you for educating me, as the information that you have shared in many cases was not in the history books....
>
> I charge myself with accountability for this knowledge that I have obtained from your program and I will do my best to pass on the knowledge that I have and share it with as many people as possible....

The Color of Love

A similar, and equally moving letter, came from Sunny Chandler of Lancaster, California, about her experiences married to a black man:

Dear Dr. Price:

I have been listening to your teaching on racism since its conception. Each week I have been tempted to write you, each week I learned something new about myself, each week I put off writing, and truth be known, I was afraid you just might read my letter and say my name for the whole world to hear. But guess what, I want everyone to know how I used to be and that the truth made me free.

I am a white female married to a black man; my husband is a wonderful, good man.... The problem though was me, after getting settled in California, I sought employment, found a great job, but as soon as my employer became aware that I was married to a "black" I lost my job. This happened to me on a few occasions, oddly enough my employers were Jewish. I thought of all the peoples who should have had no prejudice it would have been them considering what they as a people went through during the war.

I listened to my "white" peers ask me if I was unable to get a white man..., I listened to the jokes around the office.... I viewed obscene pictures depicting the black people.... I listened as "fun" was poked at the black women and references to their size.... I listened as whites told of how stupid the black person was...and I said NOTHING!!!!!

Thanks to your program I was finally able to tell this wonderful man that I am married to my feelings and the shame I carried. Guess what? God forgave me and so did my husband. Never will I be caught up in that situation again, my mouth now speaks, and it speaks the truth. There is only one race, and that is the human race, God made all of us in His own image, and brother, that is good enough for me.

There is no question that the series stirred up mixed emotions in people, sometimes different emotions in the same person. For example, a woman from Tulsa, Oklahoma [Name withheld], wrote regarding interracial marriages:

Dear Dr. Price:

I am a divorced woman with one teenage son. I am white and was married to a black man until I divorced him because of adultery. My son is (of course) bi-racial.

This letter comes to you with much love and admiration.... You make me laugh, you make me cry, you make me get on my knees and pray. However, lately, something is different. It seems you have changed.... The last couple of times I have heard you preach you seemed cocky and bitter.... Do you realize that you no longer portray a loving servant of our Lord Jesus?

Although you continued to say — Don't take it personal — you would also say, "hurts, doesn't it, well we've been hurting for 400 years." It sounded as if you wanted to hurt white people.... I know in my heart that the Lord gave you the sermon. But He didn't give you the bitterness in which you preached it.

Please Dr. Price, please don't hate white people because of their ignorance. I don't hate black women. And black women hate the interracial dating and marriages more than anyone.

I have been called a nigger lover and a nigger bitch many times by my family and others. I know your pain.

I have seen my name written on buildings and in bathrooms saying, I was a whore. I know your pain.

I was always told I was the bad one of the family. <u>I know your pain</u>.

This woman went on to detail in her letter some other things that had happened to her — all extremely tragic and traumatic:

> My own father sexually abused my most innocent years. Before I even entered first grade. I don't just know your pain, I know a deeper pain with white men than you will ever know, Dr. Price. Yes, indeed, I know your pain and more....

> You are a fine preacher. Please don't let the bitterness you feel against Whites bring you down.

There is a difference between being righteously angry and indignant, as Jesus was in the temple, and being bitter. I plead guilty to being righteously angry and indignant, but not to being bitter against any person, and certainly not against any race as a whole. I have already discussed that in earlier chapters. Like anything though, if you come in during the middle of a sermon, or even only hear one particular lesson taken out of context, you can get the wrong idea. That is why I went out of my way to give my "disclaimer" about not intending anything personally, but I did not work that "disclaimer" into every sermon that may have been broadcast. At any rate, it is interesting, don't you think, that this woman had the spiritual perception to see that the topic was given of the Holy Spirit. Only she disagreed with some of my tone in presenting it.

There are times that we need to get righteously indignant over some of the practices that have been going on in the Church. One reason we still have to deal with them today is that people, for whatever reason, have not wanted to "rock the boat." My instructions were to rip this thing up by the roots, and sometimes that requires a little indignation, a little emotion, and a well-aimed anger. But I think you'll see that different people took different things from the messages. Note in the following letter how a couple from a southern state, commended me for *not* being bitter or using names. Although they do not say so at the beginning of their letter, it is clear from the stories they tell that the wife is white and the husband is black. Note also, though, that in their letter, dated 1998, they relate something very important, namely, that this racist teaching in the Church is still with us, today:

> Dear Dr. Price,
>
> We are writing to express how proud and inspired we are by your message in your Race, Religion and Racism series.
>
> It's funny how we even came to start watching you. We moved here [Location withheld] from Detroit almost four years ago. Since that time we have visited many churches, but can't find one that teaches us anything. So we always wind up leaving the church. There was one particular church we used to attend, which has in-directly led us to you…. This past year, we heard that he [the pastor] held a special meeting for the white youth of the church. He basically told them that it was okay to socialize with blacks during school or at church, but that the whites shouldn't call them on the phone or date, etc…. I'm not going to say we were surprised when we heard this, but rather sickened.
>
> One night while flipping through the channels, I hap-pened to catch your broadcast. You were playing the tape of the white preacher. I had never heard about that tape or that situation before, and thought it was odd how all of a sudden I heard about it in our town and on your show. I had to laugh, though, because even the pastor's (from our town) prejudice was verbatim from the TV.
>
> As I watched the broadcast that night, I was impressed with the way you addressed the situation — how you left his name out of it, and dealt with the principle and

340

not the man himself. Since that time we have watched every week, without missing, to hear what truth you will uncover. My husband and I have read and heard many of the things you quote from. We understand that the truth is too heavy for many people.

They related how on several occasions people came to their store and assumed that the wife was the owner, because she is white, and the black husband just "worked there."

I could go on telling you hundreds of stories just like this, but time will not permit. We just want to tell you to keep talking. Keep talking loud and proud.... We are helping Blacks and Whites to realize greatness within themselves. And we are proud to see you are doing the same.

I have mentioned on television that we had some members of our board leave over this series, and that some of the congregation of Crenshaw Christian Center left. But for every one of those incidents, we had letters of support from other churches and/or pastors. Such a letter came from Pastor Floyd Dautrieve of Stone Mountain, Georgia:

Dear Dr. Price:

My wife and I have been members of FICWFM [Fellowship of Inner City Word of Faith Ministries] since its inception. We moved from Oxnard, California in 1995 after serving ten years in the ministry and began New Creation Christian Fellowship, Inc., August 17, 1998.

We want you to know that we stand with you one hundred percent. We have been watching the series on "Race, Religion and Racism" and know you are doing what is right. Racism in the church must be dealt with openly.

The Board of Directors, Elders and Ministers of New Creation Christian Fellowship, Inc. all agree that we will
immediately remove all books and tapes of the ministry
in question and render no financial support... . By boy-
cotting, the ministry in question, we are saying that the
church cannot be used to enforce or perpetuate racial
bigotry.

Many other letters of support from churches came in. This letter
was from Pastor J. B. Williams of Abundant Living Faith Ministries in
Tallahassee, Florida:

Dear Dr. Price,

I am in receipt of your letter dated March 2, 1998
regarding the resignations of FICWFM Board members
[over the "Race, Religion & Racism" series]. I felt compelled
to respond because of the nature of the true issue at
hand... .

I spent the greatest life-changing, educational ministry
training for four years under your tutelage while living
in Irvine, California....

It is unfortunate that ministers of the Gospel are partial
in the Gospel. But God, in His infinite wisdom knew so
and gave us a strong admonition in the book of Timothy, not to observe nor minister the Gospel with partiality. If you had asked for a boycott because of adultery. I
am sure you would have had full support. Guardians of
the precious Word and work of God have class systems
when it comes to sin....

You have our (your members' and supporters') unques-
tioned support, not only in this matter regarding that
"ancient hatred"...we call racism, but all other Kingdom
business.

Support likewise came from Pastor Al Smith of City Church
in Chicago:

342

Dear Dr. Price:

...It dismayed me...as I watched your program to receive evidence of remarks made by [the unnamed minister whose comments began this series] that were rumored a couple of years ago. It's tragic that racism still lingers even in the upper echelon of the faith movement... .

Today I faxed [the minister] a letter outlining what I felt, a proper course of action to help bring healing to the body of Christ.

Pastor Smith then included a copy of the letter he sent to this unnamed minister, outlining four alternative points of action. The fourth was:

Confess that at the time you made the observation you felt justified in doing so, but in retrospect realize that they were unjustified, unscriptural and insensitive....

From my view, this last option is in reality your *only* option.

The pastor in question did not take Pastor Smith's advice on this matter.

Members of FICWFM (Fellowship of Inner-City Word of Faith Ministries) were contacted, and we suggested that if the minister in question did not repudiate his earlier statements, and recant, then FICWFM members should begin a boycott of this ministry's products. Not all, of course, responded favorably to this call. But consider this letter from Pastor Robert E. Johnson of Living Water Bible Church of Milwaukee, Wisconsin, regarding these developments:

Dear Dr. Price:

...When I inquired at [another FICWFM church] concerning the FICWFM Regional Conference, I was abruptly informed that "never again would their church host a FICWFM Conference." I did not wish to believe what was apparent. Prior to any real difficulty arising, there was already a falling away of those who should be most committed. In my quiet time, I went to the Lord and before you had ever disclosed to us the abdication of some [FICWFM] board members, God spoke to me. He said, "Just as Elisha had stuck with Elijah, so you stay with your man of God. Dr. Price, you are my man of God.... I am righteously indignant that those who know you...would question this principle clearly shown by yourself.

Although you have stated that you are willing to stand alone — not in my lifetime! I am with you because you are right and you are following an assignment given by the Lord.

In this same letter from Pastor Johnson, he also wrote:

...I have been immensely blessed by your teaching of the Word.... There have been superficial attempts to "reconcile," but this was mainly an emotional period of a few days and then it was back to business as usual. No real change occurred because no one dared to be "raw." Faith does not come by bad feelings or guilt or an emotional release. It comes by hearing and that hearing is predicated upon the Word of God....

Dr. Price, you are for real and it takes your no holds barred teaching approach to unearth the racist mindset, which has too long stymied the church's progress. Because of your boldness, my admiration for you has only increased immeasurably. In every generation, God grants us one who has been molded by Him to dare to lead in the difficult wilderness. Brother, God has called you for such a time as this and I dare to say I will stand shoulder to shoulder with you.

My point is not to include some of these letters just for self-congratulation. I wanted to show you that some of the same things that some people perceived as "bitterness" or "anger" in fact were exactly what other people wanted and needed in order to deal with this mess. No one knew better than Jesus that not everyone was ready for every teaching at the same time. That is why He said, **"He who has ears to hear, let him hear!"** (Matthew 11:15) and why He said of John the Baptist, in Matthew 11:14, **"And if you are willing to receive it, he is Elijah who is to come."** Jesus knew all people wouldn't "hear" and wouldn't "receive" at the same time, or in the same way.

I've asked this question before, but let me ask it again: Who do you think is smarter, God or you? If God is smarter than you, do you suppose He knew that not all people would respond to the same style of preaching? Or to the same approach? Maybe that is why he sent a Martin Luther and a John Wesley, a Billy Graham and an Oral Roberts. Maybe that is why some who heard this series heard "bitterness" but others heard the sound of shackles breaking off.

Let me close with the only entire letter I want to reprint — I have only changed it by adding paragraph divisions where there were none before. It said so much that I wanted to use all of it, because Rebecca S. Lane of Morristown, Tennessee, touches on almost every point that I made during this series:

Dear Dr. Price,

As you already know I have watched your program for many years now. For a long time, you promised us your message on racism. I am writing to thank you for your bravery and willingness to obey God's wishes for your ministry. I have looked forward to this message for a long time.

As a white person growing up in the south, it is very difficult not to be a "racist". I have always been taught that Blacks and Whites are not the same and that we should always separate ourselves from "those people". I really can't blame my parents because they were taught the very same things and their parents before them. I don't want you to think I'm making excuses for myself it's just that I haven't been to any church where the minister dares to deliver this kind of message for fear that he would lose his whole congregation.

As I got older and moved from my home, in the mountains of Tennessee, I realized that color was the only difference. I got married and have three boys of my own and I was determined to break the cycle of ignorance that my family had carried out for years. I was proud of my own self for breaking the chain. My children have many black friends and I was so very proud of myself right up until my youngest son started dating a black girl.

The moment I found out, my feelings of prejudice hit me in the face like a flood. Instead of cleaning up my heart, I had only buried the truth. I was a "racist". I know you were right when you said that's the only way to know. I had succeeded in raising my boys the right way but my own feelings were still the same. Dr. Price, I am so ashamed of myself. I really want to have a clean heart without any prejudices of any kind, but I still don't feel that I do. This is why I have been so anxious for your teachings on this subject. I hope once and for all I can rid my heart of all these things I have been taught. Please help me pray for my very soul. Thank you again for being obedient to God's Word. I hope everyone will hear it with an open heart and mind. May God bless you, your family, and your wonderful ministry. Keep up the good work.

Now, I'm not concerned about Rebecca, insofar as she seems to have a good grip on exactly where her problems lay, and what to do about them. Her letter, though, brings us back to the point where I started this series back in Volume 1 of *Race, Religion & Racism*. Throughout the series, people kept bringing up the subject of interracial dating and interracial marriage, wanting to know why I made such an issue of it. I'll repeat — I have no interest personally in white women. I have a wife, thank you, and a great one. But it seems that this is the issue that separates the sheep from the goats. People of other races can be good enough to call us friends, to "hang out with," to work with, to pray with — but when it comes to marriage, well, this is where people really test their racial prejudices. If you have no problem marrying someone of another race, and if you have no problem allowing your kids to marry someone of another race, then the truth has made you free indeed.

I hope, like many of the people who wrote, that your ideas about race and racism have been informed where necessary, and changed where needed. I hope also that you have been as blessed as I have been in giving this teaching. Praise the Lord!

I believe, without any question or doubt, that there is going to be a change effected in the body of Christ that we cannot even comprehend at this time. This was God's message to God's people. And woe to us if we don't do something with that message. The time has come for judgment to begin at the house of God. And in order to do that, it has to start with me, it has to start with you. So it's time for each one to do a little introspection, a little inner investigation to be absolutely sure that when people see you, they will know that you are His disciples, because you operate out of love. Not out of an inferiority complex, or a superiority complex, but out of a complex that's been washed in the blood of the Lamb!

Appendix A

What Muslims Believe

1.   We believe in the One God whose proper name is Allah.

2.   We believe in the Holy Quran and in the Scriptures of all the Prophets of God.

3.   We believe in the truth of the Bible, but we believe that it has been tampered with and must be reinterpreted so that man-kind will not be snared by the falsehoods that have been added to it.

4.   We believe in Allah's Prophets and the Scriptures they brought to the people.

5.   We believe in the resurrection of the dead, not in physical resurrection but mental resurrection. We believe that the so-called Negroes are most in need of mental resurrection; therefore, they will be resurrected first.

Furthermore, we believe we are the people of God's choice as it has been written that God would choose the rejected and the despised. We can find no other persons fitting this description in these last days more than the so-called Negro's [sic] in America. We believe in the resurrection of the righteous.

6.   We further believe in the judgement. We believe this first judgement will take place, as God revealed in America.

7.   We believe this is the time in history for the separation of the so-called Negro's [sic] and the so-called white Americans. We believe the black man should be freed in name as well as in fact. By this we mean that he should be freed from names im-posed upon him by his former slave-master. We believe that if we are free indeed, we should go in our own people's names, the black peoples of the earth.

8.   We believe in justice for all whether in God or not. We believe as others that we are due equal justice as human beings. We believe in equality as a nation of equals. We do not believe that we are equal with our slave-masters in the status of "Freed slaves".

We recognize and respect American citizens as independent peoples, and we respect their laws that govern this nation.

9.   We believe that the offer of integration is hypocritical and is made by those who are trying to deceive the black people into believing that their 400-year-old open enemies of freedom, justice and equality are, all of a sudden, their "friends". Furthermore, we believe that such deception is intended to prevent black people from realizing that the time in history has arrived for the separation from the whites of this nation.

If the white people are truthful about their professed friendship toward the so-called Negro, they can prove it by dividing up America with their slaves.

We do not believe that America will ever be able to furnish enough jobs for her own millions of unemployed in addition to jobs for the twenty million black people.

10.   We believe that we who declared ourselves to be righteous Muslims should not participate in wars that take the lives of humans. We do not believe this nation should force us to take part in such wars, for we have nothing to gain from it unless America agrees to give us the necessary territory wherein we may have something to fight for.

11.   We believe our women should be respected and protected as the women of other nationalities are respected and protected.

12.   We believe that Allah (God) appeared in the person of Master W. Fard Muhammad, July, 1930, the long awaited "Messiah" of the Christians, and the "Mahdi" of the Muslims.

Appendix A

We believe further and lastly that Allah is God and besides HIM there is no God and He will bring about a universal government of peace wherein we can live in peace together.

Source: This material appears on the Nation of Islam Website, http://www.seventhfam.com/temple/program/believe.htm.

Appendix B

Comments of the Honorable
Minister Louis Farrakhan

(From "Farrakhan: Charismatic Beacon or Cult Leader,"
Courtesy of Plummer Associates

"...Even the prophets of God are not the best examples. They are good examples, good examples, but the best example of what man is and of what man and woman can become, is in the personage of the Man called Jesus Christ. 'What? I didn't expect to hear that in a Muslim mosque. I thought that you people were Muhammadans!' When you look at Muhammad, the Muslims are making the same mistake that the Christians are making. The Muslims are saying Muhammad of 1,400 years ago is the seal of the prophets. Yes, a billion Muslims believe that. Well, the question is, is your belief true? You are just like the Christians. They are looking back 2,000 years ago for the real man, and missing the man who comes today. Muslims [are] looking 1,400 years ago to the Prophet Muhammad, and missing the real man, he prefigured.

Now, listen, if the scholars of Islam and the scholars of Christianity are honest men, and honest women, then we will have to admit that both the Jesus of 2,000 years ago and the Muhammad of 1,400 years ago did not fulfill all the signs of the one they prefigured. Jesus, 2,000 years ago, was overcome by the powers of wickedness, and his community has been turned upside down. So it is with the Muslims. If Jesus of 2,000 years ago and the Muhammad of 1,400 years ago fulfilled the scriptures that are given to the fulfiller, when you seal something, you approve it or you close it. If you approve

Appendix B

it, that means that the life of Jesus and Muhammad would fulfill in every aspect what the prophet assigns of...that last one gave us in their lives. The fulfiller doesn't look like the prophet. The fulfiller verifies the prophet as prophet. You call the prophets liars if the fulfiller does not come to do what the prophets said he would do. If you think that your man, 1,400 years ago as an orthodox Muslim, or 2,000 years [ago] as a Christian fulfilled it all, then there is no need for us to be here today. Because the work of the fulfiller would have ushered in a brand-new world and civilization. It has not happened yet; it's coming now — to seal up the book.

****

"...you're the people that Jesus is going to be raised among. He's not a white man, believe it nor not. He's one of your own brothers. Now I'm going to prove it and I'm going home, and happy Easter to you too! He wasn't born in Bethlehem of Judea, he was born in Sandersville, Georgia. . . . The book says, can any good come out of Nazareth? It ain't likely that something good is going to come out of black folks, that's why the Scriptures says, can any good come out of Nazareth? He's a man; you didn't understand him, we didn't either. Little humble, meek man, walked among us for 40 years laying a foundation. The Bible closes in the Old Testament, "Behold, before the great and dreadful day of the Lord, I will send you (who?) Elijah."

What does Elijah mean?. . . . It means God. Some say, "God is with us." Emmanuel means, "God is with us." Elijah means God. Eli! When Jesus was on the cross, they said he said "Eli, Eli, Lama Sabacthani." My God! So you got God, God. Jah, Jah, Jah is the name of God, so when you have Eli-Jah you have "God, my God! My God, God!" Elijah the prophet, now the Bible says, Elijah would turn the hearts of the children to their fathers, and the fathers hearts to the children. When you close the Old Testament, you open the New Testament with the genealogy of Jesus. But the Old Testament closes saying Elijah is coming. God, my God is coming! Then you open up with the genealogy of Jesus. So who is Jesus, who is Elijah? Jesus and Elijah, one and the same!

****

"We were scanning the horizon, looking for Elijah Muhammad to return. I was scanning with you, but I didn't know that at the end of my three years down, when I rose up, Elijah would rise up in me. I am that Elijah that was to come and now is. That Elijah that says God is not to come but He's present. What is your function, Elijah? To turn the children, and their hearts back to the father. Who is your father? Elijah Muhammad is the father of this knowledge, and you were turned away from him. But Elijah comes to do what? Elijah must first come and restore all things. You can only restore what was taken away. What was taken away from you in your fall? It is this little Elijah that is restoring it back to you, that you may rise again. . . . I'm not talking about myself, because it's not good. But I'm not really talking about myself; I'm talking about something that God has done for you, for me, for us. White people want to know why so many black people are moved by Farrakhan. What is it about Farrakhan that he touches the essence of black people? That even if they don't agree with everything that he says, nobody meets him and remains the same. What is it about him? People say he's an orator. Yes, I'm that. But orators don't transform human life. I'm more than an orator with good oration. I came before you today with no notes. Nothing is written; it is all coming from within....

I want you to look at your brother [i.e., pointing to himself], this Easter, who while he is speaking to you, is in the first phase of his crucifixion. Were you there when they crucified my Lord? We're always there. We usually take part in it. . . . You're looking for Jesus. I'm telling you as your brother, I'm the son of my father...because when he speaks he opens their eyes by God's

354

permission. When he speaks, he unstops their ears by God's permission. When he speaks if you listen to what I say and say what you hear me say, God will put a tongue in your mouth and you that were dumb yesterday, but you speak with wisdom today, if you speak after what I say. Whether you like it or not, I'm your connecting link to the Honorable Elijah Muhammad. To deny me is to deny Him! To accept me is to accept him! You will never be successful, even in what he taught you, if you don't connect me in there, then the power to (...?) the word won't be with you. This is not vanity. I'm among you man, open up your eyes and look and see what God is doing in the midst of you....

My job is to hook you up with the Christ. "Now Farrakhan, how can you hook somebody up to Christ if you ain't hooked up?" Check me out! If I'm not hooked up, then nobody in America or in the world is hooked up. I'm more hooked up to Christ than the Pope is. . . . I'm hanging on a cross right now. I'm on Calvary right now. "Aw, come on, Farrakhan, let's not be melodramatic." Any other black leader catching this kind of hell? Not one! No! I'm beginning to hang here now and it's around the first hour. They want to strip me of my robe or followers...the more I suffer, the more our people are raised in consciousness. Just by their beating on me and me being able to take it, black people beginning to say, "What are they beating on that man for? What are they...? I mean, and people are getting angry now. Well, what's raising you? It is the cross. It is my suffering that is undeserved. I did nothing to deserve this. But it is out of my love for Him and for you that I am suffering. And I'm ready to go all the way, because I know that by my stripes every one of you will be healed. You don't have to look anywhere for your Jesus, I represent Him!. . . . This journey to that hour when he says, it is finished; it don't mean he died; it means I have done what you brought me into the world to do. It's finished! I've ran my course, and now it's laid up for me the crown and I'm going to get my crown. And what is my crown? You will see me again! Man, I'm so happy,

I'm so happy, that my blessed mother who is not alive to see her son today, but that blessed black woman may (...?) for Mary again, laid a foundation in her son. I was born to die for you. I love the thought of dying for you.

****

"...That 75 percent of what you read in the Bible referring to Jesus is referring to a future man. And 25 percent of what you read is referring to the man of 2,000 years ago who is considered a type. But the real question is, Who is Jesus? Where will you find Him? This, the scholars are going to have to sit down and meet on. If the scholars agree that the Jesus of 2,000 years ago prefigured or gave of us a picture of the real Jesus then the historical Jesus is not the real Jesus. But the real Jesus is the one that the historical Jesus prefigured or gives us a type of. The historical Jesus was not the Messiah! The prophetic Jesus is the Messiah. The historical Jesus prefigured the Messiah and that's why the Jews have never accepted the historical Jesus; they continue to look for the Messiah. They are not wrong...."

Bibliography

This bibliography is not a complete record of all the works and sources consulted in the researching and writing of this book. It only indicates the substance and range of reading upon which the ideas and text were formed and is intended to serve as a convenience for those who wish to pursue the study of this subject further.

Ali, Abdullah Ysef, *The Meaning of the Glorious Koran*, 2 Vols. (Cairo: Dar Al-Kitab Al-Masri, 1934).

"Andrew Jackson Beard," in *A Salute to Black Scientists and Inventors*, Vol. 2 (Chicago: Empak Enterprises and Richard L. Green, n.d.), 6.

Anti-Defamation League home page. For background information select "Press releases" for ADL Backgrounder papers. http://www.adl.org/presrele/breaking-news.asp.

Blank, Jonah, "The Muslim Mainstream: Islam is Growing Fast in America and its Members Defy Stereotypes." *http://www.usnews.com/usnewsissue/980720/20isla.htm*

Blum, Edward and Marc Levin, "Islam Challenges Black Churches," *USA Today*, July 19, 2000.

Brookes, Warren, *The Economy in Mind* (New York: Universe, 1982).

Cadbury, Henry J., "Negro Membership in the Society of Friends," *Journal of Negro History*, Vol. 21, no. 2, April 1936, 151-213.

Calhoun, John C., *A Disquisition on Government* (Columbia: A. S. Johnston, 1851.)

Churches and Church Membership in the United States, 1990 (Marsh Hill, N.C.: Glenmary Research Center, 1991).

Clegg, Claude Andrew, III, *An Original Man: The Life and Times of Elijah Muhammad* (New York: St. Martin's, 1997).

Creative Fire, by the Editors of Time-Life Books, African Americans, Voices of Triumph Series (Alexandria, Va.: Time-Life Books, 1994).

Davis, David Brion, *Slavery and Human Progress* (New York: Oxford, 1984).

D'Souza, Dinesh, *The End of Racism: Principles for a Multiracial Society* (New York: Free Press, 1995).

Ellison, Ralph, *Invisible Man* (New York: Vintage, 1995 [1952]).

Evans, Anthony T., *Are Blacks Spiritually Inferior to Whites?* (Wenonah, N.J.: Renaissance Publishers, 1992).

Evanzz, Karl, *The Messenger: The Rise and Fall of Elijah Muhammad* (New York: Pantheon, 1999).

"Farrakhan: Charismatic Beacon or Cult Leader?" Christian Television Network, c1996, videocassette.

Finkelman, Paul, *Slavery and the Founders: Race and Liberty in the Age of Jefferson*, 2d ed. (Armonk, N.Y.: M. E. Sharpe, c2001).

Fitzhugh, George, *Cannibals All! Or, Slaves Without Masters*, edited by C. Vann Woodward (Cambridge: Belknap Press, 1960 [1857]).

Fogel, Robert William, *Without Consent or Contract: the Rise and Fall of American Slavery* (New York: W. W. Norton, 1989).

Folsom, Burton, "Real McCoy Showed Depth of Black Enterprise," *Detroit News*, February 28, 1996.

Gilder, George, *Wealth and Poverty* (New York: Basic Books, 1981).

Hadaway, C. Kirk and Penny Long Marler, "Did You Really Go to Church This Week? Behind the Poll Data," *The Christian Century*, vol. 115, no. 14, May 6, 1998, 472-475.

Hamidullah, Muhammad, *Introduction to Islam*, 5th ed. (Chicago: Kazi Publications, 1981).

Bibliography

Kahn, Muhammad Mushin, *The Translation of the Meanings of Sahih Al-Bukhari: Arabic-English*, 9 vols. (New Delhi: Kitab-Bhavan, 1984).

Kenzer, Robert C., "The Black Business Community in Post Civil War Virginia," *Southern Studies*, new series, 4 (Fall 1993), 229-252.

The Koran, translated by N. J. Dawood (London and New York: Penguin, 1999 [1916]).

Lamar, Howard R., ed., *The New Encyclopedia of the American West* (New Haven: Yale University Press, 1998).

Leadership, by the Editors of Time-Life Books, African Americans, Voices of Triumph Series (Alexandria, Va.: Time-Life Books, 1994).

Lewis, Bernard, *Race and Slavery in the Middle East* (Oxford: Oxford University Press, 1990).

Lincoln, C. Eric, *The Black Muslims in America*, 3rd ed. (Grand Rapids: William B. Eerdmans Publishing Company, 1994 [1961]).

Locke, John, *An Essay Concerning Human Understanding*, abridged and edited by A. S. Pringle-Pattison (Oxford: Clarendon Press, 1924).

Malcolm X, *The Autobiography of Malcolm X*, with the assistance of Alex Haley (New York: Ballantine, 1973 [1964]).

McKenzie, Stephen L., *All God's Children: A Biblical Critique of Racism* (Louisville, Ky.: Westminster John Knox Press, 1997).

Muhammad, Elijah, *Message to the Blackman in America*, 1997. Reprint, Messenger Elijah Muhammad Propagation Society (MEMPS), 1965.

Perseverance, by the Editors of Time-Life Books, African Americans, Voices of Triumph Series (Alexandria, Va.: Time-Life Books, 1993).

Pipes, Daniel, "How Elijah Muhammad Won," *Commentary*, vol. 109, no. 6. June 2000, 31-36.

Potter, Joan with Constance Clayton, *African-American Firsts* (Elizabethtown, New York: Pinto Press, 1994).

Price, Frederick K. C., *Race, Religion & Racism, Vol. Two, Perverting the Gospel to Subjugate a People* (Los Angeles: Faith One Publishing, 2000).

Rogers, J. A., *Sex and Race: Negro-Caucausian Mixing in All Ages and All Lands*, vol. 1, 9th ed. (St. Petersburg, Fla.: Helga M. Rogers, 1967).

Rogers, J. A., *Sex and Race: A History of White, Negro, and Indian Miscegenation in the Two Americas,* vol. 2. (St. Petersburg, Fla.: Helga M. Rogers, 1970).

Schweikart, Larry, *The Entrepreneurial Adventure: A History of Business in the United States* (Ft. Worth: Harcourt, 2000).

Smith, H. Shelton, *In His Image, But . . . Racism in Southern Religion, 1780-1910* (Durham, N.C.: Duke University Press, 1972).

Smith, William, *Dictionary of the Bible* (Nashville: T. Nelson, 1986).

Strong, James, *The Exhaustive Concordance of the Bible* (Peabody, Mass.: Hendrickson Publishers, 1990).

Taber, Clarence W., *Taber's Cyclopedic Medical Dictionary,* 14th ed., edited by Clayton Thomas. (Philadelphia: F. A. Davis, 1981).

Walker, Juliet K., *Free Frank: A Black Pioneer on the Antebellum Frontier* (Lexington: University Press of Kentucky, 1983).

"Where Slavery Isn't History, in War-ravaged Sudan, a Still Bustling Trade in Human Chattel," *Washington Post*, October 17, 1993, section C-3.

Wiecek, William, *The Sources of Antislavery Constitutionalism in America, 1760-1848* (Ithaca: Cornell University Press, 1977).

Wilson, Elinor, *Jim Beckwourth: Black Mountain Man and War Chief of the Crows* (Norman: University of Oklahoma Press, 1972).

Index

The italicized *n* following page numbers refers to information to be found in footnotes; *nn* refers to more than one footnote on a page.

black Jews, 275-278, 281
Black Muslim movement, 3-4n,
    3-5
Black Muslims
  history of, 5n
  number in America, 1-2, 5
  See also Farrakhan, Louis;
    Muhammad, Elijah; Nation
    of Islam (NOI)
The Black Muslims in America
    (Lincoln), 5n
Black separatism, 4n, 51-52n,
    64-65
Blacks
  achievements of persons of
    color, 299-320
  in the Bible, 262-298
  illegitimacy rates, 300n, 300
  spiritual inferiority myth, 311
  stereotyping of, 236, 300
  and welfare, 300n, 300
  See also black entrepreneurs;
    black inferiority; black Jews
Blank, Jonah, 1n
Blum, Edward, 1n
body of man, as separate from
    spirit and soul, 25-26, 76-
    82
Boone, Sarah, 302, 317
born again, 41-42, 162, 168-
    169, 211-214
  horizontal vs. vertical birth,
    212
Brookes, Warren, 300n
Burr, John, 318
Burridge, Lee, 318

Cadbury, Henry J., 55n
Cain, Herman, 306-307, 308
Calhoun, John C., 144n
Cannibals All! Or, Slaves Without
    Masters (Fitzhugh), 144n
Carson, Benjamin S., 303-304
Carver, George Washington, 299
census, in the Bible, 11

church attendance, 5
Civil Rights Movement, 4n, 51n
Clayton, Constance, 300n
Clegg, Claude Andrew, III, 6n,
    51-52n
curse of Ham. See under Ham
    (son of Noah)
Cush (son of Ham)
  meaning of Cush, 271, 285
  sons of, 272
Cyrene (city), 293-294

Dakes Annotated Reference Bible,
    vii, 190
Dar Ul-Islam, 4
David and Bathsheba, 238-242
Davis, David Brion, 154
Dawood, N. J., 91, 190
"A Day of Absence" [story of black
    achievements], 317-320
death/sleep principle, 60-61
devil
  angels of the, 70
  as a spirit, 70
devils/demons
  and belief in God and Jesus,
    167, 188
  white race as devils, 8, 50, 86-
    87
Dictionary of the Bible (Smith),
    293
A Disquisition on Government
    (Calhoun), 144n
Downing, Philip, 319
Drew, Charles R., 303, 319
Drew, Timothy. See Ali, Drew
    (Timothy Drew)
D'Souza, Dinesh, 144n
Dusable, Juan, 305
dust of the earth, mankind and,
    75-76

Ebed-Melech (Ethiopian), 285-
    289
The Economy in Mind (Brookes),
    300n

Index

El Beshir, Gen. Omar Hassan, 157
Elijah (prophet), Islam vs. Christian view of, 169-177, 184
Ellison, Ralph, 299
Emancipation Proclamation, 307
The End of Racism: Principles for a Multiracial Society (D'Souza), 144n, 144
The Entrepreneurial Adventure: A History of Business in the United States (Schweikart), 300n
Ephraim (son of Jacob), 279-280
An Essay Concerning Human Understanding (Locke), 14
eternal life, black Muslim vs. Christian beliefs, 70-82
Ethiopia, meaning of word, 285
Evans, Anthony T., 311
Evanzz, Karl, 6n, 51-52n
Ever Increasing Faith, vii, 264, 321
everlasting life. See life after death; resurrection of the dead
The Exhaustive Concordance of the Bible (Strong), 252

faith, and sight, 14-15
fall of America, 32-33
false gods, 24
false prophets, 28-33, 164
Fard, Wallace D. See Muhammad, Wallace Fard ("W.F.")
Farrakhan: Charismatic Beacon or Cult Leader? (videocassette), 162-163, 203; excerpt from, 352-356
Farrakhan, Louis, 4n, 5
  on being the Messiah/Jesus, 165-166, 178-181, 203-204
  on black slavery in the Sudan, 157-158

Farrakhan, Louis (continued)
  comments of, 352-356
  on Elijah the prophet, 169-170
  on historical vs. prophetic Jesus, 181-192, 196-197, 199-200, 203-235
  on Jesus and Muhammad, 167-168
  and the "mothership" or "mother wheel," 9-10n
  on wasting time with the Scriptures, 197-198
  See also Nation of Islam (NOI)
Finkelman, Paul, 145n
Fitzhugh, George, 144n
"Five Percenters," 4
Fogel, Robert, 155
forgiveness
  of sins, 102-104, 221
  without forgetfulness, 326-327
free will, 133, 142, 151-152

Gammel, Joseph, 318
geneaologies
  and color in the Bible, 265-298
  of Jesus Christ in Luke, 245-247
  of Jesus Christ in Matthew, 243-245
geneaology, use of the term, 259
generation, meaning of, 259
Gilder, George, 300n
God
  as an everlasting/living God, 21-24
  as the Creator, 21, 23, 24
  existence of today denied, 21-24
  as a man, Islam belief in, 6-8, 15-16, 20-21, 25-27, 36, 66-67
  same as Jehovah/Allah refuted, viii, 2, 6, 39, 66-67, 88, 117

Scriptural Index

All biblical quotes are taken from the *New King James Version* unless otherwise noted.

Scriptural Index

About the Author

Dr. Frederick K.C. Price is the founder and pastor of Crenshaw Christian Center, in Los Angeles, California. He is known worldwide as a teacher of the biblical principles of faith, healing, prosperity, and the Holy Spirit. During his more than 47 years in ministry, countless lives have been changed by his dynamic and insightful teachings that truly "tell it like it is."

His television program, *Ever Increasing Faith*, has been broadcast throughout the world for more than 20 years and airs in 15 of the 20 largest markets in America, reaching an audience of more than 15 million households each week. His radio program is heard on stations across the world, including Europe via short-wave radio.

Dr. Price is the author of more than 50 popular books teaching practical application of biblical principles. He pastors one of America's largest church congregations, with a membership of 20,000. The church sanctuary, the FaithDome, is among the most notable and largest in the nation, with seating capacity of more than 10,000.

In 1990, Dr. Price founded the Fellowship of Inner-City Word of Faith Ministries (FICWFM). Members of FICWFM include more than 300 churches from all over the United States and various countries. The Fellowship, which meets regionally throughout the year and hosts an annual convention, is not a denomination. Its mission is to provide fellowship, leadership, guidance, and a spiritual covering for those desiring a standard of excellence in ministry. The ministers share their methods, as well as experiences commonly faced by ministries in the inner cities. Their focus is how to apply the "Word of Faith" to solve their challenges.

Dr. Price holds an honorary Doctorate of Divinity degree from Oral Roberts University and an honorary diploma from Rhema Bible Training Center.

On September 6, 2000, Dr. Price was the first black pastor to speak at Town Hall Los Angeles. In 1998, he was the recipient of two prestigious awards: He received the Horatio Alger Award, which

375

is bestowed each year upon ten "outstanding Americans who exemplify inspirational success, triumph over adversity, and an uncommon commitment to helping others ...." He also received in 1998 Southern Christian Leadership Conference's Kelly Miller Smith Interfaith Award. This award is given to clergy who have made the most significant contribution through religious expression affecting the nation and the world.

Books by
Frederick K.C. Price, D.D.

THE PURPOSE OF PROSPERITY

INTEGRITY
The Guarantee for Success

HIGHER FINANCE
How to Live Debt-Free

RACE, RELIGION & RACISM, VOLUME 1
A Bold Encounter With Division in the Church

RACE, RELIGION & RACISM, VOLUME 2
Perverting the Gospel to Subjugate a People

THE TRUTH ABOUT . . . THE BIBLE

THE TRUTH ABOUT . . . DEATH

THE TRUTH ABOUT . . . DISASTERS

THE TRUTH ABOUT . . . FATE

THE TRUTH ABOUT . . . FEAR

THE TRUTH ABOUT . . . HOMOSEXUALITY

THE TRUTH ABOUT . . . RACE

THE TRUTH ABOUT . . . WORRY

THE TRUTH ABOUT . . . GIVING

LIVING IN HOSTILE TERRITORY
A Survival Guide for the Overcoming Christian

DR. PRICE'S GOLDEN NUGGETS
A Treasury of Wisdom for Both Ministers and Laypeople

BUILDING ON A FIRM FOUNDATION

FIVE LITTLE FOXES OF FAITH

THE HOLY SPIRIT:
The Helper We All Need

THE CHRISTIAN FAMILY:
Practical Insight for Family Living

IDENTIFIED WITH CHRIST:
A Complete Cycle From Defeat to Victory

THE CHASTENING OF THE LORD

TESTING THE SPIRITS

BEWARE! THE LIES OF SATAN

THE WAY, THE WALK,
AND THE WARFARE OF THE BELIEVER
(A Verse-by-Verse Study on the Book of Ephesians)

THREE KEYS TO POSITIVE CONFESSION

THE PROMISED LAND
(A New Era for the Body of Christ)

A NEW LAW FOR A NEW PEOPLE

THE VICTORIOUS, OVERCOMING LIFE
(A Verse-by-Verse Study on the Book of Colossians)

NAME IT AND CLAIM IT!
The Power of Positive Confession

PRACTICAL SUGGESTIONS FOR
SUCCESSFUL MINISTRY

Books by Frederick K.C. Price, D.D.

WALKING IN GOD'S WORD
Through His Promises

HOMOSEXUALITY:
State of Birth or State of Mind?

CONCERNING THOSE WHO HAVE FALLEN ASLEEP

THE ORIGIN OF SATAN

LIVING IN THE REALM OF THE SPIRIT

HOW TO BELIEVE GOD FOR A MATE

THANK GOD FOR EVERYTHING?

FAITH, FOOLISHNESS, OR PRESUMPTION?

THE HOLY SPIRIT —
The Missing Ingredient

NOW FAITH IS

HOW TO OBTAIN STRONG FAITH
Six Principles

IS HEALING FOR ALL?

HOW FAITH WORKS

FAITH'S GREATEST ENEMIES

To receive Dr. Price's book and tape catalog
or be placed on the EIF mailing list,
please call:

(800) 927-3436

*Books are also available
at local bookstores everywhere.*

For more information, please write:

**Crenshaw Christian Center
P.O. Box 90000
Los Angeles, CA 90009**

or check your local TV listing:

**Ever Increasing Faith
Television Program**

or visit our Website:

www.faithdome.org